COLORS

COLORS

The Ancient African Connection to the
Founding of America and the Making of
the Crips and Bloods

WILLIE HILL
LINDA JENKINS

ARPress
ILLUMINATING IDEAS
EMPOWERING VOICES

ARPress
45 Dan Road Suite 5
Canton MA 02021

Hotline: 1(800) 220-7660
Fax: 1(855) 752-6001

Ordering Information:
Quantity sales. Special discounts are available on quantity purchases by corporations, associations, and others. For details, contact the publisher at the address above.

Printed in the United States of America.

ISBN-13:   Paperback   979-8-89389-689-3
                eBook   979-8-89389-690-9

Library of Congress Control Number: 2024923811

DEDICATION

This book is dedicated to

To all the Incarcerated Parents who, despite being 'Rehabilitated', still find themselves incarcerated, unjustly being warehoused out-of-sight-out-of-mind and forgotten for no just reason except to serve the diabolical purpose of keeping people of real inherent substance hidden behind the Prison Walls of the "Divided but not Conquered".

Willie Hill, B-58763

Also,

A special Shout-Out to all my Ex-Cellie's who Graciously Endured (Or not), My Anti-Social Attitude During the Writing of this book. Fore, as I always used to acknowledge; "Creative Writing is a solitary endeavor, total self-indulgence an absolute prerequisite to any possible success".

In which case, any anticipated success will be due, for the most part on account of that rare acceptance from People, (in general), who endured my reclusive nature while being forced to share space with me in mutual peace.

God Bless One and All!

Will Hill

ACKNOWLEDGEMENT

In Loving Memory

Of

"LINDA JENKINS"

The Dearest Friend I have ever felt,
Without ever meeting,
(May her saintly SOUL Rest in peace)

ALSO

All my love and appreciation go out to the dearest most
cherished Lady In my life, and I do mean, LADY!

"Joyce Crowther"

Whom without her, (Joy), Selfless kindness I could
never have managed accomplishing what I did.

And,

Of course, this is for my mother, who have always been there
for me although this book is the only thing I've done that I pray
will give her reason to finally be proud of her only Son?

"Lela Mae Hill"

You already know Ma, this is for you, with Love.

Love,

Willie

ALSO

There are some other Individuals that in some way made this book possible, yet with time being a factor because after all the final publication is long overdue, I might miss a few but you know who you are and will hopefully forgive until book #2, I thank you all the same for now;

Lavern "Bonnie" Winding

('Thanks for Everything, Kala-Kala!)'

Bessie Lockett

David Lockett Jr.

Ardis Lockett

Cassie Hart

Barbara Wilson

Wardell Lane

Dwane "New Baby" Newman

Rev. Sharon Reddick

Debbie Jackson

Larry McFarland

Dr. Terry Day

Dr. Farr

Dr. Ray Fong

Mary Ratcliff

Mrs. Shirley Lamar

Claudia G. Schumann

Dwayne Jones

Getahun Weldeselassie

Sendeku Kassie

Yobyonas

INTRODUCTION

More ten 30 years ago I hand wrote and compiled a 550 page hand written manuscript during my 15 years 4-month long prison term spent behind the Walls of the **California Department of Corrections and Rehabilitation**, (CDCR), 1983-1998, on several Prison yards, "**San Quentin**", "**Folsom, Old** and **New**", *(A, B, and C, Yards)*, "**Soledad**", *(North, Central and South Yards)*, "**Vacaville**", "**DVI**" *(Tracy)*, and "**Fire Camp**", *(#4, Francisquito)*.

And finally paroling in 1998 from "**California Men's Colony**" *(CMC-East)*.

A dear friend, an ex-English School teacher named Linda Jenkins, (May her saintly soul rest in peace), was kind enough to spend more than two years, in her spare time on weekends and often during the week knights After returning home from working a full day and a half on two jobs her main profession was that of an executive secretary to a busy hands-on work-alcoholic, President/Owner of an exclusive NASA contracted Steel Manufacturing Co, in Pennsylvania, one of only two specialty steel makers in the world that make the metal for the Space Shuttle.

Linda's other job following a usual 12-hour day working overtime into the night, she would then make her way across town and put time in caring for patents at the local Hospice Retreat, and on top of that on weekends she Volunteered her tireless little busy body Mentoring young Juveniles that for one reason or another got caught-up and locked up in the Youth Arm of the 21st century Prison Industrial Complex.

The point is Linda had a lot on her plate yet she voluntarily committed herself, or, as she use to say; "challenged" herself to the pain-staking task of typing, editing preparing and eventually transformed my 600 page chicken-scratch hand written manuscript into a 500 page edited and typed manuscript, according to publishers requirements'.

The irony is that Linda never failed reminding me our mission was to enlighten not only the Youth but Parents as well to what our mission was that, even though she was a "rookie Editor", (*her own words*), and I knew, as I know now, that I'm a rookie Writer, however within the *story* line itself she noticed my frequent mention of real-life unsung historical heroes of all COLORS and my revealing tales of untold (true), legendary events will prove to be a game changer, in its own time. And, for two decades now Linda's premonition has been my inspiration and calling card that, "Our Baby", *is going to be a game changer, in its time!*

"Our Baby", is the pet name that Linda use to call the manuscript during our, painstaking, 2 plus yearlong collaborating by mail and by short limited phone conversations, with me from a Folsom Prison Cell in California, and she from her little red brick house in suburban White Oaks PA. Linda use to say that, "even in the event she and I happen to not be here to see the change happen, it didn't matter to her, because Linda was convinced the story was ordained by God of her faith, and that she and I were just vessels being used to make a changing impact on the red-blue, Crip-Blood rivalry, which at the time of our collaborating the manuscript, *Flagging,* was popular with the Crips and Bloods, and rival Mexican gangs here in California. And, Linda was really sure that one day "our baby" would become a welcomed addition to the Grade School System as a History Curriculum within the California Department of Education as well as the on both sides of the "Wall", especially behind the Walls of the California Department of Corrections and Rehabilitation where I spent 15 years, (1983-1998), of a 23 year prison sentence wholeheartedly devoted to reading, researching, studying, creating and with pen to paper, more often with tiny pencil, and on any kind of paper on hand at any given time in whichever prison environment I happen to be in I always found a way to keep writing and the necessary means to keeping sending what I wrote through the mail to Linda in White Oaks PA, No matter what.

And everything I wrote Linda took time to add her magic pen transcribing and complimenting my every word and expression until finally through our two-way assembly line my Postal Mail we compiled "our Baby" into a Book Manuscript. Which Linda so graciously had *Copy Righted* under **"MORNING STAR". Aka "COLORS AAC".**

In regard to the stories potential of helping end the misconstrued rivalry between the **Crips** and **Bloods**, the bottom line is that all the ancient massages from all the God's invented by man say; "The truth shall set you free".

THE Mission Objective that I discovered bestowed upon me decades ago limited me with only the insatiable obsession to write the Story as instructed which by the grace of God and Linda's unselfish assistance we got it done.

One thing is for certain I'm not sure if the mission would have gotten done had Linda not appeared in my life when she did. As I was only sitting on a bunch of handwritten Notes and rough-draft short story Narratives about the African *His-Story,* (African-American creation /foundation Myth) of the Two Lost Houses of King Narmer the Thrice Great and the sacred COLOR Triade surrounding the untold Story about the real significance of UNITING, The **Two Lands**, Upper and Lower Nile Valley Land of the Gods, Symbolic of the Blue-rag/Red-rag, Crip-Blood Rivalry, and "There will be no peace in the Hen House until the red and blue Roosters stop squabbling in the Barnyard".

Linda was a real Godsend. How we started our collaboration on the Manuscripts in the first place was Divine Providence as it was a life-changing moment for me that, during our *pen paling* relationship, Linda commented on the first few hand-written chapters of my story which I sent her out of her curiosity for what I told her was my hobby, "writing". Quote, *"Willie, I'm really taken by your African story, I'm sure Tuuwee and Luba Zandi's adventure will become even more exciting. Can't wait to read more. In fact you mentioned being near finished writing. With your permission of course, I'd like to challenge myself, just to see if I, a middle aged, middle class suburban white lady, can take your African story, 'chicken scratch',*

(: (big smile), into a manuscript that, (Jesus willing), will meet publishers requirements. I promise to do my best not to take anything away from your underline objective, I gather, which is to show the Crips and Bloods their symbolic Infamus Legacy as does not not have to remain negative because it is not set in stone and for the sake of the next generation youth they should use their ability to rewrite their history by bring some positive elment to their Legacy. And I gather you wish to help with your marvilas story Willie, im so proud of you my good friend.

And I promise my Editing shell not go beyond the technical errors. How 'bout that?" Unquote.

And so, here it is over 2 decades later and Linda's challenge to herself and promise to me has finally materialized into a complete finished book, ready to be introduced to society in general, but particularly the **Department of Education**, on both sides of the Wall, for acceptance into the **Grade School System**, as a History Curriculum, and in general my work is aimed at; *"paying it forward"*, what I was somehow chosen to be blessed with. Not just any old book with potential of becoming a successful marketable Product, but a history book with the potential of becoming a Grade-School Curriculum. That is the Goal that Linda and I shared, to produce a book that will **Be Useful** not only to our-**S**elves but to **S**ociety as well. And so, here comes; "BUSS COLORS", AAC.

I recall another favorite 'Pet Term' Linda use to refer to "Our Baby", she would say the book should be considered; *"Illuminating fuel for the Think Tank"*, "Serious thought for serious Thinkers".

In other words a conversation key for opening dialogue between rival Societies of COLOR, in order to find common ground in which to discuss ways and means by which to bring about much needed healing to a wounded Nation of COLOR;

WILLIE HILL

"COLORS"

The Ancient African Connection to the founding of America and the making of the Crips and Bloods."

It's a story linking present-day Crips and Bloods with two ancient African warrior tribes called the Cuuzan and the Ikeely, who worshipped the colors red and blue for religious and ritualistic reasons. Respectively, these colors held supernatural powers in the minds of these two tribes.

This action-packed story takes place in Central Africa during the 1800s at the peak onslaught of European and Arab colonization, at the time when millions of Africans were enslaved and/or forced to disown their ancestral religious practice and adopt the Islamic faith either by persuasion or at the point of a sword. We all know the part bad European Christians played during this horrendous period of history. But how familiar are you with the role the Arab Muslim fundamentalists played?

The culprit in the story is a Muslim leader of an army of Arab fighters under the spell of this evil-minded caliph named Mustafa the Plunder. This particular Muslim conqueror had a twisted agenda to force the Islamic religion on people. He sent his invading army out on missions to conquer all of Africa that hadn't already been infiltrated. To seize mineral-rich land and convert all the indigenous people living on the land to Islam by friendly persuasion or at the point of the sword.

However, the Cuuzan and Ikeele were not easy prey. They both were mighty warrior tribes, friendly neighbors who shared the same water holes and the same hunting grounds, and above all else, they both honored the ancient path of allegiance their ancient forefathers made swearing to defend each other's homeland and each other against any and all threats, to the death.

Unbeknown to so-called Street Gangs today who patronize the Colors red and blue as their patriotic Flags is the Symbolic connection those two enigmatic colors have to an ancient Alchemist Curse called Sacred Violence.

According to secretly held Disciplines in esoteric Alchemy, practitioners of the "Forbidden Pair", (Two thirds of a secret Holy Color-Triad) are those who pay homage to one sacred color, (red or blue) while harboring contempt for the other, with the exclusion of the all-important catalyst, (Third) color White is in stark violation of the deadly Curse that ancient African Alchemist warn with these metaphorical words; "Be warned all those among the Ruling Class Few that posse knowledge of the Curse of the Forbidden Pair (or not).

To read these wards any further will bestow the knowledge upon the Reader, For the ruling class Hierarchy to selfishly employ the forbidden Pair upon the Subservient Class Mass' to divide and control the whole of a society and you will witness uncontrollable Sacred Violence, The key to the curse is that there can never be peace in the hen house while the blue and red Rooster's squabble in the barnyard".

Ultimately the misrepresentation of these sacred colors will doom, (Transform) unwitting Practitioners into becoming inadvertent "Host-Perpetrators" of the contagious Social Disease of "Sacred Violence".

As written in the ancient secret Alchemist Disciplines, "those who abuse the secrete knowledge shell witness Perpetual Social unrest and unprecedented violence of a nature for each crisis will prove greater than the other and will blanket family, Community, and the entire Nation, beginning with the arrival and landing of two young African warriors aboard an illegal slave ship named the Duchess that arrived in North America from Africa landing off the shores of New Orleans in the mid-1800s leading up to the first American Civil War. The first gang truffe war that proved to be unprecedented violent unequal in American history to this very day.

The landing of these two African warriors sworn allies according to their African ancestral Tradition they were a united sacred Pair bound together in chains a young Cuuzan warrior crown prince name Tuuwee Cuuzan and Luba Zandi an equally young warrior apprentice of a neighboring African tribe and joint Territorial Allies with the Cuuzan name the Ikeeli.

Tuuwee and Luba were the best of friends; chained together side by side, two disciples of their respective religious tribal customs forcefully uprooted from their homeland and planted in a foreign land thousands of miles away, with nothing but the tattered rage on their backs. But what they did come with was firmly embedded in each of their hearts—their sacred tribe customs involving the colors red and blue, religious customs that were as tolerant of each other as red and blue are conforming colors. Yet today, several generations after the initial landing of these two friends and their respective color-worshipping customs, their legacy of friendship and reverence for each other's religious customs have spouted out of control into quarrelsome deadly groups of American gangsters, most notably the Crips and Bloods street gangs.

If any one reason for the peculiar division between these two color-worshipping groups can be unraveled, we will have to go back in time to the moment and place where Tuuwee and Luba first arrived in America, when slave and slave master first met to wed in an unholy matrimony of torturous servitude and greedy convenience.

12 smartly dressed white men, all of them rich Southern flesh buyers, wearing shinny silk and plush beaver skin top hats, and carring gold plated walking canes, looking like peacocks on a chicken farm standing around an auction block platform in the midst of a dirty fish smelling seaport as musty smelling dock workers went about their daily chores loading and unloading merchant ships totoly oblivious of the elevated just high enough off the ground for the rich southern gentleman to get a good view of the fresh shipment of human product.

Owning domesticated Slaves as poperty was still legal in 14 of the 50 states of America at the time. Pure greed, and lack of respect for existing slave laws drove these plantation owners to this filty fish smelling back loading dock were once a week or so a load of illegal raw natives, usually more dead than alive would arrive.

The crowd of flush buyers, looking like peacocks on a chicken farm gathered around on elevated auction platform as dock workers wearing greasy overalls went about their daily labors loading and unloading cargo ships and horse driven flatbed wagons totally imbigerous of the fancy dressed congregation of rich southern gentlemen. And, in turn, the group of Southern Aristicrates egnored their dirty low class waterfront work force. Only one thing was on the mind of these rich slave buyers, out bidding the next fellow for the cream of the human crop that was about to be off loaded from the newly arrived slave ship called the "Duchess".

Most of these men were big production plation owners, and what they wanted was healthy and strong looking Black males and females, who they call, Bucks and Wenches. (What they called male and female slaves). that show signs of having at least 15 years of production, laboring in the cotton, tobacco, and sugarcane fields.

Tuuwee and Luba were herded from the ship onto the docks of New Orleans in 1850. They were put on the auction block chained together. The bidding hardly began before they became bought pieces of property of a wealthy sugar plantation owner, ironically named Jay Fullove. Luba Zandi's overbearing head of red dreadlocked hair the size of ropes was too much of an intimidating sight that Jay Fullove ordered his crew of brutish henchmen to cut Luba's hair right there on the spot. Of course Luba Zandi resisted and was beaten unmercifully as the henchmen commanded the young Ikeelian to ether submit to the will of his new master or die.

They had taken the young Ikeelian from his home and family, and now they wanted to strip him bare. The symble of his manhood was his red hair. It was the silent, but bold expression of his warrior pride his badge of honor, his only symbolic connection to his god, as he know it to be.

Tuuwee Cuuzan knowing that his friend would rather die than allow his hair to be cut, stepped in and stoutheartedly absorbed that death blow meant for his friend. And when the slave master saw that one was willing to die for the other, and he realized the strong devotion between them had to do with their peculiar colors that Fullove knew were associated with Trible "Marking". what southern Slavers called "Nigger Comradery" and of course Fullove decided to separate Tuuwee and Luba immediately with these momentous words: "Gentlemen," Jay Fullove began shouting to the other Slavers, "we have just witnessed an occurrence unbefitting of niggars. Rather, they are tamed niggers or wild. I myself refuse to have any semblance of niggard comradery behavior in my stable. Therefore, if any party is interested, the blue niggard I just purchased is now up for resell at the low price of half what I myself just paid. But mind you, this offer is good only to a buyer from outside the good Southern state of Louisiana. My reasoning is simple. These two niggers should never be allowed to be together in the same state, least of all the same plantation."

For the shrewd minded owner of hundreds of black slaves; Jay Fullove happen to be familiar with with African supperstise belief in esoteric ritual practiced by African Alchemist who mark their bodies in certain ways that act as power conductor that can supposedly channel certain spiritual energy such an act of loyalty between slaves that he had just witnessed, such comradery behavior on the part of two African's, noticeably of two different tribes, was unheard of and peculiarly troubling and by no means was it to be tolerated. Comradery between slaves had to be stamped out at the roots, before it grows into something that plantation owners fear most, UNITY among their slaves.

In the end the blue warrior prince of the mighty Cuuzan, and the red head Ikeely warrior were separated as a sacred "Forebitten Pair" Right there on the cargo docks of New Orleans, where the wretched American legacy of the Red and Blue began and the "Curse of Sacred Violence" came alive.

With the unfortunate landing of these two enslaved young CuuIkee natives and the wicket actions of the slave master, Jay Fullove, to separate Tuuwee and Luba Zandi on account of their sacred alliance surrounding those two colors red and blue two thrids of the sacred Narmer Triade in violation of the forbidden Pair resulting in the deadly Curse being inadvertently brought to life with far reaching negative effects of a Divisive Nature that spawn the Nation with the Social Disease of sacred violence now rooted deep in the psyche of American society from the concrete jungle streets gangs of the inner cities to the gangster Politicians in the White House and the gang bangers all through the halls of Congress the separatist antagonist verbal gang Turf War is wagging on from the very top of the so-called "Bright Shining City on the Hill" all the way down to our inner city concrete jungle Elementary School Yards you can hear the hateful negative divisive mind-set of our Political Leaders (and the single most highest Civil Moral Authority and role model in the land, the President) in the conscious mind of our children at play, "You wearing blue I shouldn't play with you". And "I'd rather be dead then caught wearing red".

So-called St. gangs today that posse a strong reverence toward the pair of enigmatic colors red and blue, and yet no one have a clue as to why this is true? Because truth-be-told, there is a well held secrete reason behind the strange alluring fixation people have for those two colors, secrete reasons being kept hidden by the Ruling Class Few, from the subservient Class Mass's for reasons being revealed in, "Morning Star", aka "Colors the ancient African connection to the Founding of America and the making of the Crips and Bloods".

All most people know about those two provocative colors is that symbolically as a pair they signify "rivalry". Universally they are misrepresented as opposition forces, one color pitted against the other in all things, from opposing game pieces on a checker board to real life drama on the world stage playing out as we speak in the political arena between the red-rag Republicans in the White House and the blue-rag Democrats of the House Congress, the two highest Civil Moral Authorities in the Land and yet through the naked Eyes of the world Audience (and our uninformed children), our fearless Political leaders are no more than gangster counterparts to the Crips and Bloods.

And thus, our Nations gang turf waring just keep raging on, from the inner city concrete jungle streets of hell, to the heaven bound "Bright Shining City on the Hill". With no apparent end in sight until the pair of "Forbidden Colors", Red and Blue are United with their conductor color White. And then and only then will the truth be revealed why the two mightiest superpower nations the United States and her mother Nation the United Kingdom both identify and embrace the sacred "Code of the Universe", (In Word), "United".

As the old school saying goes; "Be True To The Game And The Game Will Be True To You".

"Hold True to the "Holy Triade", the sacred colors red, white and blue or else the Game will be played on you". What is not taught in school about, "Old Glory", (The United States Flag), and The "Union Jack", (The United Kingdom Flag), is that there is that deeper esoteric meaning behind Superpower Nations patronizing those sacred 3 colors red, white and blue. And that the forbidden practice of promoting and perpetrating the use of just two sacred colors without the stabilizing conductor color will make for a dangerous "Divisive Pair" of opposing forces, unleased will bring about the destruction of sacred violence on the 'Perpetrator' and the whole Nation.

The secret clandestine meaning is in the telling of the untold story about the ancient Cuuzan and the Ikeely, symbolic counterparts to the Crips and Bloods by their mutual association and peculiar fixation and devotion toward a pair of COLORS red and blue.

The Two long Lost Houses of King Narmer The Thrice Great, The famous Unifier of the historical Two Lands (of The Gods) Upper and Lower ancient Kuush, (Todays Egypt).

Worth noting here is the untold legend about the ancient Prehistorical origins of the popular COLOR-Triad (combination) red, white and blue and why so many Countries (twenty-nine today), use these Colors in their National Flags, the secrete span the corridors of time all the way back to the founding of the first Earth-bound Civilization and the so-called First Egyptian Dynasty, (3050 BC). Victory over the rebel break-away Kuusite Colony in the Northern Lower Nile Valley that became the Egypt, and the capture of the Red Crown of the God Seth, was the result of Narmer following a vison by the Muugi, (High Priest) Herockas who informed The Southern King of Kings of Upper Nile Valley, Narmer that the blue-skinned God Osiris would assure Narmers victory over the Egyptians if he would don his Royal Guards with Blue headdress and send them into battle, they would be victorious.

And sure, enough Narmer obeyed the Muugi's message from Osiris and outfitted his entire Military force with blue headdress and under the command of his Brother the crown prince and renown General of his Elite Royal Blue Guards named Cuupreous, Narmer himself led the all or nothing famous military campaign that captured the Egyptian red crown and United the Land into one.

And when the smoke cleared all that was seen standing on the red blood-stained battlefield were blue headed warriors with Narmer wearing his White Crown, the red crown in hand as he stood proud in his royal chariot driven by a team of white horses.

King Narmer, "The Thrice Great", whom the Greek scholars upon learning of this renown Kuushite/Thinisan Nomarch who indigenous Scribes dubbed 3-times a Great King, and after spying Narmer's fabulous Empire coined the term **Pharaoh** a title the Greeks coined in honor of the man's achievement not so much the man. Because although the wearer of the title is revered as just another King or Emperor because the term merely means "Great House" in Greek. But Narmer's true deserved title "The Thrice Great means *3 times* that of any expression of Reverence.

Obviously, the Greeks couldn't bring themselves to title any mere Mortal "three-times" that of a man. Not to mention exalting someone above the title of their young superhero, **Alexander 'the' Great**, their favorite young 23-year-old conquering Gang Banger. Who at the ripe young age of 24-years had himself crowned Pharaoh after conquering Egypt, the final jewel in his personal crown?

And even though he obviously would have loved to have worn the real sacred blue-stone incrusted red and white Double Crown of Narmer the Thrice Great, instead Alexander had to settle for an amalgamation of the Double Crown, a red and white "Shmty", with blue trim. Because the original Narmer Double Crown with the sacred blue stone of Osiris has been lost to history, like Narmer's true Title.

Yet it was the Great Greek student of the Egyptian Mysteries, Aristotle, Alexander's Mentor who went to great lengths to make sure no Title will undermine that of a 'King-Pharaoh', by convincing his Greek countrymen to have all records expunged of any mention of Narmer's true homegrown Title "The Thrice, (3-times) Great". All monuments and edifices wherever found were scrubbed clean of Narmer's name to the point that Narmer's name is hardly visible anywhere even his burial tomb is questionable.

Nations ever since have glorified the COLORS red, white, and blue as their national flags. And every Nation-State has a fabulous Creation/Foundation Myth surrounding their patriotic flag. Of course, we also know that the British Colonist brought the red, white, and blue to America with the landing of the mixed races of **Anglo/Saxon** from the **Old Greco/Roman** European World to the newly found World in the Western Hemisphere they named the **Americas.**

What we don't know, because until now it's been an inadvertently well-kept secret is that the "red and blue color phenomenon" also arrived by way of the Slave Ship the Duchess.

The Ancient African connection to these mystic colors came to America with two young enslaved African warriors named Tuuwee Cuuzan, a warrior prince of a tribe called the Cuuzan and an equally young warrior apprentice named Luba Zandi, who was a member of an allied neighboring tribe to the Cuuzan called the Ikeely. The 19th century Dynasty of the two long lost Houses of Narmer.

These two young CuuIkee warriors were best of friends, Tuuwee and Luba Zandi were caught up in a masterfully Designed scheme to rid the Brown Dragon from the land, but an unsuspecting glitch in the execution caused Tuuwee and Luba Zandi to lose their precious freedom during what was called the **Dragon Wars.** A war of armed resistance against the viscous incursion and forced religious conversion by a renegade army of Muslim fundamentalists under the leadership of a blood thirsty fanatical Muslim warlord named Mustapha "The Plunderer". Mustapha and his murdering army of Arab horsemen called Brown Dragons swept into the land of the blacks from across the hot desert sands of the Sahara Desert. Ancient, indigenous scribes and historians record that the Brown Dragons came like mad demons on horseback whaling swords and attacking towns and villages without mercy. They claimed their mission was Holy, converting the week, conquering or killing the strong and enslaving the rest.

By the same token and with no less viciousness, the invading White Dragons, of the Christian persuasion crossed the Atlantic Ocean to launce their ungodly campaign of conquest, conversion, and enslavement of the African people.

But then, from out of the heartland 0f central Africa where neither the Brown nor the White Dragon Imperialist forces had not yet managed to penetrate, rape, robb, divided and conquer the last of the diehard Tribes that refused to be Colonized a United Resistance Force of neighboring warrior tribes set aside their individual local squabbling to save Africa from a much bigger problem.

The sound of African Drums was the first to carry the news like the starting bell it announced the epic history making drama to come filling the air and UNITED forces together to turn back the Colonial Invaders during the last historical; "Scramble for Africa", in a final decisive do-or-die battle to prevent the last far-Eastern corner of African homeland from being conquered and colonized.

The Black Dragon Freedom Fighters", (BDF), was the name given to what became the 'Great Alliance', The Lost Narmer Federation that was the Mighty Ikeely and the Fearless Cuuzan.

Since ancient times they lived side by side togather in a mineral rich territory where they shared the same water hole and the same hunting grounds. And swore a pact with one another that they would protect the land and each other against any enemy or engrossment into their joint territorial homelands.

The Ikeely and Cuuzan where equally domineering warrior tribes, yet diplomatically they were as complementary of each other as red, and blue are matching colors. In fact, they both are devout practitioners of peculiar religious practice involving the ritualistic use of the colors, red and blue.

The Ikeely are a fierce mountain dwelling warrior tribe who live on a forbidden mountain of gold in a hidden well-fortified city said to be made of gold. The Ikeely Mountains overlook the rich fertile river valley domain of the fearsome Cuuzan. a vast garden of Eden rolling green foothills and patches of industrial farmland as far as the eye can see and yet there were untapped dance patchts of rain forest teaming with wildlife bordering Africa's most powerful river, and deepest river in the world, which is todays Mighty Congo. And then there's the fibulas Kingdom of the Cuuzan and its magnificent Royal Palace and temple complex surrounded by the 5 tributary Kingdoms and their individual tributary towns and villages. The entire river valley was the size of Florida

. And it was all under the control of the Cuuzan, all except the Ikeely Mt.

Valley tribes people have a popular saying that the Ikeely warriors were so hostile that God confined them up there to protect the rest of the world from their unbridled aggressive behavior.

The Ikeely are named after a legendary warrior known as the Red Lion, (Ikee Junga), to whom we can only imagine had to have been a great warrior.

Ikee, was named the Red Lion because of his fire red heir, which was twisted into rope size dreadlocks that hung beyond his stout shoulders. Shoulders said to have been stronger than 3 men and toughened by many hard-fought skirmishes on the battlefield, victories, one and all. Legend further state that Ikee Junga would hunt male lions with his bare hands. He'd wrestle the lion to the ground and hog tie the beast with his long red ropes. That's an over exaggeration, of course. But any lesser of a 'tall tale, about the mighty deeds of Ikee Junga, would be to underrate the strength and courage of this renowned warrior.

So renowned was the red head warrior that tribal forefathers adopted the devout custom of dying all male infant's hair red, from the moment of birth the male's hair is routinely cured with never cutting it and keeping their hair twisted into dreadlocks. As boys grew into men, one premier attribute that defined an Ikeely warrior's manhood was how long and how red they could cultivate their hair. The passionate belief is that the redder and longer the Ikeely male's hair, the more strength and courage the males receive from the mighty Ikee, whom the tribal forefathers deified, as tribal War God.

The other half of the dynamic Cuu-Ikee Duo The Cuuzan are a warrior tribe that occupies a vast territory down below in the Valley region boarding a mighty river, which was first called the Cuuzan River until many centures later it became the Congo River today. The ancient river valley Cuuzan, like their mountain dwelling neighbores, the Ikeely, also have a devout reverence for worshiping a color that they consider sacred, the color "Blue". The Cuuzan are practitioners of a peculiar custom, whereby Cuuzan warrior's smear their bodies with a specially treated blue chalk prior to embarking on certain perilous hunting expeditions, and before going into combat against an enemy tribe. The Muugi,(High Priest), performs a mass prayer ceremony. The warriors, covered in a light blue chalk from the neck down, all gather together in the main square. A hunting party as small as 3 hunters, or in the case of impending warfare with an enemy tribe, hundreds of Cuuzan soldiers, prior to making their exit from the village, assemble before a tall alter where the Muugi, (High Priest) stand before the assembly and delivers a blanket prayer, the sacred ritual of consecration. From his place on the alter, overlooking the sea of blue coated warriors, the Muugi recite an ancient esoteric prayer which is believed to empower the blue chalk.

The spellbinding prayer, coupled with the strong psychological belief in the protective and strength enduring power of the blue chalk incites the Cuuzan warriors with a fearless sense of invincibility, nothing can harm his blue coated body. No fighting man ever went into battle with the utter fearlessness of a "spellbound" Cuuzan warrior. Donned in his blue impregnable coat of armor, the Cuuzan is transformed into the ultimate warrior.

Of the five other indigenous tribal Kingdoms spread throughout the Cuuzan Valley, the Cuuzan and the Ikeely were the two undisputed superpowers who reign supreme over a vast Mountain-River-Valley Domain called;"United CuuIkee Nation".

Singers sang romantic Songs, Poets gave fabulous verse and Writers told Epic Story's about the 'Lost Narmer Federation' of these two Unknown Great Black Civilizations before their illustrious His-Stories, (African/American Creation-Foundation Myths), were forced underground. As in "absent entirely from the pages of contemporary His-Story, (Greco/Roman Creation-Foundation Myth), Books.

But, as it is written, "All things hidden, in the dark and kept secret, will eventually come to light for all to see".

And sure enough today if you know where to look songs are still being sang all over again about the mighty Ikeely and the fearless Cuuzan. And Storytellers still lend superb Narrative about the fabulous joint ventures of the legendary BDF and the CuuIkee Alliance. In addition, modern day Poets today refuse to let the world forget the Untold Great Dragon War:

"From out across the western ocean a great White Dragon arrived in Africa on an in-coming wind, One stroke of the White Dragons mighty wings brought on tidal waves of deception and exploitation, submerging the land of plenty and the African people underneath a sea of greed and upheaval, the wings of the White Dragon stretched far and wide across the land of plenty sweeping Africans off their feet and on their knees from where they were reduced to having to beg for their own land back.

The other religious wing of the White Dragon blocked out the sunlight and overshadowed African religious ancestral worship and other African religious beliefs and rituals never to be practiced again.

Then... from out across the Eastern Desert of the Sierra and a Mighty Brown Dragon crawled unto the African homeland, bearing two heads and breathing fire and burning sand, One breath from the two-faced Brown Dragon's fire breathing mouth scorched and burned to the ground the greatest Libratery there ever was setting ablaze ancestral land, all in their wake they through in the flames burning to the ground the illustrious history and Great achievements of the African Woman and man, Another fiery breath from the mouth of the second head on the Brown Dragon and fiery sandstorms of distortion were born, false claims to great works that wasn't theirs, they claimed as they tried to plunge the children of the sun into a permanent darkness of falsehood and ignorance, As African kingdoms, and great African works of art, burned in the flames, shameless forgeries rose from the ashes, master works were claimed by others, foreign imposters forged their names to the magnificent wonders of the African man.

But then came a mighty rumbling from out across the untouched heartland, and a Black Dragon appeared to take a stand. The Black Dragon was the Epic unsung Great Alliance between the Untold Mighty Ikeely and the Fearless Cuuzan", The untold ancient African counterparts to the modern-day Crips and Bloods.

Thus was the arrival and birth of the red-and-blue phenomenon. It came to America with the landing of these two bests of friends and original patron worshippers of devout customs that represented unification. Yet today, their legacy of friendship and mutual respect and reverence for each other's religious practice, which was a positive affiliation as opposed to having a negative implication, has been literally commandeered and turned into an instrument of "divide and conquer."

Colors

The Ancient African Connection to the Crips and Bloods Willie Hill

Oral historians recount how seven African kings agreed to meet under one roof to discuss and make a momentous decision on the fate of their respective tribes, people, and homeland. Some of these kings were territorial rivals; others shared bitter differences because of long-standing tribal feuds which were so old that their cause had long since been forgotten.

But in the early 1800s, in a vast region of West Central Africa, seven dominant tribes put aside their trivial hatreds and real-estate squabbles and agreed to assemble for the first time. An age-old enemy force, which had already succeeded in the conquest and colonization of most of Western Africa, along the Atlantic coast, was staging armed invasions and other subversive campaigns in an effort to conquer the interior lands as well. The tribes were in the position of reaching their own accord and making ready their defenses or trusting their fate to the hands of the oncoming enemy.

White European invaders were overrunning the west coast of Africa at an alarming pace. What was needed to quell the onslaught was a massive, aggressive, united defense force to stand up to these great white invaders who sprang from the sea and swept through the lands like hungry sharks on a mad feeding foray.

King Nuumyu of the Cuuzan and King Owana of the Ikeely was the organizers and driving force behind the emergency summit conference. King Nuumyu's and King (One Eye), Owana's visionary approach convinced the other tribal leaders that each of their respective tribal homelands faced definite annihilation if drastic, practical steps weren't taken at once. It became apparent to Nuumyu and One Eye early on that the great Brown Dragon was on a mission to devour the land of any and all useful minerals and precious resources. Gold and diamonds attracted the Arabs most of all, and One Eye knew they were hot for the Ikeely Mountains and its surrounding territories in the River Valley belonging to the Cuuzan other prominent tribes were rich in such valuable stones.

The weaker tribes in East Central region had been targeted first by the invaders. Whole tribes, who individually tried to fight back in defense of their homeland, ultimately wound up either fleeing from the land or dying at the hands of the Mustapha The Plunder. Some tribes, however, thought that submission was the answer to survival, and these most naïve natives unwittingly surrendered themselves, along with their lands, to the marauders. The price they paid for submission was tremendous. They found themselves in chains, under armed guard, and digging in the earth from dawn to dusk for gold and diamonds until their fingers bled. All this to benefit their captors. After the land was thoroughly raped of its natural resources, the native men, women, and children, most more dead than alive, were marched off in chains to the sea to be swallowed up and never heard from again.

The notion that the Arabs could be destroyed or forcefully driven back to the sea was just that—a notion—and wishful thinking on the part of any African native so far it seemed. The invaders had guns and canons, awesome magic that struck fear in the hearts of even the most fearless African warrior.

The only notion worth considering was strictly a defensive one. King Nuumyu's vision was to build a fort city. This was necessary, he believed, if he and his tribe were to be left with the task of defending Cuuzanland. His vision, on the larger scale, which he hoped to sell to the other six kings, was so huge that it hadn't been attempted since ancient times. King Nuumyu envisioned an empire of tribal states, the merging of the seven dominant tribes into an economic and military alliance. The allied kings would carve out a specific territory: the richest and most fertile land. They would establish a governing body and create a constitution which would guarantee each tribe an equal degree of autonomy. They would incorporate their warriors into a single fighting force to defend the "united" homeland against all foreign attackers.

Africa was on its last leg, during the historical so-called "Scramble for Africa" the CuuIkee Territory was the one remaining domino still standing in the wake of conquered Black Empires falling one by one to the unstoppable infiltration of the renegade Muslim warlord Mustafa the Plunderer and his merciless Arab fighters.

The CuuIkee Territory was so named for the Cuuzan and and Ikeeli, the two undisputed dominate superpower tribes in the Mountian-River-Valley Region of Central-East Africa.

By pre-His-Story written account, It, The BDF, was historically the Greatest Affiliation of all time between allied African Tribes, during the untold period in Africa called the "Congo Valley Dragon War". The monumental war of Imperial conquest by Arab and European invaders and the defense of ancestral African homelands by the "Black Dragon Freedom Fighters", the war that saved the last holdout Nation from the jaws of Colonialism.

Unsung in Western Society, Yet, ancient African indigenous Writers and Historians wrote epic tales about the heroic exploits surrounding what they dubbed the Great CuuIkee Alliance.

Celebrated Singers sang songs praising the deeds of the Cuuzan and the Ikeely, and Poets to this very day refuse to let the world forget the Legendary Great Dragon Wars.

"From out across the western ocean a great White Dragon arrived in Africa on an in-coming wind, One stroke of the White Dragons mighty wings brought on tidal waves of deception and exploitation, submerging the land of plenty and the African people underneath a sea of greed and upheaval, The powerful religious wing of the White Dragon blocked out the light of the sun and overshadowed African ancestral worship and other African religious beliefs and ritual practice.

Then... from out across the Eastern desert a mighty brown dragon crawled unto the african homeland, bearing two heads and breathing fire and burning sand, One breath from the two-faced Brown Dragon's fire breathing mouth scorched and set ablaze the land, burning to the ground the illustrious history and achievements of the African man, Another fiery breath from the mouth of the 2nd face on the brown Dragon and fiery sandstorms of distortion were born, false claims to great works that wasn't theirs, they hoped to plunge the children of the sun, into a permanent darkness of falsehood and ignorance As African kingdoms, and great African works of art, burned in the flames, shameless forgeries rose from the ashes and laid claim to the wonders of the African man.

Then came a mighty rumbling from out across the untouched heartland, and a Black Dragon appeared to take a stand. The Black Dragon was the mighty Ikeely and the fearless Cuuzan.

The defensive battles won were all heroic encounters earning the mighty BDF much praise through-out the land. However, the victories were counterproductive too costly to the young male population keeping up a no-win war. Nuumyu and Owana realized nothing short of total inhalation of the enemy would totally stop the waring.

And so Nuumyu and Owana decided on an all-out Offensive Strike and with the blessing of the High Prist, called a Muugi, (Godman), the Orical was consulted and a plan put in motion that would ether drive the Arabs into the sea once and for all or it would bury forever the mighty CuuIkee?

The BDF, was historically the Greatest Affiliation of all time between allied African Tribes, during the untold period in Africa called the "Congo Valley Dragon War". The monumental war of Imperial conquest by Arab and European invaders and the defense of ancestral African homelands by the "Black Dragon Freedom Fighters", the war that saved the last holdout Nation from the jaws of Colonialism.

Unsung in Western Society, Yet ancient African indigenous Writers and Historians wrote epic tales about the heroic exploits surrounding what they dubbed the Great CuuIkee Alliance.

However, hours before that consequential summit conference of the seven kings had taken place, another . . . almost equally momentous . . . event was held involving one of the largest and most influential tribes of the seven: the Cuuzan.

It was midmorning—hot, dry, and not a cloud in the sky to block the scorching sun. A cloud of another sort rose from the earth's floor. A reddish dust cloud hovered among the ranks of a moving wave of black bodies. The Cuuzan natives slowly exited the village and marched their way across the dusty African plain.

There was a separate group of marchers: about 130 native men, women, and children. They were actually horseshoed in the middle of the other villagers. This smaller group led pack animals laden down with travel gear and personal possessions they could carry. They were leaving . . . they were the "exodus." The group surrounding them were grieving relatives, friends, and well-wishers who had turned out to get one last look at those who were going into exile and forbidden to ever return. The mass escort chanted a farewell song as the marchers headed toward the border frontier of Cuuzanland.

The exodus was comprised mostly of women and children along with a support group of warriors. A number of the women were pregnant, and an equal number, who didn't carry their burden in their bellies, carried newborns inside hammocks strapped to their backs. Small children, unable to walk, rode on the backs of pack animals and inside wagons. Those children whose little legs could run were used as shepherds, herding chickens, pigs, and goats. The small number of men in the ranks tended to the cattle and camels. These men carried nothing on their person except weapons. They were Cuuzan warriors who happened to be a part of the exodus because, as warriors, they were bred to follow orders. These warriors were bound by a king's decree to protect and provide for the women and children and to serve the exiled leader of this exodus—Muusamali, King Nuumyu's brother.

Muusamali, clutching the front of a lion skin mantle which he wore in the fashion reserved for kings and tribal elders, walked at the forefront of the exodus. Muusamali's stroll was proud in spite of the dark gloomy cloud of shame and dishonor hanging over his head. He walked as if he were taller than his already towering 6'3" figure. Thrust into a role he neither subscribed to or condoned, Muusamali stared straight ahead, his face set in stone. He fought to conceal the bitter anguish he felt in his heart. He had allowed himself to be so easily coerced into abandoning his homeland. And in so doing, he was also allowing his name to be tarnished forever.

All things considered, Muusamali played his role well as though following some planned script, a script for which he would have rather died than accept. Except for one thing: the script's creator was his brother, King Nuumyu, the one man on earth whom he revered enough to lay down his own life.

Walking at Muusamali's side was his beautiful wife, Puulu. She was eight months pregnant with their first child. Yet, uncomfortable as she felt, she refused to ride in a wagon, choosing instead to walk on her own at least as far as the border crossing.

As Puulu walked along, matching stride for stride with her husband, she also tried to display a stone-faced expression to match Muusamali's. But Puulu's efforts to appear nonchalant were unconvincing. Anyone who knew her realized that, inside, her heart was crying painful tears. Although she avoided eye contact with friends and relatives as she filed past, fixing her gaze straight ahead like Muusamali, every so often Puulu could be observed stealing quick peeks from the corner of her eye at the surrounding crowd. Those who caught her glances waved at her furiously. But Puulu would merely look away. It was the only proper thing to do in keeping with her role as the faithful wife. Even beneath this role-playing, she was genuinely devoted to Muusamali. She shadowed him in everything he did and believed in him without question. Even before Puulu's father pledged her in marriage to Muusamali when she was sixteen years old, she worshipped the very ground he walked on. Puulu's father tried to console his daughter with his choice for her husband, for Muusamali was not what one would call a handsome man. He promised her that young Muusamali, in all his apparent unattractiveness, was destined to become someone great. He would grow out of his ugliness and also grow out from under the shadow of his older brother, Crown Prince Nuumyu, heir to the Cuuzan throne. What Puulu found in Muusamali was manliness without the extra fanfare, which only served to make other women take an interest in something she wanted to keep exclusively for herself.

On Puulu's other side walked a daring figure. Not exactly towering in size like Muusamali, but a proud man and an obviously seasoned warrior. He was Zuuox, chief escort and guard along with the thirty-five other warriors delegated by the king to accompany the exodus into the new land. It was their solemn role to provide the pilgrims with protection and assistance while building a new kingdom with Muusamali as king. By all outward appearances, especially on the part of Zuuox, the two leaders did not care for each other's company. Zuuox made no effort at concealing his bitterness about being forced to leave the homeland, especially at this point in time. The homeland was being threatened with attack from the dreaded White Dragons; war was inevitable. Zuuox was a warrior, born and bred to fight. He wasn't trained to run and hide as he was now compelled to do by king's decree.

Muusamali was deeply intimidated by Zuuox's unhappiness. Muusamali suspected that Zuuox would never swear a warrior's allegiance to him, something which Zuuox was expected to do in a formal ceremony in front of the entire Cuuzan people within minutes from now.

According to Cuuzan custom, the brother of the king was allotted the right to secede from the tribe at will and start a new society of his own choosing. He was guaranteed enough women, children, and soldiers to fashion a clan and enough provisions to give him a favorable start in the new homeland.

It was also tribal custom that a certain ceremony be conducted at the border. Just as the king's brother is exiting the homeland of the reigning king, that brother officially becomes king of the exiled clan. At that point, the chief warrior accompanying the exiled clan is expected to pledge an oath of obedience to the exiled king, precisely on the border.

Muusamali couldn't conceive of Zuuox going through with this ceremony once the procession finally reached the border crossing. Muusamali wasn't aware that Zuuox knew more about the true purpose of the exodus than he ever should have known. The true facts were reserved strictly for the king and his brother.

Zuuox was, indeed, a loyal devoted soldier who would have gladly given his life for the royal family. Along with the security of the tribe, Zuuox's sole purpose in life was to serve the king and the king's family. But being a curious man by nature, the sudden and unexpected split between King Nuumyu and his favorite brother Muusamali didn't sit right with him, and it brought about a burning curiosity in his mind which compelled him to pay special attention to certain matters which otherwise would have been quickly dismissed.

As King Nuumyu's personal bodyguard, Zuuox was often present while the king conducted private sessions with certain elders of the governing council or visiting dignitaries. Never, in his twenty years of service to the king, had he been directed to leave the room upon the arrival of any guest, except on one momentous occasion. It was the last private meeting between King Nuumyu and Muusamali on the morning preceding the exodus.

Muusamali was summoned to the king's chambers for a one-on-one meeting, and Zuuox was politely excused from the room.

However, the mud-packed walls of the king's chamber didn't afford the king much privacy. Alone in the next room, Zuuox couldn't resist the temptation to lend an ear to listen to the compelling conversation between the king and his favorite brother. It was a clandestine conversation which set the stage for the infamous exodus.

The king sat proud and straight on his fur-covered throne. Muusamali stood before him holding a proud posture of his own. As he paced with both hands clasped behind his back, he said to the king, "I should choose my own warriors . . . those whom I feel will best serve me with the degree of loyalty I can absolutely trust. Your personal warrior guards are a poor choice. They were trained and bred to serve you, my king. Besides, Zuuox hates me. He despises me for this act of self-exile in the face of war. This mission of ours on which I am about to embark does me no justice except that it puts me in the light of being a coward! And we both know that Zuuox has nothing but scorn for any act of cowardice."

"Your mission, Muusamali, by your own choice. Do not forget!" the king said in a stern yet patient voice. "This exodus is your decision and yours alone. The people must believe that and only that! You must keep in mind that I had nothing at all to do with your exile other than my permitting it to happen. My permission, and my decree, which allows you to go and take a number of the tribe with you, is based upon tribal custom. I have no choice in the matter but to give you my blessing and to forbid you from ever returning. No one is to ever know it is I who initiated this move!

"As far as your reputation, it has to be sacrificed in order to assure that this mission is a secret and a success. The masses must believe that you chose to flee the homeland rather than stay and fight with your kinsmen. As the king's brother, you alone are afforded the right to leave at any time. And in so doing, with war on the horizon, it is only natural that the masses will loathe your decision. Zuuox and the other warriors are no exception. Complete secrecy is absolutely necessary if the plan is to work to a successful conclusion.

"Little do the people know that the future of the Cuuzan could quite possibly be leaving here with you . . . into exile. The children are our future. I've arranged for the youngest portion, the cream of the crop, to go into exile with you. These children who will accompany you must remain of pure blood to maturity. They must remain free from exposure to the whitewash that is spreading like wildfire, threatening to overrun our beloved homeland.

"It is your noble task, Muusamali, to seek out land that is still pure black and unaffected by the whitewash. You and your thirty-five warriors, warriors who are sworn to serve you, must work together and raise a strong generation of Cuuzan. You must populate the new territory and always live apart from the homeland. Teach your clan and future generations to repeat the same thing that's being played out here today. Break off a root from the tree and plant it in a faraway land; a land that is pure black. The survival of the Cuuzan depends on what you, and I have secretly set this in motion by way of this exodus. This will work out to a right and just conclusion. It must work. The Cuuzan must not perish. We must multiply!"

King Nuumyu paused and leaned forward in his chair. His dark black complexion made the whites of his piercing eyes shine as he solemnly fixed them on Muusamali and continued. "Your fears and suspicions about Zuuox's loyalty are premature, my brother. Obviously Zuuox and the other warriors I've assigned to accompany you are unhappy about being forced to leave their families and comrades behind, especially with signs of war looming over the homeland. Just remember, Zuuox lives to serve and honor one thing: the oath of a Cuuzan warrior. Zuuox's devotion is blind. Once he swears a warrior's allegiance to you as his king, he will see nothing else but your safety and that of the clan's. As commander-in-chief, the other warriors will follow Zuuox with the same devotion as Zuuox shows you. So, before you pass a negative judgment on Zuuox's faith, let's wait and see if Zuuox's pledges a warrior's allegiance to you at the appointed hour. If he does, then you can have faith in his word. I would stake my life on Zuuox's word.

"Now, I see still more discontent on your face, my beloved brother. Speak and let us examine your doubts and fears. Even though your destiny is sealed, you are entitled to speak your mind in order to bring your thinking in line with mine."

"Indeed your consideration, my king, is well taken. Know that for you and the true purpose of this exodus, I will gladly sacrifice whatever reputation I've sowed over my short lifetime. I always did strive to be a positive force for the good of the tribe."

"And your presence has always been felt in a positive way, Muusamali. You will surely be missed."

"Oh, but how terribly will I be remembered? Whatever small amount of reverence I managed for myself while living in your eminent shadow will now be wiped clean by this self-exile," Muusamali said as he freed one of his hands from his behind back to thoughtfully rub his chin—contemplating each word before he spoke it.

"But you've just spoken of your willingness to sacrifice all for the cause," King Nuumyu said.

"Correct. But something inside me compels me to make this one last plea. At this juncture, my king, I'm tempted to risk being looked upon as a true and genuine coward, a coward in the eyes of the one person in the world whom I would rather die at his feet than to leave him with this vision."

"Don't bite your tongue on my account. Remember, I've known you all your life. I know you're no coward, Muusamali."

"Well then, wouldn't it be appropriate, my king, if we just confided in the counsel of the elders and the common people of our true intent? Can we not tell them that my leaving the homeland with a portion of the women, children, and warriors is for the purpose of assuring the continuing existence of the Cuuzan? It is such a noble and wise move on your part. Why clothe it in such a shameful disguise as having your brother branded a coward, exiled from his homeland forever?" Muusamali paused and once again clamped both hands behind his back as he looked pleadingly into the eyes of his older brother.

King Nuumyu studied his brother for a moment and then spoke in a soft, calm voice. "God forbid we should plant any seed in the mind of the common masses, or of the elders or any warrior, that running away is the answer to our problem," King Nuumyu began. "The mere suggestion that a Cuuzan should run and hide is forbidden! Your exile is appropriately looked upon as a disgraceful act and, thus, you and your clan will be condemned—forever banished. No Cuuzan should ever be inspired to imitate your actions. Can't you see, Muusamali? If we condone your behavior openly and allow for the exodus to be anything but disgraceful, we will likely open the floodgate for a huge number of our people to desert the land. On the other hand, if we who remain behind are annihilated and our homeland overrun, then there will always be your exiled clan living elsewhere. It's insurance! Insurance for the continued existence of the mighty Cuuzan! No, my beloved brother, we must discourage anyone from ever thinking in terms of desertion. At any cost, desertion must not be allowed. Do you understand, Muusamali?"

"I understand, my king."

"Always remember, Muusamali, once you and your clan have safely left and staked your claim to a new homeland, you must remain forever removed from Cuuzanland. Your clan must understand that returning to Cuuzanland, under any circumstances, is forbidden. Our fate is our own, as it is with your clan. You are Cuuzan and will always be in our hearts. Continue to be strong and dominate as a tribe with the purpose in mind to preserve and multiply our race throughout the world."

After a short pause, Zuuox heard Muusamali acknowledge the king and accept the secret undertaking without further discussion. The brothers embraced for the last time and parted ways.

The next morning, the group of 130 exiles crossed the open clearing surrounded by more than five-hundred grieving tribespeople who had gathered to bid their farewells. King Nuumyu and his younger brother, Duugawdu, stood off in the distance atop a hill overlooking the multitudes of their people.

King Nuumyu watched with intense interest as the exodus party with Muusamali, Zuuox, and Puulu in front led the marchers to the border crossing site. The younger brother, Duugawdu, wore what appeared to be an angry expression on his bearded face.

Muusamali, marching alone, caught sight of his brothers standing strong and erect on the distant hill. King Nuumyu's animal-skin mantle blew softly in the breeze. He made an imposing figure with his full mane of black, woolly hair. He allowed his bushy crop to fly naturally in the breeze and this reminded Muusamali of the lion he so much admired. His younger brother, Duugawdu, was the image of a wild and restless black panther, subdued and kept in line only by virtue of his respect and admiration for his elder brothers King Nuumyu and Crown Prince Muusamali.

The sight of King Nuumyu and the rambunctious young Duugawdu steeled Muusamali's resolve and gave him a certain amount of self-confidence. It was Muusamali's deep personal conviction that he would overcome the false stigma placed upon him by settling this exiled clan in a new homeland and raising them up to be a mighty tribal nation unto themselves.

As Muusamali thought about Duugawdu, who was two years his junior, he wholeheartedly wished that he could have revealed to him the truth about the exodus. They had always been close. But lately Duugawdu had completely ignored Muusamali. He hadn't even bothered to say goodbye. In fact, his presence on the hill was the first time Muusamali had seen him since word of the exodus had become public knowledge. He was convinced, at this point, that Duugawdu was hurt and ashamed to know him, let alone acknowledge the fact they were brothers.

Muusamali continued his private musings and hoped his little brother would be consoled by the fact that, as long as King Nuumyu fathered no sons, he was now the crown prince of the tribe. Nuumyu fathering sons was unlikely given the fact he had sired only female children by a number of different wives. Because of Muusamali's departure and the fact that he was sonless, that left Duugawdu next in line to inherit the throne of his homeland tribe of the Cuuzan.

Muusamali thought about his twin sister, Muutata, who insisted she accompany him into exile in spite of his pleas to the contrary. If only Duugawdu had shown that kind of unconditional brotherly love—his heart would not carry the heavy burden it now did.

Finally, the group of 130 exiles reached that all-important point which marked the Cuuzan tribe's territorial threshold. Muusamali pulled up and stopped. Puulu, Zuuox, and the remainder of the front ranks came to rest following his lead.

Slowly, the surrounding wave of dark milling bodies began to subside with a rippling effect, and the mass of Cuuzan natives came to a halt. The singing died out, and the only distraction breaking the silence came from an area at the center of the crowd. It rose from the tiny child-shepherds scrambling at the core to bring a few squealing piglets into line.

Slowly, Muusamali tuned to face Zuuox. Zuuox, however, avoided his gaze, looking past him and into the open space over his shoulder as if he were on some other journey far removed from the hot, dusty, plains where his body now stood on the border of Cuuzanland. Zuuox could feel Muusamali's eyes penetrating the side of his fact, yet he remained unmoved and appeared to be in deep thought.

Muusamali waited patiently for Zuuox to drop to his knees before him and pledge the warriors' allegiance to his new king. He doubled-checked his stance to make certain he was across the territorial threshold where, by Cuuzan custom, he was now king of the exiled clan.

King Nuumyu and the tribe were silently watching and waiting for the reckoning of this very moment—envisioning its uncertainty along with Muusamali. Puulu stood quietly at Muusamali's side, solemn in her composure. Even in her balloon-like state of being eight months pregnant, she looked fit and robust. Her ebony eyes, fixed on Zuuox, had a sleepy look about them—not from fatigue but rather from impatience. She, like the others, knew what was expected of Zuuox. While her husband had grown numb and subdued, Puulu was irritated by the delay, and her feelings showed on her soft, pretty face as she stared at Zuuox with a sheepish contempt.

Finally, Zuuox's attention was drawn back to the present by movement among the crowd. As his hawklike eyes shifted and brought the scene into focus, he saw one of his warriors quietly working his way through the sea of bodies toward the center of the arena. The warrior, carrying only spears and waterskin, stopped and silently stood before Zuuox. Then there was more movement as another warrior stepped from the crowd, then another, and yet another, all with the quiet grace of cats. One by one, Zuuox's comrades appeared, filtering through the crowd and stepping into the center square, until all thirty-five warriors were present. All eyes were fixed on their leader, Zuuox.

Zuuox was now on the hot seat. He expected this moment to be a test of his cool head under pressure. But he didn't count on his friends and comrades stepping forward making the pressure even more intense. Zuuox had a tough, potentially self-destructive choice to make. And he had little room to make it with thirty-five hardened warriors breathing down his neck. These warriors revered Zuuox for his hard-line stance and waited to see if their fearless leader would bow down before a man who bore the disgraceful mark of a coward on his back.

Zuuox turned and faced Muusamali head-on. The presence of King Nuumyu, visible over Muusamali's shoulder, standing on the hilltop, was not overlooked by Zuuox. He felt it was only fitting for the king to witness the unorthodox move he was about to make. Zuuox's eyes met Muusamali's for just a few seconds. Then, without warning, Zuuox turned and faced Puulu. Clutching his spear as it rested with the butt on the ground and the point aimed skyward, he slowly dropped to one knee and held out his right hand to Puulu. As she stared at Zuuox's outstretched hand, she held her own hands close to her blossoming belly as if she were being asked to touch a snake. She finally looked over at her husband, Muusamali. But Muusamali didn't even bother to look at her. Instead, he remained calm and collected. Almost too calm. He studied Zuuox with an intense expression.

"Take my hand, Puulu," Zuuox said in his deep commanding voice, "that I may give forth my oath of allegiance through you to the unborn prince and future king of the Cuuzan exile."

Puulu wasn't sure just what to do. She looked desperately to her husband and searched his face for some kind of reaction that she might draw on. But Muusamali avoided Puulu's imploring eyes as his attention was fixed on Zuuox. Zuuox, meanwhile, kept looking at Puulu. His expression was insistent. His outstretched hand with the palm up seemed to be pleading with her to take hold. Those witnessing this event stood by holding their breath in silent wonder.

It was Muusamali who, finally, flinched. First, the tense wrinkles stamped across his forehead suddenly disappeared. He pried his eyes away from Zuuox and turned them to his frightened wife. Puulu met his gaze with a mixture of relief and fear. She watched as Muusamali nodded his head in an obvious gesture of approval for what Zuuox was suggesting. But Puulu was hesitant as she stared at Muusamali in disbelief. Again, Muusamali nodded and attempted to put on a half-hearted smile to assure his wife that he was confident in his decision.

Puulu gathered her posture by taking a deep breath. She turned to Zuuox and, without further hesitation, eased her tiny hand forward placing it inside Zuuox's giant grasp. Zuuox bowed his head at Puulu's feet. As he held Puulu's trembling hand, he recited the Cuuzan warrior's oath of obedience . . . directing it to the unborn prince and future king of the exiled Cuuzan who, at the moment, resided in the belly of Puulu. Zuuox added a special emphasis as he pledged his life and service to the yet-unborn king to include the royal family as a whole.

The entire oath took less than two minutes. As Zuuox rose to his feet, he released Puulu's fragile little hand as gently as he could. His faced remained set-in stone. But as his eyes met Puulu's, she noticed a sparkle of tenderness and a look of sincerity which gave her a jolt in her stomach.

Zuuox turned to Muusamali. Briefly the two exchanged looks. Both wanting to avoid the other, their eyes drifted apart. Zuuox scanned the satisfied faces of his comrades before he looked upon the hilltop where King Nuumyu stood peering down at him. The king's expression couldn't be read from that distance, but, somehow, Zuuox was confident that the king was more pleased by his surprise actions than he was disappointed.

Everyone's attention was focused on the hilltop. All eyes were fixed on the king, and not a word was spoken. After a hushed moment, King Nuumyu turned and gracefully started to descend from the hill.

As if the king's departure from the hilltop was some silent signal, the singing suddenly commenced, and the sound of thousands of stomping feet filled the air. It was a perfect mix of soft thunder and swelling, blended voices. The crowd rocked from side to side, gracefully slid into a dance step, and sang in soulful harmony: "Farewell, my beloved, forever you'll be missed." The soul-stirring accord created a marching rhythm that aroused Muusamali and his clan of exiles into action.

Slowly, the 130 exiles began to pick up and move out following Muusamali's, Zuuox's, and Puulu's lead. The exiles moved reluctantly, but they all knew they had to go. The stimulating rhythm produced by the singing and foot stomping was much-needed fuel for their emotional engines and was driving them forward.

The exodus made their way slowly across the border and headed out into the open plains. The singing masses inched forward behind them, swaying from side to side and keeping with the dance step. The scene of ebony bodies ceased their onward advance at the border. They stood and watched, continued to rock from side to side, still involved with the beat and motion of their dance. They sadly and tearfully watched the exiled clan depart. They sang even louder. "Farewell, my beloved, forever you'll be missed."

As Muusamali and Zuuox walked along, they set the pace for the procession of ox-driven wagons, domestic cattle, livestock, women and children, and the thirty-five hardened and unhappy warriors.

Puulu was joined now by two women. They walked at her side waiting to attend to her every need and were several steps behind Muusamali and Zuuox. Puulu watched as the two men turned their heads to each other and allowed their eyes to meet. Silently, without missing a step, Muusamali and Zuuox held each other's gaze for several minutes in a thoughtful fixation. As she watched, Puulu could feel the energy pulsating from both men. Not some malignant, ill-intentioned force. Rather, a breaking down of tension which produced a certain sense of benevolence between two old friends and comrades. As children, they had been the closest of friends until power, ambition, and duties associated with tribal politics came between them. And the strained circumstances surrounding the exodus weren't helping matters any.

But now, as they trekked across the barren African plains headed toward uncertainty, they both had the presence of mind to realize and accept the fact that, as leaders of the tribe, they had a responsibility to set aside their differences and think in terms of the tribe's survival.

Zuuox, who secretly knew about the true clandestine nature of the exodus, held a certain reverence for Muusamali which he didn't dare divulge. In Zuuox's view, only a brave man would willingly sacrifice his hard-earned reputation and good name by accepting such a disgraceful mission. Muusamali didn't deserve disgrace. In fact, Zuuox wanted to reach over and pat him on the back. But for the mission to be successful and to carry it out exactly as the king wished, Zuuox was forced to keep what he knew a guarded secret. Zuuox could never reveal his knowledge about the mission without it becoming known that he eavesdropped on the king's conversation with Muusamali. This was a dishonorable act which Zuuox would not be able to live down.

Muusamali thought about Zuuox's unprecedented move at the border. It revealed a part of Zuuox which Muusamali didn't know existed. Zuuox displayed a gift of foresight and shrewd diplomacy which only his renowned battlefield prowess could match. Muusamali understood Zuuox's move for all it was worth, all the subtle, far-reaching implications. As commander-in-chief of thirty-five warriors, Zuuox had the burden of not only maintaining a macho image but also fulfilling a duty to keep the morale up among the warriors to ensure the tribe's safety and harmony as a people.

For the moment, Muusamali was content with Zuuox's decision to swear his allegiance and that of the other thirty-five warriors to the unborn prince. It allowed Zuuox to save face in the presence of his peers and, indirectly, gave Muusamali kingship in a nominal sense. Muusamali had the good sense and patience to leave well enough alone . . . for the time being. But if Zuuox really figured that Muusamali would actually accept the figurehead role of king of the tribe once the child was born, be it a boy or a girl, then Zuuox was as naive as he was shrewd.

Five days into the exodus, a man-child was born to Puulu and Muusamali. Muusamali was somewhat dismayed that the child turned out to be a boy. The birth of a girl would have entirely nullified the validity of Zuuox's border move. Puulu, as any mother, was impartial about the infant's sex. But knowing her husband's ambitions and how determined he was to be rightfully recognized as king of the tribe and to rule without sharing the king's throne with their infant son, she empathized with her husband.

Puulu, faithful wife that she was shadowing her husband in everything he did and felt, pretended that her hopes would also be dampened if she gave birth to a boy. But on the morning of the delivery, that all changed.

It was in the early-dawn hours as the sun was just starting to rise in the sky. Puulu lay on her back panting and still in some pain, yet she also felt a pleasant and most welcomed relief. The baby had been born! She was staring at the heavens when she caught sight of the morning star, the only one still visible in the clear, first-light sky. Such a tiny sparkle in the midst of endless space—all alone—sparkling and shining brightly as if it were fighting for its very existence, she thought.

Muusamali lay down beside her and cradled their newborn in his arms for her to see. The child was kicking his small feet and waving his wee arms—but was otherwise as quiet as the dawn itself. As quiet as the last remaining star in the morning sky.

"Look over your shoulder, my husband, up in the sky," Puulu said with a warm radiance about her. Muusamali pulled the infant gently to his chest and followed his wife's gaze. He recognized the phenomenon in the sky, the sun just barely peeking its nose over the horizon and the last star in the sky still glowing brightly as ever. Such a sight occurred frequently on clear mornings such as this. Puulu turned to look upon her dear baby. "You are my son. My sun!" she said and quickly added, "I wish to name our child Tuuwee, which means 'morning star.'"

There was rejoicing and celebration among the exiles over the birth of Morning Star. They slaughtered a lamb, prepared a feast, and danced the day and night away on the great open plains of the Bomu. If not for Zuuox pledging his allegiance to the yet-unborn prince at the border crossing, he would have been much more elated with the birth of his first son. As it was, at best he seemed to be "fatherly proud" by Tuuwee's arrival. However, he was clearly annoyed at the constant attention Zuuox showered on the child.

The Cuuzan exiles' quest was to reach a certain land called Halmahera. It was located on the far northern side of the Sudd Swamp. Halmahera was legendary for its vast unexplored rainforests. It was thought to be far out of reach for the white and Arab landgrabbers in that it had no valuable minerals which attracted the wealth-seekers from Europe and Asia.

More than anything, the Cuuzan exiles wanted to find a land they could homestead. If necessary, it was not beyond the warriors' nature to infiltrate occupied territory, conquer the weak, and dominate the area inasmuch the same way as their forefathers had done through their violent penetration and aggressive takeover of what was currently Cuuzanland.

To reach Halmahera, the exiles were prepared to make an arduous journey straight through the heart of the deadly Sudd Swamp. The Sudd was said to be a two-hundred-mile ordeal.

After three days on the plains of Bomu, crossing the great canyon area, they came to the jungle rainforest region called Kinshasa. Kinshasa was a vast tropical paradise separating the hot, dry hell of the Maradi Plains to the north. According to some tribes, Kinshasa was another name for "hell's well." Other tribes like the Gatooma pygmies called it the "garden of the gods."

The Kinshasa region was a lowland basin, surrounded by the upland Bomu and Maradi plains. The Kinshasa jungle, like the Sudd Swamp on the northern end of Maradi, was the recipient of flood waters during the rainy season. The waters would drain down from the Maradi Plains in the north and seem to overtake the land. Sometimes the entire Kinshasa jungle found itself covered with three feet or more of water, for weeks on end. Slowly it would recede, leaving behind a large lake filled to overflowing. The lake was called Runyum, after the goddess of plenty and a deity worshipped by the Gatooma, a pygmy tribe in the region.

The Gatooma pygmies have a belief about Kinshasa's hot climate. They claim that the floodwaters which drain off the Maradi provide "hell's well" with the necessary moisture to keep it from bursting into flames.

Unlike the Sudd Swamp region, the Kinshasa jungle teemed with exotic tropical fruit trees, a cluster of which sat just to the west of Lake Runyum. To the east was an area of thick green vegetation and palm fronds so dense with growth that the Gatoomas dug caves into its thick green walls. A massive tunnel network was also fashioned, which ran like interconnecting mazes to all portions of the surrounding jungle. The tunnels were especially plentiful in one particular area to the west. Here they were used by the Gatooma pygmies as escape routes into the dense and remote jungle where secret underground hideaways were located upland.

As the exiles entered the Kinshasa jungle, Zuuox and a party of two dozen warriors ventured off to scout the area. They quietly crept up on Runyum Lake and encountered a group of naked Gatoomas basking in the sun, munching fruit, and playing water games in the lake. Upon spotting the Cuuzan intruders, they dropped what they were doing and ran straight for the getaway tunnels hidden inside the thick walls of jungle brush.

Not all the Gatoomas ran away. Those who didn't soon saw that Zuuox and his comrades were not raiders but merely thirsty travelers who were looking a drink of water and not a fight.

Zuuox and his scouting party were able to gain the confidence of the docile group over a short period. Within hours, a friendship developed. And in a week's time, the Cuuzan exiles were living among the Gatoomas as if they had been friends and neighbors for years.

The Gatoomas' main source of food was a fish called the mudskipper, monkey meat, fruit, nuts, and vegetables. Kinshasa was a land of great abundance.

To the Cuuzan, a warrior clan from a land where territory was often obtained by force and protected by means of constant warfare with neighboring tribes, the Kinshasa natives were the friendliest, most peaceable people they had ever encountered. They never dreamed such people existed. The kindly nature of the pygmies disarmed the Cuuzan and forced them to confront their own deep-seated desire to live a simple, carefree existence.

It was soon understood that the one drawback to the jungle paradise, and the only force the natives feared, was the same force which had driven the Cuuzan from their homeland—European and Arab slave hunters who periodically ventured into the area in search of native blacks who might be easily taken and enslaved. The Gatooma pygmies, however, were not an easy prey although they were a nonviolent people and wouldn't fight unless cornered. Their first line of defense was to avoid any visible threat. If that was not possible, they would run away, either straight into the swamp or into the maze of tunnels which had secret passages leading into the swamp. The maze had other tunnels, decoy shafts not so generous to the passersby, rigged with deadly booby traps for unsuspecting pursuers.

Deep inside the swamp interior was the natives' second line of defense. Numerous underground bunkers had been installed, scattered far and wide in secret locations on the high-altitude enclaves. The natives would crawl inside the bunkers and remain there until the threat had passed. This run-and-hide philosophy worked well against the white slave hunters who avoided the severity of the swamp region. But occasionally, black mercenaries would be hired by the slave hunters to pursue the fleeing natives with bloodhounds all the way to the underground bunkers. The greedy mercenaries foolish enough to corner the natives at their bunker would find themselves stonewalled and bombarded by a storm of poisonous darts from the natives' blowguns. The blowguns, long and hollowed-out portions of bamboo, were used as a weapon to hunt monkey and other small animals. But with their backs to the wall and the sound of the bloodhound in the air, the natives, in protecting their women and children, would have no other recourse but to break out their poison darts and fight both man and dog to the bitter end. This end was usually demonstrated by the man, more dead than alive, dragging himself and his dog out of the swamp. Dogs hit by a dart would die from the poison after a very short while. Men, however, with healthy bodies and constant care, could potentially survive the deadly fever but could also easily lapse into an irreversible coma.

The jungle paradise of Kinshasa was also frequently visited by other outsiders such as the Cuuzan who utilized it for its natural usefulness in providing freshwater and nutritious fruits and vegetables. Arab merchants, caravanning from the east, made Kinshasa a favorite stopping point for rest and relaxation on their way to and from the marketplace at Timbuktu. Desert tribespeople of the northeastern Sahara made yearly trips to the Runyum Lake during the drought season. These desert nomads would show up with caravans of camels loaded with water barrels and waterskins. The Kinshasa natives would help the weary travelers tend to their camels and fill their water holders.

The severe flooding that occurred every year was what made Kinshasa unattractive for homesteading and for farming crops. The native people who chose to live there were content with their life and their home around the swamp. They were simple hunters, killing only what was required to feed their families each day. They had strong family ties and lived a carefree life.

Muusamali found the natives' lifestyle to be an important asset to his group, who were not at all accustomed to nomadic life. To the Cuuzan's credit, they learned quickly and easily. They made a smooth transition from herdsmen and farmers who occasionally went on a hunting expedition to full-scale hunters who had to hunt to eat.

In mingling with the pygmies, the Cuuzan warriors improved upon their one-dimensional hunting skills, and the women learned new ways of homebuilding and housekeeping. By nature, the Cuuzan warriors were spear hunters who had perfected the age-old technique of running down game, such as antelope and zebra, in teams out on the open plain. They were now learning methods of trapping wild boar, shooting monkeys out of the trees with blowguns, and tracking big cats in the jungle terrain with nets made from woven fronds and brush.

Zuuox and the other warriors provided meat and skins in abundance for the whole clan. They were zealous hunters and kept the Cuuzan women busy skinning, cleaning, and cooking the animal meat. The women prepared and cooked their meat every morning and every evening. The surplus, which was plentiful, was dried and stored, and, when traveling merchants came through on their layovers, the Cuuzan traded meats and fruits for exotic spices and other rare delicacies, many of which they were sampling for the first time. The women also put to good use the abundance of animal skins. They learned from the Kinshasa native women how to build portable homes out of the hide and leather. They quickly learned how to make leather tents which allowed for quick dismantling and easy carrying.

All the while the Cuuzan were sojourning with the Kinshasa natives and learning their new, beneficial skills on how to live like them, they kept alive their yearning to reach the "land of promise," the land on the other side of the Sudd Swamp.

Eight months passed quickly. Winter brought the heavy rains. Massive flooding began once again as sheets of water rolled down from the Maradi and Bomu uplands to carpet the floor of Kinshasa. The Cuuzan exiles said their goodbyes to the Gatooma pygmies, whose yearly migration took them west into the hill country of the Bomu. The Cuuzan set out to the north in their quest to cross the Sudd Swamp in search of the land called Halmahera.

Their expedition took them across the Maradi Plains, a grassland region with sloping hills, scattered trees, and many roaming herds of wildebeest, zebra, giraffe, and antelope. The trek across the Maradi took a day and a half, at which point they reached the Sudd Swamp region of the infamous Sudd. They journeyed to a region of the swamp which took about a day to reach. The area was densely populated with giant Reseda trees. Their thirty-foot-high branches were littered with moss, which blocked out most of the sunlight. The floor of the area was two-thirds water, while the other third was dotted with islands of dry ground which, in those places where the sun shone through, consistently produced lush green growth.

The Cuuzan exiles settled on one of the bigger islands, intending to stay only for a short time. They were still of a mind to go in search of their utopia farther north on through the Sudd Swamp.

During their sojourn inside the Sudd, the Cuuzan met and befriended yet another breed of nomadic tribespeople, swampdwellers, masters of the no-man's-land who had long ago fled their original dry homeland, surrendering it to the Arab forces that swarmed into East Africa from Asia.

These swampdwellers had a lot in common with the Cuuzan exiles. They chose to flee their homeland rather than stay and risk being annihilated. But the swampdwellers had taken their choice one step further in determining not to place themselves on any valuable property. They did not want to be confronted by enemies or wealth-seekers, forcing them to fight or be killed, or to be once again challenged by the greedy. So the swampdwellers elected to live in the Sudd among poisonous snakes, man-eating insects, and crocodiles, where nothing of real value existed. Living in this way, they reasoned, would not attract the murderous landgrabbers that had already driven them from their East African homeland.

The Cuuzan exiles adapted well to the swamp thanks to these swampdwelling tribes who were just as open-minded and hospitable as the Kinshasa natives. The swampdwellers eagerly taught the Cuuzan all the secrets of swamp survival just as the Kinshasa natives accustomed them to jungle life.

The idea about going in search of some utopia was put off year after year. For a decade, the only journeying the Cuuzan did outside the swamp was their occasional two-day trek to the Kinshasa jungle. During that first decade, the Cuuzan made yearly hunting trips in Kinshasa. The Gatooma pygmies, however, began to go into hiding for long periods of time. They would surface out of necessity only to hunt and to transport water back to their secret dwellings. The reason—like all fertile areas on the African continent—the Kinshasa paradise was eventually sniffed out by fleeing refugees and other exiles escaping the all-out onslaught of European and Arabian invaders.

Several greedy warrior clans of Africans who discovered the Kinshasa jungle enclave didn't believe in mutual sharing. They refused to respect anyone's right to the water hole during drought seasons. They were prepared to fight and indeed, more often than not, did so.

The Foliose warriors were one such clan. Pushed out of their central region homeland by European expansion, they settled on the Bomu Plains and began monopolizing Kinshasa as their personal garden and freshwater well. Soon, other warrior tribes with aggressive mentalities moved into the area and an unending struggle for domination of Kinshasa ensued.

Kinshasa became a battleground where only the strongest and fiercest clans dare come. Whenever two tribes met in Kinshasa, they fought each other.

The Gatooma pygmies refused to be driven from their homeland. However, they were forced to adapt to the lifestyle of hermits, hiding from everything except their own shadows. They even avoided their friends, the Cuuzan.

The Cuuzan, being self-sufficient on their swamp island refuge, didn't have to rely on the Kinshasa Lake as did the desert-dwelling tribes of the Northern Sahara. The Cuuzan could afford to forego their yearly migration to Kinshasa. But nevertheless, Zuuox and his comrades were not to be denied an occasional visit to the lake during hunting expeditions.

The Cuuzan warriors were adequate fighters, and whenever they visited Kinshasa, they came in such large numbers that any other tribe in the area avoided provoking them into a fight. But any visitors whose numbers were small were forced to stand their ground and fight. The skirmishes were often severe but were rarely fatal encounters. Using spears, shields, and battle clubs, the wannabe users of the water hole would engage in battle with whichever group was standing guard over the area on any given day. They were quick to oppose all comers. The combatants would engage in conflict until either one group or the other gave up and ran in defeat or until members of the visiting group managed to fill their waterskins while still managing to fend off the other's attacks. Once the skins were filled and ready for travel, the fighting would cease. The verbal attacks, however, could go on and on. Each group would shout death threats and warnings to the other that the next battle would be their last!

Over a period of nineteen years, the Cuuzan exiles made a complete social transition from dry land farmers to swamp-dwelling hunters. They didn't, however, deviate one iota from their religious dogma or ritualist practices.

The Cuuzan were a very spiritual and highly ritualistic people. They paid homage to five demigods, along with their principal god, Cuuz. During their favor-asking rituals, the Cuuzan slaughtered live animals to appease their god and demigods. The status of the god being solicited, or the size of the required favor determined how large or how small the sacrificial animal would be. The mightier the beast, the greater the favor.

The Cuuzan's ritualistic ceremonies were a one-man exhibition centered around the one particular dance priest performing at the blood altar with a live beast. The spectacles were nighttime affairs performed under a full moon and by the light of huge bonfires. The ceremonies were loaded with all the trappings of a magic act and conducted with high emotion and spellbinding fanfare of well-trained, charismatic dance priests called the Huzza.

There were five dance priests among the Cuuzan. Each carried the sacred title of Huzza doctor. These Huzzas were looked upon and revered as divine agents of the gods, blessed with the mystic ability to communicate the people's wishes and needs to the deities.

Huzzas were chosen by divine appointment at birth, accompanied by unusual signs in the sky coupled with strange and unusual phenomenon on earth during the time when certain pregnant women were in labor. The chosen infant was trained by the reigning Huzza. Every Huzza had one or two of these chosen infants under his wing who remained the protégé of his master until the master's death or removal from office.

There was a Huzza doctor who healed the sick and fought off evil spirits with fresh blood using an esoteric dance routine. He was Ruuski, one of the eldest of the elders in the tribe. Zuuox, chief among the ranks of the warriors, also held the title of Huzza doctor. His sacred dance routine and act of slaughtering a wild beast at the sacrificial altar was meant to appease the war god, Cuu-ba, for special blessing prior to going into battle.

There was Muutus, the Earth Huzza, who danced in the fields among the crops and offered blood to the earth in exchange for a plentiful harvest. The all-important, favor-asking ritual sacrifice, and most spectacular ceremony of them all, went to the supreme deity—the Sun god Cuuz. To the Cuuzan, the sun was the all-prevailing symbol and manifestation of omnipotence. It was the totality of god's power touching everything and blanketing the entire earth with life-sustaining energy. The sun was the source, the Cuuzan considered, which gave them their beautiful black skin. In fact, their very name was derived from it, meaning "children of the sun." The duty of paying homage to Cuuz, this most awesome of powers, was allocated to the Chief Huzza, King Muusamali, and his protégé the crown prince . . . young Tuuwee.

Tuuwee was barely nineteen years old when his father and mentor, Muusamali, called upon him to conduct his very first ritual ceremony. It was to be a solo performance. The occasion was the most important sacrificial rite of them all. It held monumental significance in Tuuwee's life. This was an important step which Zuuox and some other elders considered too much too soon for Tuuwee. Failure could damage Tuuwee's self-esteem and be disastrous toward his image among his peers and tribespeople. Yet on the other hand, if Tuuwee succeeded in putting on a good performance so early in his life, the result could catapult his popularity and boost the people's confidence in his ability to be king.

Muusamali had insisted that this was Tuuwee's year to garnish his body with flashy decorations and animal skins. He was to adorn his face with ceremonial paint and be thrust into the spectator arena with a live, full-grown hyena.

The ceremony took two weeks of preparation. Zuuox and the other warriors traveled all the way to the Maradi Plains where they tracked and captured a 190-pound spotted hyena, then transported it alive and kicking back to their swamp island.

Meanwhile, the women prepared the arena, turning the village square into an elaborate outdoor theater. They built a sacrificial altar, a wooden 10' × 15' platform mounted six feet off the ground and installed on wooden stilts. A twelve-step stairway led up to the platform's stage where the waist-high altar table sat in the center. The altar was covered with animal skins and furs.

The moon was full, making for a clear, heavenly spring night in the swamp. The Cuuzan island village was filled with the sounds of merriment. The entire tribe was out in cheerful force, assembled in a wide circle surrounding a dozen or so female dancers kicking up dust and giving a seductive tribute to Cuuz.

The women's naked bodies were richly decorated in blue body paint. Their wrists and ankles were adorned with fluffy fur bands. These women strutted and danced to the beat of the bongo drums, hollow drag sticks, and maracas. The musicians were seven young boys sitting in a circle facing each other. Each was moving his body and bobbing his head to their own soulful rhythm.

The men were standing on the sidelines stomping their feet to the beat and cheering the women on, as these same women had done to them earlier. The men had just finished their tribute to Cuuz. This consisted of a spectacular stick fight dance in which a dozen warriors, with their faces painted blue and bodies garnished with blue chalk, paired off and did mock combat. This was all done in keeping with the beat of the drums. They moved in unison to the slow, intense dance routine. Their ceremonial weapons were ornate and beautifully sculpted pieces. The spears, brilliantly painted in blue, gave off a florescent glow as they sliced through the air. Their shields, also decorated and immaculately polished, were embellished with colorful, artistic portraits of hawks, eagles, and other magnificent creatures of the wild.

The village square was engulfed by the light of seven huge bon fires spread out in a wide circle surrounding the outer-most perimeter. Large torches were mounted on tall poles and burned throughout the village.

Off in the distance, sitting all alone like a hangman's gallows waiting for the crowd to deliver up its victim, stood the six-foot wooden platform which held the sacrificial altar of Cuuz. Three men were seen busily attending to the richly decorated structure. An old man was supervising two youngsters. The young men were carefully placing tiny sticks of firewood inside four large black kettles. The kettles were mounted on poles overhead, each atop one of the four pillars supporting the platform. The sticks were of a special type—from the Kasa tree—which, when cured with a certain incense and set on fire, gave off a sweet-smelling aroma which was thought to delight the gods and persuade them to be open-minded and agreeable to the will of man.

The women dancers were the last act before the main event: the sacrificial offering of the beast. The hyena, the primary event, was secluded inside a canvas-covered cage which sat in a darkened corner in the near distance. For days, the wild hyena had been fed plenty of fresh meat and put through vigorous scrimmages of teasing and cruel goading. This was all done in an effort to fatten him up, make him a ferocious force to be reckoned with, and a most worthy prize for the almighty Cuuz.

The dance festivities were winding down as the altar platform was being prepared for Tuuwee's emergence from the hut where he was being readied for what was yet to come.

Puulu, Tuuwee's mother, was present, along with one of his stepmothers, Nuufy. Of course, Zuuox, the chief warrior, and Kuula, Tuuwee's cousin and best friend, were also there.

Tuuwee was standing on his feet in the center of the brightly lit hut. His long slender legs spread wide. His muscular arms were hanging by his side and extended outward from his body. Tuuwee's entire frame had become a human canvass covered with a blue chalk and water mixture. Zuuox, exhibiting one of the artistic skills for which he was so renowned, spent hours transforming his human canvas into a masterpiece of finger art. Using only his fingertips, Zuuox carved up Tuuwee's body into bold vertical and horizontal patterns than ran over his body like a maze of broken railroad tracks.

Tuuwee had been deadly silent throughout the arduous process. He was mentally occupied, playing out in his mind's eye his upcoming dance routine and barehanded bout with the beast, all in successful sequence according to his training. He was about to put years of training into actual practice and all too soon as far as some people were concerned. He was scared to death—frightened of failing, frightened of dying—yet still anxious to get out there and prove himself.

"Tuuwee, you look better this year, your first, than did your father last year which was probably his fortieth year conducting the ceremony," Kuula said from his place at the door. Occasionally Kuula, who was a robust twenty-year-old warrior, would crack open the door and peer out into the night toward the sound of the drums and the excitement taking place in the village square. He was both watching and waiting for the female dancers to finish.

"He looks better than any Huzza priest has looked, all painted up, since we departed our beloved homeland and settled here in this mosquito's nest." Puulu joined in from the corner of the room where she was sitting on a stool covered by a large leopard-skin cape draped over her lap. The cape was part of Tuuwee's costume, and Puulu was grooming it to bring out more of its shiny luster. She continued to stroke the hide with her brush in one hand and swat mosquitos with the other.

"Your son looks wonderful in his paint, I admit. But our husband, the king, is in a league of his own. He is king, after all, and the king has no equal. Has everyone in this room forgotten that?" Nuufy remarked with a stern look on her pretty young face. She was going about her task patrolling Tuuwee's body. As her searching eyes would discover a mosquito, she would carefully sneak up on it with her thumb and forefinger, plucking the pesky insect from Tuuwee's frame without disturbing Zuuox.

No one answered Nuufy because everyone in the room knew she was incapable of keeping any criticism of Muusamali to herself, and to speak so highly of Tuuwee was to criticize the king. So for a short while, they all remained silent, preoccupied with their own thoughts.

Zuuox went about his work on the final stage of creating his masterpiece on Tuuwee's face. It was a handsome face, a broad nose, full lips, and prominent cheekbones which served to highlight his deep-set eyes. Those eyes would gently rest their gaze upon you yet, even in their softness, would seem to penetrate your very soul.

At 6'2", Tuuwee stood shoulder-to-shoulder with Zuuox. He was not quite as wide and meaty as Zuuox's 235-pound frame. Tuuwee was leaner and more wiry and his upper torso muscular. His shoulders were square and his legs long like a creature born to run.

"There," Zuuox announced as he stepped back and marveled at his handiwork on Tuuwee's face, painted deep blue with yellow zebra stripes. "You are ready to knock the gods' dead!"

"Mother!" Tuuwee turned to Puulu and held out his arms for her to view his body's canvass. "Cuuz will be pleased," Puulu answered, letting her hands rest in her lap. Her face revealed her total fascination as she added, "The young ladies will be falling down with desire." Puulu was speaking about the fact that a painted warrior was an irresistible attraction to a Cuuzan female. Among other rituals, the warriors used paint when courting the women of the tribe. To charm prospective wives, warriors donned their bodies with breathtaking artwork and pranced before the particular lady of interest for hours—even days—until he was chosen.

"Oh stop it!" Nuufy shouted as she stood up and swatted a mosquito from her arm. "The important thing is for Tuuwee to give a flawless performance tonight. That's what will please the gods. And if he isn't perfect"—Nuufy paused and looked directly at Tuuwee—"the hyena will chew him up and the gods will express their disappointment by punishing us all!"

"Okay, okay, everybody out except Tuuwee and me," Zuuox said. Tuuwee stared back at his stepmother with open contempt. Instead of speaking, he revealed a toothy grin as he gazed deep into Nuufy's eyes. Apparently Tuuwee knew what would work best to irritate his father's youngest wife. And true enough, Nuufy stomped her feet and abruptly stormed out the door. Kuula, as he held the door open for her, gave her the same smile. In response, Nuufy put her nose in the air and quickly hurried out.

Puulu stood up and, holding the cape in one hand, reached up with the other and placed her palm on the side of Tuuwee's ear. Barely touching his body paint, she said, "Pay no mind to a jealous heart."

"I will show her and my father what a flawless performance is," Tuuwee grumbled back, sure of his own abilities. "Of course you will," Puulu replied and then handed Tuuwee his cape. "I have all the faith in the world in my son." With that, Puulu smiled and turned away. She waved her goodbyes to Zuuox and, as she was about to go through the door, she turned and touched Kuula on the arm and then left.

As he closed the door behind her, Kuula looked at Zuuox. Zuuox stepped over to the young warrior's side as Kuula continued almost defiantly, "I wish to stay with Tuuwee up until he enters the arena, Zuuox!"

"I know, I know," Zuuox answered calmly as he placed a hand on Kuula's broad shoulders. "But I have a much more important task for you. As Tuuwee's trusted and most loyal companion, I want you to go out there and be our eyes and ears. When the hyena is removed from its cage and is tied to the stake, Tuuwee and I will be depending on you to double-check the rope knots and make sure no one touches them after your final inspection. Do you understand?"

Kuula looked over at Tuuwee, who nodded his head in agreement then said, "Save a seat for me!"

Kuula smiled at his cousin then turned back toward Zuuox. "I won't let Tuuwee or you down," he whispered. With those words, the tall lanky warrior slipped out the door.

Zuuox held the door open for a moment as he listened to the sound of bongo drums, tambourines, and drag sticks kicking out their soulful rhythm. Judging by the beat, he knew that the time was fast approaching for Tuuwee to make his entrance.

Zuuox hurried over and took the leopardskin cape from Tuuwee's hand and said, "Come." As he walked over to the table in the center of the room, Tuuwee followed. There he picked up a small leather pouch. Carefully, Zuuox spread the cape out onto the table revealing a large square pocket hidden inside. Slowly, Zuuox untied the drawstring on the pouch. He then held the mouth of it open for Tuuwee's inspection. As Tuuwee leaned forward, examining the contents, Zuuox said, "This is your blind dust. I will empty some of the dust from the pouch into the cape's secret compartment," and Zuuox began pouring the fine, granular dust into the hidden pocket. "Halfway into my dance, I grab a handful!" Tuuwee offered. "No," Zuuox said flatly. "You don't just grab a handful like a bumbling anteater digging in the ground. You must 'will up' the fox in you and use the grace and cunning of the fox to finesse the dust from the hidden pocket into your hand. No one in the crowd must see you, not even me. Remember, Tuuwee, it is very important that the tools you use remain out of sight. A Huzza's tools are instruments of the gods. They are secret agents to be used only by the chosen and not meant to be seen by anyone except another Huzza."

Zuuox picked up another pouch, loosened the drawstrings, and turned it upside down. A ring and a small wooden valve fell onto the table. Zuuox picked up the ring. It was large and bulky and held a breakaway cap at its center. Zuuox held the ring between the fingers of his one hand, using the other to open the cap. Once opened, it revealed a razor-sharp blade about an inch long and shaped like a miniature pyramid.

Zuuox reached down and picked up the corked wooden valve. Sticking the cork between his teeth, he twisted the valve free from its confines. With the ring in his right hand and the valve in his left, he dipped the blade of the ring into the wooden valve. He carefully pulled the ring free and once completed, it was covered with a poisonous sap called urucu. To the natives, urucu meant "waking dead." Just a tiny amount in the bloodstream had the potential to render the 190-pound hyena unconscious.

Zuuox held the ring in the air about eight inches from his lips. He began to blow on its point. Soon the wet sap dried into a white film, coating the pointed pyramid blade.

Calmly Zuuox replaced the cap over the blade at the ring's center and turned to Tuuwee, who had been watching Zuuox's every move. "Wait until the last minute before you uncap the ring," Zuuox said as he slipped the ring on Tuuwee's right finger. Tuuwee knew exactly what to do. As he admired the ring, he took his other hand and slowly turned the ring over so that the cap concealing the poison was positioned toward the palm of his hand. "The longer you keep the cap on, the less chance you will have of sticking yourself with its point. The urucu poison is very strong. And the hyena is a large, very strong beast. So, you must be careful of both the hyena and the poison."

Zuuox picked up the cape and gently draped it over Tuuwee's shoulders. Zuuox stepped around Tuuwee and now stood in front of him. He took hold of two leather straps attached to the cape's collar and slowly began to secure it around Tuuwee's neck. Done, Zuuox stepped back and looked over his work. Zuuox was pleased with what he saw, and Tuuwee was elated at the satisfied look in Zuuox's eyes. All of Tuuwee's life, he strived to meet Zuuox's approval, more so than any other elder of the tribe including his own father. But Tuuwee realized his exquisitely decorated body at which Zuuox marveled was all Zuuox's doing. The test of Tuuwee's masculinity was still to come.

"Thank you, oh mighty Cuuz," said Zuuox as he began the Cuuzan prayer to the supreme god. As Zuuox paused, Tuuwee picked up the next verse and looked fondly into Zuuox's eyes. "For blessing me with life, health, and wisdom this day as in yesterdays and every day still yet to come." Tuuwee paused and Zuuox continued, "And thank you, great Cuuz," he said, stepping over and putting a hand on Tuuwee's shoulder. Together they walked toward the door and continued to recite the prayer in unison, "For allowing me the strength and courage to be a brave warrior and worthy protector and provider for our beloved tribe, this day as in yesterdays and in every day still yet to come. And please, oh mighty Cuuz, continue to protect me and guide me through life. And I promise to protect and respect your divine presence which is in my soul and everywhere upon the earth.

"In the name of all the mighty Cuuzan warriors before me and their great deeds, I too remain in your service, your child under the sun."

The hyena was fitted with a leather muzzle and spirited from the cage by a dozen warriors. It was tied between two stakes which had been hammered deep into the ground. The stakes were positioned at the base of the stairs leading up to the altar platform. The platform was alive with four fires burning incense wood inside large mounted kettles.

Several strong ropes extended from each of the stakes and were attached to the hyena's neck and midsection. The ropes were drawn tight thus keeping the hyena on its feet in a stationary position between the two stakes which stood less than seven feet apart. The leather straps were removed along with the muzzle, giving the hyena full freedom in its powerful jaws.

Kuula was the closest person, standing near the disgruntled hyena. The hyena's head was down, and an angry hump was visible on its back. It watched the goings-on with red, bloodshot eyes and was growing more irritated and enraged by the minute. The tribespeople of Cuuzan, close to 150 adults and 50 or so children, kept their distance. The one exception was a few young boys who occasionally tried to tease the hyena with sticks and rocks, only to have Kuula chase them away with his long spear.

The crowd of eager spectators were painted for the occasion and wore their favorite jewelry and best animal skins. They were awaiting the main event and had formed themselves into a gauntlet of sorts. Two rows of clustering bodies stood facing each other, permitting a ten-foot-wide isle to run between them. Sixty yards stretched from the altar platform where the hyena stood to Zuuox's hut which sat in the dark, just on the fringe of the village square.

The drums and drag sticks were kicking out a slow, steady beat as the two rows of spectators clapped their hands and rocked back and forth on their feet. As one row would sway to the right, the other rocked left. Their gleeful black faces displayed shiny white teeth which beamed at one another across the man-made aisleway. They waved happily at one another and shouted playful remarks.

Some members of the crowd sang a soft chant, the words of which beckoned for the appointed Huzza dance priest to come forth and represent them before the great god Cuuz.

Tuuwee emerged from the hut with Zuuox at his side. Everything, the drums and drag sticks included, came to a standstill. Tuuwee froze in his tracks. The painted glory of his towering muscular form stood motionless. Suddenly he was afraid. The sight of more than a 150 staring faces all focused on him was unnerving the first time out. Tuuwee felt the beads of sweat bursting forth on his brow, and the moisture from his underarms was great.

Tuuwee looked up the aisle of black faces and staring white eyes and saw where the hyena waited for him, angrier than before. Then Tuuwee looked to the left of where the hyena was positioned and saw Kuula, who was still at his post, waiting until the last minute before abandoning his assignment.

The sight of Kuula had a way of settling Tuuwee's jitters. Tuuwee could make out enough of Kuula's face to detect a smile of confidence, such as only Kuula could give. All the other faces staring at him appeared to be dead serious and waiting for a tragedy to occur.

As Tuuwee watched Kuula in the distance, he took a moment and recounted a time when they were young boys together, playing a dangerous game of chicken in the Swamp Lake, a lake infested with crocodiles. It was a game not meant for those with slow feet or weak nerves. The dare was to race across a shallow portion of the lake, from one bank to the next, without being bitten by either crocodile or poisonous snake. Snake bites were the most frequent injury but, in general, were as common as the "common cold" in the Sudd Swamp. Crocodiles . . . they were another matter entirely. They had the ability to snap off a leg with one bite. That's what made the game so daring for Tuuwee, Kuula, and the other boys, all ranging in age from seven to ten at the time.

Usually it never failed, but a crocodile would charge after the intruders venturing to cross their lake. Tuuwee remembered his first dare. He stood alone on one bank, and Kuula, with six other boys, stood on the other side watching him, waiting for the tragedy to happen. Even then, Kuula stood apart from the rest in his facial expressions and physical size.

The lake was only three feet deep at the upper end where Tuuwee was to make his run. But in areas toward the center, the soft mud was capable of slowing a crosser's momentum or causing him to fall.

From bank to bank there were some seventy yards of shallow water to cross. The closest crocodile was twenty yards away on a dry mound near the center of the lake, basking in the sun. Already, several other crocodiles just on the other side of the mound in deeper water were slowly swimming their way toward the shallow side where Tuuwee was poised to cross.

"Hurry, Tuuwee, before the crocodiles get a jump on you!" Kuula cautioned from the other side. Kuula had already braved his crossing several days earlier and had given Tuuwee a detailed description of what to expect and where the lake's soft spots were.

Tuuwee took a deep breath and lit out across the lake like a bat out of hell. He didn't remember touching the floor of the shallow water—that's how fast his little feet were traveling. And how numb his mind was from fear.

Tuuwee reached the other side in one happy piece. It was obvious that he had beaten Kuula's time. Kuula had held the fastest record prior to Tuuwee's run. Yet it was a jubilant Kuula who was the first to race over and embrace his cousin. The other boys soon joined in patting Tuuwee on the back. Tuuwee was amazed at his own foot speed. He was overwhelmed with the feeling of triumph, so much so that as the others jumped up and down and shouted his glory, Tuuwee turned away and raced back into the water. He was well on his way to the other side once again, when the others looked up and saw him.

Again, Tuuwee was so quick on his feet that the crocodiles didn't bother to give chase. But as Tuuwee reached the other bank, he was bitten on the leg by a venomous snake, and for a week he was in bed with a high fever and diarrhea.

Tuuwee's recounting of that triumphant occasion on "crocodile lake," minus the last-minute snakebite, was a confidence builder. Coupled with the sight of Kuula standing near the hyena, Tuuwee suddenly found his lost resolve which he had worked so hard to put in place prior to leaving the hut.

Tuuwee heard Zuuox's whisper, "Cuuz is with you." With that, he relaxed his body and felt the earth's electrifying presence beneath his bare feet. He raised his head to the sky and gazed into the full moon, allowing its pulsating energy to penetrate his entire being. The mental image of an eagle in flight overwhelmed him. A sense of knowing that he was one with the earth and the moon engulfed him. And as this power of earth and moon flowed through him, giving him power to become an earth unto himself, Tuuwee slipped into a deep trance which brought him into perfect harmony with the eagle in his spirit.

With the crowd looking on in silent awe, Tuuwee griped the edge of the cape with both hands. Suddenly, and with a quick burst of intensity, he threw his arms into the air, spreading the capelike wings. He then lunged forward and raced up the aisle with his cape flying in the air behind him. He ran straight toward the hyena. The crowd quickly broke ranks and closed the aisle behind Tuuwee, cheering and clapping as they formed their half-circle.

The hyena became hysterical as Tuuwee approached, snarling and bucking wildly. The ropes contained the hyena's movements as Tuuwee came to within a few feet of its snapping jaws before pulling up and stopping. Tuuwee's sudden halt brought the hyena to a pause. It stared at Tuuwee with angry, bloodshot, death-defying eyes enraged by the possibilities in front of him. Tuuwee's own expression as he glared at the hyena was intense, hinging on savagery to match the animal's own magnetism.

The crowd grew quiet as it assembled into a horseshoe formation around Tuuwee, the hyena, and the altar platform. The drums and drag sticks struck up a beat, and Tuuwee started to move. Like a man possessed, or in a dream, Tuuwee began dancing to the rhythm of the drums, all the while looking at the hyena as though it were his only audience.

Tuuwee and the hyena were the main attraction. Tuuwee was the focal point of every breath his audience took. His dance routine was considered enchantment in motion. He was expected to put this testy hyena to sleep using only the hypnotic power of the magic dance, an esoteric dance known only to the Huzza.

The first five minutes, Tuuwee warmed to the hyena, dancing slowly before it as if it were a delicate object of seduction. He was graceful and his every move demonstrated his intense feeling of the moment. He seemed to be one with the drumbeat. Yet his body glided effortlessly with each stroke of the drag stick.

As the dance wore on, Tuuwee's intensity escalated, causing murmurs of wonderment to spread through the crowd. As Tuuwee danced, his entire focus was centered upon the hyena, and, in turn, the hyena followed Tuuwee's every move, his steely eyes fixed upon him in fascination.

Tuuwee's motions grew slowly wilder, though still a graceful yet controlled version of a wild fling. As he kicked up dirt coming out of a triple spin, the crowd gasped in appreciation, an indication of its approval.

Tuuwee danced his way closer to the hyena, his arms and legs snapping vigorously to the rhythm of the drums. The hyena snarled angrily at him. Tuuwee was undaunted and continued his dance even closer than before.

Tuuwee stared in the hyena's face for several minutes, waving his hands in front of it, tasting its reactions. The hyena snapped at Tuuwee's hands, and Tuuwee took mental notes at how far the ropes allowed it to lunge. It was important for Tuuwee to know how much play was in the ropes.

Tuuwee backed off from the hyena and began executing a series of acrobatic leaps and turns, showing superb agility. He would run in a wide circle leaping high into the air and spin while yet airborne. This was all done in synchronization with the beating drums. His high-flying routine gave him the control to push the crowd further back, away from the hyena. It worked magnificently. Each time he came out of an airborne spin-around, he landed right at the feet of those in the front row of his well-pleased spectators. This would invariably cause them to loudly gasp and back up quickly, driving the spectators at the rear back further as well.

At one point, Tuuwee landed in front of his father, who was standing with his arms folded, his entire body draped with animal skins. Those in the front row flanking Muusamali, including both Puulu and Zuuox, quickly backed up. But Muusamali took his own sweet time. He was now left alone standing close to three feet in front of the others. As Tuuwee's dance routine carried him toward the center of the arena, Muusamali turned his back on him and slowly walked over next to Puulu where he resumed his original position. Zuuox, standing several feet away on the far side of Puulu and Nuufy, watched with keen interest.

It was time for Tuuwee to reach into his bag of tricks to take his dance to its climax. Tuuwee aligned himself square with the hyena. There was some twenty-five feet of open space between him and the waiting animal. The crowd held its collective breath, anticipating some daredevil stunt. The drums and drag sticks subsided. Tuuwee was breathing hard and sweating profusely. He threw up his arms, gripping the capelike wings. He raced toward the hyena, pretending he was an eagle swooping down upon its prey. Tuuwee stopped five feet from the hyena and leaped high into the air. His momentum carried him smoothly through the air as the cape beat the wind behind him. As he landed, he dropped to one knee, all in a single motion, and dared to push his face to within inches of the hyena's jaws, jaws which were making vicious attempts to reach Tuuwee's head. The crowd was awed by his bold display of courage and showmanship.

Tuuwee kept his face to within inches of the hyena's sharp teeth and crushing jaws. Each time the hyena snapped at his nose, he felt the beast's hot breath on his face and the disgusting moisture from its spittle. This was the time when Tuuwee was supposed to pull back. But instead, he held his death-defying pose some moments longer than usual—longer, in fact, than any veteran Huzza priest would have done. The crowd was spellbound, dreading that any moment one of the ropes would give way and Tuuwee would have his whole face mangled.

Tuuwee continued to kneel with his nose before the hyena, facing the onset of the inevitable. He kept his focus on the next task at hand. Carefully and slyly, he reached his left hand inside the secret pocket of the cape. He grabbed a handful of the finely powdered blind dust. Removing his hand, he was supposed to make his move to blow the fistful of the powdered dust into the hyena's eyes. And as the dust rendered the hyena momentarily blind, Tuuwee would be afforded the opportunity to utilize the poison-tipped ring on his right hand and reach in and nick the hyena on its neck. With the poisonous concoction in the hyena's system, it would take only a matter of minutes before it was rendered unconscious—unconscious but still very much alive. Meanwhile, Tuuwee would dance before the hyena in his most seductive fashion. As the hyena slowly succumbed to the effects of the poison, it would appear to the spectators that Tuuwee's dance was the real magic which put this wild, ferocious beast to sleep. Afterward, the unconscious hyena would be carried up the stairs and put onto the altar. It was then that Tuuwee would bring the ceremony to its climax by slitting the hyena's throat. He would then present a cup of its fresh, warm blood to Cuuz, the almighty, as a gift offering.

Tuuwee had conducted the ceremony in a most superb fashion up to this point. No one, not even his father Muusamali, could doubt that Cuuz was not completely satisfied with Tuuwee's dancing, Tuuwee had given the kind of dance tribute which would compel the gods to grant any favor the tribe asked. Having such ability and charisma to give the appearance of pleasing the gods through dance is what made kings and Huzza priests great in the minds of the tribal people.

It was said that an overly gifted ability on the part of the king's son to please the common people with his ritual dance would occasionally promote the son to king before his appointed time. And Tuuwee was obviously of a mind to do just that. Instead of following through with the practiced script of throwing the blind dust into the hyena's eyes, Tuuwee abruptly rose to his feet. With the dust powder gripped tightly in his fist, he began dancing once more. The drummers quickly caught on and provided him with their forceful beat.

Zuuox, knowing that Tuuwee had deviated from the routine they had rehearsed so many times together, took on a worried expression as he watched from his place in the front row. Muusamali, on the other hand, standing several feet down from Zuuox, displayed a look of renewed interest. As he watched, a devilish smirk played on his lips.

The rest of the crowd looked on with sure confidence. They felt Tuuwee was in full control of this situation. But little did Tuuwee's beloved tribespeople know that he was operating more on reckless emotion than intellectual calculation. Tuuwee wanted to prolong the ceremony, perhaps to make his father eat his heart out with envy. Or perhaps Tuuwee was simply just too caught up in the feelings of triumph and glory to slow his winning role.

Whatever the motivation, Tuuwee continued another five minutes before surrendering his dance and positioning himself before the hyena. This time, Tuuwee was standing within three feet of the hyena, and he threw up his arms without raising the cape. As he stared down at the hyena, Tuuwee's entire body began to shake. All this was done in keeping with the beat of the drums. Tuuwee kept his fist raised high in the air, in triumph! He took one step forward and then another, as though he were some trembling mechanical robot. His eyes remained fixed on the hyena. The closer Tuuwee got, the more enraged the hyena became. It shook and twisted violently against the binding ropes. One break in the rope, a slipped knot, would mean the hyena's snapping jaws would be close enough to Tuuwee to do major damage. Yet Tuuwee stood there for some moments, exposing his vulnerability to the hyena's sharp teeth. Then, abruptly, Tuuwee stopped his movement. The drums ceased and the crowd fell silent.

With his arms and legs positioned spread eagle before the hyena, Tuuwee began to drop ever so slowly to the ground. As he came to rest on his knees, he brought his hands down into his lap. Tuuwee kept his eyes fixed on the hyena's eyes. They were to be his first target, the unsuspecting recipient of the blind dust which he clutched in his left hand. Once completed, Tuuwee would uncap the poison-tipped ring and proceed with the most dangerous phase of all: slipping the ring past the hyena's jaws and forcefully puncturing the hyena's neck with the poison.

The hyena was crouched in a stalking position, watching Tuuwee with its head bowed and the hairs on its back standing on end. Its lips were curled back exposing its sharp fangs. There was less than fifteen inches now between Tuuwee's face and the hyena's waiting jaws. As Tuuwee steadily grew closer, the hyena growled and became more menacing and aggressive than before.

It was essential that Tuuwee get as close to the hyena as possible to blow the dust powder from his hands into its eyes. He used the cape to shield his clandestine activity from the watching audience. As he hunched his shoulders high in the air, he carefully and discreetly brought his left hand up to his mouth. The hyena made a lightning quick lunge at Tuuwee's hand. The crowd gasped in terror. But the ropes tightened and held, causing the hyena's snapping jaws to stop short of Tuuwee's hand by mere inches. Tuuwee hardly blinked. His nerves and reflexes were like cold steel against the hyena's feeble attempts.

At the same moment, the hyena settled back into its deadly crouching posture to await its next opportunity, Tuuwee felt his opportunity had arrived. Quickly, he opened his fist to blow the dust into the hyena's eyes. He was shocked at what he discovered. Because of all his activity and sweating, the dust powder had turned into mud in his hands!

Tuuwee's brain went dead. He stared at the muddy goo in horror and disbelief! Out of sheer desperation, he kept his outstretched hand lingering in front of the hyena's face. More out of reflex than thought, he aimed his hand toward the hyena's eyes and blew into his hand as hard as he could. The caked-up powder didn't budge. But his motion in doing this carried him closer to the hyena than he planned. That was all the hyena needed. It lunged toward him and clamped Tuuwee's little finger in his mouth. Its sharp teeth severed the member cleanly and quicker than a blink of the eye.

It all happened in an instant. Tuuwee experienced very little pain. It was the blood and eerie coldness which Tuuwee felt at the place where his warm finger had once been that brought the realization to him of what had occurred. Tuuwee seemed to have slipped into a state of forced denial.

Suddenly, Tuuwee leaped to his feet and began dancing once again. The drummers quickly provided him with a beat and Tuuwee continued as though all was well.

The surrounding tribespeople, unaware of Tuuwee's injury, looked on in amazement. The crowd was astonished at his stamina. He had been dancing passionately for some time. The crowd was equally gratified by Tuuwee's eagerness to please them. This made them even more unsuspecting of the mishap which had just taken place.

However, there were several others in the crowd of onlookers, such as Zuuox and Muusamali and other high priests, who knew all the aspects of Tuuwee's dance routine. These elite members were aware of his injury from the start. Nevertheless, for the most part they stayed calm out of respect of Tuuwee's responsibility to deal with any situation which might arise.

Tuuwee danced with renewed intensity, intensity which was lacking before. He didn't appear to be conscious of his missing finger even though blood was gushing forth like a waterfall.

As though drawn by a powerful magnet, Tuuwee danced his way over to where his father, Muusamali, stood. Positioned directly in front of him, Tuuwee's movements grew wilder. He danced as if he were dancing "at" Muusamali instead of "for" him. As wild and violent as his movements became, he was still graceful, methodical, and perfectly in step with the rhythm of the drums.

Tuuwee's and Muusamali's eyes were locked, compellingly so, as if by some bewitching force. Muusamali stood tall and erect, his arms crossing over his chest. His head remained slightly bowed, giving his bloodshot eyes the appearance of staring at Tuuwee from over top of his thick eyebrows. Those eyes were almost as fierce as the hyena's!

Tuuwee danced closer and closer to Muusamali. His dance continued to grow more and more intense, like graceful violence in motion, seductive rage about to explode. By this time, the audience had become both nervous and spellbound. Tuuwee taking his dance suddenly before Muusamali's face, or, as the audience saw it, "in the king's face," was a nightmare unfolding.

Zuuox became uneasy and began a slow sidestep maneuver, working his way along the front row of spectators toward Muusamali.

Tuuwee was dancing four feet in front of Muusamali now, and it became apparent to everyone that Tuuwee was indeed seriously injured. Red blotches of blood now dotted his body's artwork, and his full hand and wrist were colored crimson. Drops of blood, as he waved his hand through the air and continued his body motion, flew through the air and managed to land on Muusamali's arm. Muusamali, however, didn't budge. He continued to lay-in-wait, watching Tuuwee's every move with his sharp, patient eyes. An arrogant expression of defiance marked his face, a fearless look which bespoke his confidence in his ability to defend himself from anything or anyone.

The look in Tuuwee's eyes as he danced was that of an angry and immature young man, a young man possessed of a menacing and misguided impulse of dire proportions. He brought his right hand up to his mouth where he clinched the ring between his teeth and bit off the guard cap. The razor-sharp tip, laced with its poison, was exposed. Tuuwee managed this in one smooth motion, all the while keeping perfect rhythm to the soulful beat of the drums and drag sticks.

Suddenly, Muusamali raised a hand in the air, and the drums ceased. This brought Tuuwee to an abrupt halt, and he stood silent and limp, both hands hanging by his side. He stared at his father with hate-filled eyes. Muusamali was undaunted, and he met Tuuwee's gaze with an inflamed expression of his own.

Tuuwee was mad enough to strike his father with the poison-tipped ring. He wanted so badly, but somehow, without the sound of the drumbeat and the dance to keep his adrenaline flowing, Tuuwee's whole body suddenly grew very tired. His arms were as heavy as logs. His left hand, hanging freely by his side, was discharging blood at a frightening clip. The surrounding onlookers remained silent, watching in awe and waiting for the reaction of their king, Muusamali.

Tuuwee felt as though he was a worthless failure, a failure with no strength left to move his arms. The feelings plaguing him were only compounded by the fearless and almost casual expression stamped on Muusamali's face. At that moment, realizing he was helpless to react, he wanted nothing more than to turn his back on Muusamali. But Muusamali's eyes were like a powerful vacuum sucking out the last portion of energy from Tuuwee's weakened body.

In desperation, Tuuwee willed his legs to turn and walk away. But they failed him miserably. As he tried to leave, his legs gave out and he dropped to his knees. His upper torso remained erect, but he wavered from side to side as though in a drunken daze. He fought valiantly to stay conscious, but the effects of the blood loss were slowly closing the blinds on his senses.

Tuuwee's upper body suddenly titled forward, sending him crashing to the ground, facedown.

Zuuox carried Tuuwee's limp body in his arms to Puulu's hut. As he gently laid him into bed, Tuuwee began to gain consciousness. He found it difficult to focus his eyes and to readjust his mind to the present. But one look into Zuuox's face and he was able to relax while still shaking the cobwebs from his mind. Slowly, the dreaded details of the ceremony drifted into focus.

"I failed before the eyes of the people, Zuuox!" Tuuwee said as he stared at the mud-brick ceiling. Tuuwee didn't want to look at his maimed bloody hand to which Zuuox was busy tending, applying a tourniquet to his wrist.

"No one failure will deem you less a man, Tuuwee. The true test of a man is his ability to gain strength and wisdom from his failures. And life will present you with many more misfortunes to test your manhood. So do not dwell upon this minor one."

"But now I have only nine fingers to deal with future trials, Zuuox. The beast did manage to take one finger, did he not?"

"Yes, my prince. Only one and the littlest one of the lots."

"Good." Tuuwee sighed, slowly closed his eyes, and drifted off to sleep.

No more than a minute had passed when Tuuwee heard the voice of Ruuski, the Huzza doctor, as he entered the room. Puulu and Nuufy entered behind him. Ruuski approached Tuuwee's bedside and immediately began barking orders about gathering sewing needles, boiling water, and making sure the poker was red hot.

Tuuwee's heart began pounding in his chest. His forehead grew moist with perspiration. He tightly closed his eyes, dreading the look upon the old, hardened Huzza doctor's face and his tools of pain. Suddenly, Tuuwee felt both of his arms and legs being gripped. He was being pinned securely to the bed and was helpless to move. He opened his eyes to find Zuuox holding his wrist while Puulu and Nuufy each held a leg.

The old Huzza doctor stood over him holding a large leather sack which was open at the mouth. Without warning, Ruuski bared down on Tuuwee, slipping the mouth of the sack over his head. Tuuwee knew not to panic. He was well acquainted with the procedures being implemented against him. He was being sedated with chiluk, a strong herbal concoction used by the Huzza doctors as a sleeping anesthetic. Chiluk produced a painful stinging sensation upon initial contact with the nostrils, which was why it was necessary to pin Tuuwee down. The inside of the leather sack was coated with chiluk, and it would remain over Tuuwee's head so that he could breathe the fumes continuously while Ruuski operated on his hand.

Tuuwee went through a moment of violent convulsions as Zuuox, Puulu, and Nuufy struggled to keep him down. Finally, he settled and then consciously relaxed his body and began breathing deeply. He was finally allowing the chiluk to freely take hold and he welcomed its numbing effect. A sensational feeling of serenity swept away all his pain and anguish. A sweet, blissful peace overwhelmed him, and the thoughts which earlier tortured him were thankfully gone.

From his newfound high seat of awareness, Tuuwee discovered an overwhelming perception of power. A strange sense of being one with the whole sum total of all that existed consumed Tuuwee's consciousness. He suddenly realized that he wasn't just the morning star, as the name which his mother gave him indicated. Tuuwee now felt that he was the morning itself! He was one with the source of all light, the sun. He was not some reflection, neither in space, time, nor on the earth.

As the chiluk's super invigorating influence increased, Tuuwee's self-esteem skyrocketed. His imagination went wild, and suddenly he realized that he no longer wanted to be a humble prince of an exiled tribe living in a swampy hellhole at the end of the world.

Tuuwee began to see a vision in his mind's eye. He was standing atop a high altar platform overlooking a great multitude of Cuuzan natives, one hundred times the number living in the swamp. Standing on the platform with him was the real king of the Cuuzan, ruler of the motherland, Tuuwee's uncle King Nuumyu. The occasion marked the traditional passing of the king's crown. The retiring king, Nuumyu, was anointing Tuuwee the new king and ruler of Cuuzanland. Tuuwee also received the king's blessing, a sacred honor reserved for the king's most favorite son or nephew.

Tuuwee's vision coincided with a certain prophesy of Zuuox's. Several times Zuuox had told him that he was destined for greatness in a faraway land. He said that Tuuwee's destiny was linked to the motherland.

As Tuuwee's vision turned cloudy and sleep slowly crept in on him, he promised himself that someday he would surely go in pursuit of his true destiny, in search of the greatness of which Zuuox had prophesied. Doing this, of course, would mean violating tribal law and breaking his father's strictest decree forbidding anyone from attempting to advocate desertion. If anyone were caught in their attempt to quit the clan and return to the motherland, the penalty was death!

Tuuwee finally succumbed to the effects of the powerful anesthesia of the chiluk potion. Hours after the crude stitching operation on his hand

and the removal of the chiluk sack from his head, Tuuwee still hadn't regained consciousness. Ruuski worked frantically around the clock trying everything he knew to bring Tuuwee back. He even used the assistance of his young Huzza protégé Cuunga. Ruuski and Cuunga put on a noisy, all-night vigil. As Ruuski danced and chanted loudly, Cuunga pounded the congo drum in Tuuwee's ear.

All of Ruuski's efforts were to no avail. Tuuwee laid in a coma for two days and two nights. There was no predicting how much longer he would remain suspended in time, lingering between life and death. The chiluk was much like the herbal concoction urucu. Both were very effective in serving their primary purpose. But the dangerous side-effects were very obscure. Although the secret formula for making the chiluk had been passed down through the elite ranks of the Huzza priests for untold generation, no Huzza had succeeded in smoothing out all its flaws. And given the complexity of making the chemical's components, making and harvesting certain mushroom fungus, and fusing several varieties of herbs and roots along with certain snake venom and insect larva, no sure recipe could possibly be drawn. Nothing could ensure the consistency of the chiluk's effect on the fragile human nervous system. The creation of a chemical antidote was never even attempted by any of the former Huzzas. Thus, Ruuski's noisy remedy was the only game in town.

The success rate of the chiluk was high enough; nine out of ten people awakened within minutes after the sack had been removed from their head. That was why the Huzza doctors so readily gambled on the treatment. Even when complications set in, such as Tuuwee's present condition, the coma would normally last one day. A week was the longest Ruuski could remember anyone staying under the chiluk's spell.

Tuuwee laid on his back in a bed positioned in the center of the spacious hut. Puulu and Nuufy stood quietly in one corner, while Zuuox and Kuula remained like two statues in another. Several candles gave the room an eerie cast. Cuunga sat on a stool with a drum between his legs several inches from Tuuwee's head. The boy looked fatigued as he continued to pound his measured beat. Ruuski stood over Tuuwee with a large ostrich feather in one hand and a ring of bones, dried shells, and animal teeth in the other. Tuuwee had a zebra hide draped over his lower body, while the remaining portion of his naked torso was covered with a shiny ointment. Ruuski ran the ostrich feather up and down Tuuwee's body. At the same time, he shook the noisy ring of bones in Tuuwee's face.

Muusamali hadn't paid a visit to his son's bedside the entire time. Then, on the third night, he and a warrior named Suubala showed up at the front door of the hut. Muusamali, customarily overdressed in his catskin outfit and carrying his white-bone staff, stepped lively into the room following Suubala's lead. Everyone in the room turned their attention toward him. Everyone, that is, except Cuunga, whose head was hung to his chest half-asleep. Cuunga's hand would slowly raise barely a foot above the drum wedged between his legs. Then it would fall lazily back down to hit the drum with a dull thump. It took him quite some time to repeat this procedure over and over again. Ruuski had to tap the young man on the shoulder before he realized the king was in the room and he snapped to alertness, acknowledging his presence.

Muusamali barely glanced at Tuuwee before he then turned and looked at Ruuski and asked, "Has my son not come around yet?"

"Not yet, but we are working on him. He could regain consciousness any minute now," Ruuski answered with a straight face."

"You sound sure of yourself," Muusamali replied.

"On only one occasion did I lose a patient, and she was sixty years old with a gangrenous leg which I'd just removed. I'm sure she died from loss of blood and not the chiluk." Ruuski paused and waved his ostrich feather over Tuuwee's motionless body. He went on, "I've had patients sleep for seven days and nights like this. And I still managed to bring them back to full consciousness, and in the best of health. Yes, I am sure that Tuuwee will recover any minute now."

"Good," Muusamali said. "Your expertise and service are needed elsewhere. Suubala's wife is having hard labor. I'm sure you were told, yet you fail to make your presence known."

Ruuski looked over at Suubala. Someone had told an untruth. Ruuski's expression was that of shock. Suubala returned the look with one of indifference. Ruuski tried to shake it off as he said, "I did pay a visit to Suubala's hut and examined his pregnant wife." Ruuski paused to tone down his voice, which was becoming increasingly agitated. He realized he was excited and talking much too loudly. Suubala's rank among the warriors was second only to that of Zuuox. But his status and influence with the king was second to none. To talk down to Suubala was to show disrespect for the king himself.

In a submissive tone of voice, Ruuski continued, "I found Suubala's wife to be stable and far from being in any danger. Besides, the two midwives are quite capable of dealing with her hard labor. Kolara and Idris are the same midwives who successfully delivered not one, but two of your oversized, spirited bucks," Ruuski said, smiling in an effort to make light of the situation. However, no one in the room looked amused, least of all Muusamali, who shot back, "Kolara herself is an old woman and not up to the task. And Idris is fatigued from too many sleepless nights. Your services are required."

With that, Muusamali turned his back on Ruuski, Zuuox, and Kuula and headed toward the door. Suubala rushed ahead of him reaching the door first. He swung it open and allowed Muusamali to pass through.

But Zuuox's thundering voice froze Muusamali in his tracks. "Ruuski's services are required right here!" Muusamali kept his eyes fixed on Suubala as he asked in an excruciatingly slow manner, "I take it that was Zuuox who spoke?" Suubala, looking over Muusamali's shoulder directly at Zuuox, nodded.

"Ruuski," Muusamali snapped, "I have spoken on the matter. Now take heed." Before Ruuski could answer, Zuuox spoke up. "No, you take heed! Ruuski shall not leave this place until the prince has awakened."

In a burst of fury, Muusamali spun around on Zuuox. He glared at Zuuox saying, "And how will you dare try to stop me when I proceed to drag this old man out of here by his heels?" "It will not be with words, my king." Zuuox answered, looking Muusamali square in the eye.

Suddenly, from another corner of the room came the cry, "What are you doing?" Puulu stepped from the shadows and faced her husband. "That's my only child laying near death. Whether you know it or not, I hang by the very same thread of life as does he. If you allow Tuuwee to die, you will kill me as well. For this I swear, I will kill myself the minute his heart stops beating."

Muusamali stared at her with a look of complete disbelief. His favorite, most devoted and obedient wife was actually speaking out of line and, worse yet, speaking against him.

Muusamali searched her face for some sign of rationality. All he saw was a defiant urgency in her expression. Her eyes revealed a deadly earnest. Those eyes, usually calm and warm, were now passionate in their plea. Muusamali had never seen Puulu this way. He was spellbound. The room was so quiet that Suubala's heavy breathing could be heard in the corner where Zuuox and Kuula were standing.

Kuula displayed a worried expression for both Tuuwee and Puulu. Puulu was his aunt. Muusamali's twin sister was Kuula's mother and Kuula was torn. Puulu had just committed one of the worst offenses against a husband. And not just any husband but the king himself! Kuula pitied her and feared he was about to witness Puulu's great suffering. There was nothing he could do but hope that the king spared her life.

Zuuox's pity was felt in another way. He feared that Puulu would suffer the worst punishment Muusamali could muster. And all because of him. But Zuuox had no intention of standing by and watching the inevitable. His head was already on the chopping block by standing up for Tuuwee. If it was his destiny to lose his head to Muusamali's axe for that infraction, then it mattered not what else he did or said.

But Puulu had ideas of her own. And they didn't necessarily involve her or anyone else meeting a disastrous end. Her main objective now was to prevent a deadly fight between Muusamali and Zuuox. Puulu trembled with fear as she felt Muusamali's piercing eyes bore through her with a sharpness equal to his spear. Even so, she mustered enough strength and self-control to keep a straight face and steady voice.

"God and the great spirits are guiding my actions. A mother's love for her one and only child is something you wouldn't understand, my husband. You already have seven children by your other wives. And you, dear Suubala, you have more than that!"

"Eight," Suubala bolted out with pride. Then he dropped his eyes to the floor, embarrassed by his sudden outburst.

"Please, my husband," Puulu went on in a pleading, insistent tone, "Ruuski is Tuuwee's only hope of waking. Do not take him from our dying son to go and sit with a pregnant woman who is no stranger to giving birth. I beg you to walk out of here the way you came. Do not start a fight that would likely be the death of Tuuwee and others. If you grant me this one request, I would be willing to make a vow. In the event that Suubala's wife should lose her child because of Ruuski's absence, I pledge an oath that I will—"

"No!" Muusamali snapped. His left hand sprung up like a striking cobra but landed as softly as a butterfly. Two of his fingers met Puulu's lips, gently freezing the words in her mouth. "Say no more," Muusamali warned in a chilling voice. He leaned his burly face closer to Puulu's perfectly molded petite face. "From this day on, you hold that careless tongue until I tell you to rattle it or I will cut it out and feed it to the chickens. Is that clear?"

Puulu's heart winced with dread. She knew Muusamali's wrath could be swift and deadly if he were pushed too far. She nodded her head in agreement and closed her eyes, not knowing what to expect next.

Muusamali turned away from her and faced Zuuox. The two men, each with burning hostility for the other, fearlessly held each other's gaze. Neither flinched, and both appeared ready for a physical confrontation, a confrontation they both craved yet had avoided for twenty years. Each had determined to outlive the other naturally, without gambling on the unpredictable outcome of a physical duel which, by tradition, would be fought with their most select weapons. The result of such a dispute would mean the death of one or the other or both of these valiant men.

"I declare you responsible, Zuuox," Muusamali thundered, waving his bone club back and forth. "While Ruuski resides in this room and refuses to leave, I hold you personally accountable for any mishap which might befall Suubala's wife or unborn child." With that, Muusamali turned and stormed out the door.

Suubala hesitated just a moment. He and Zuuox exchanged looks of mutual respect and an unspoken comradery which warriors felt for their own kind. For the most part, Zuuox and Suubala were rivals, forcibly pitted against each other by virtue of Muusamali's shrewd scheming. Muusamali shunned Zuuox, the number one warrior, and openly courted Suubala, the next bravest and second most renowned warrior of the tribe.

Suubala, in granting Muusamali his soul, had in essence alienated himself from Zuuox and most of the other warriors who were his childhood friends. About two-thirds of the warriors vehemently refused to acknowledge any authority above their chief commander, Zuuox. The other third, allied with Suubala, believed the king's authority was paramount.

Several elders in the tribe, along with Suubala and his followers, considered Zuuox to be trouble. In secret, they believed his move at the Cuuzanland border crossing some twenty years earlier, when he pledged his warrior's oath to Tuuwee while still in his mother's womb, was a clever, long-running scheme to rule the tribe through the prince when he came of age.

Everyone except Suubala was genuinely apathetic toward the Muusamali-Zuuox feud. The tribe would hardly be affected, one way or the other, whether Muusamali continued to rule or Zuuox managed to catapult Tuuwee to the throne. The tribe would likely always remain a close-knit community.

As the two hardened warriors stared at each other, Suubala gave Zuuox his most loathsome expression. Zuuox responded with one of animosity and antagonism. Without a word, the two old friends turned their backs on each other at the same instant. As Zuuox turned and faced the wall, Suubala made his way out the door. Ruuski, Puulu and even Cuunga breathed easily once again.

Meanwhile, seven days later . . .

A thunderstorm had been steadily raging. High water carpeted the greater portion of the swamp. This was the second night of the rainstorm. The Cuuzan village, which sat on island high ground, plus a well-dug drainage system running throughout the village, ensured it would be virtually flood-free.

The villagers felt the fury of yet another of nature's elements gone amok. Fierce tempest winds! The angry gusts blew through the village at speeds that would have been a hurricane if not for the intermittent period of sudden calm when only gentle rain fell on the mud huts. Then, without warning, the tempest would return, slamming the rain violently against the hut where Tuuwee lay still motionless on his back. The rain sounded like a barrage of rocks hammering down on the soft earth. It was during one of these bursts of tempest winds and rains that Tuuwee's eyes suddenly flew open.

Puulu was seated on a stool at the side of Tuuwee's bed stringing a piece of hide using the light of a solitary candle to ease her work. Puulu brightened with excitement as Tuuwee's hand slowly reached out and touched her arm. The hand he used was the one maimed by the hyena. It was unbandaged, and the crude stitching performed by Ruuski gave it a gruesome look. But without hesitation, she immediately took the hand in hers and brought it to her lips. She kissed it and lovingly held it next to her cheek. Tears rolled from her eyes, and she looked at Tuuwee with an expression of thankfulness which only a mother could feel with such warmth and earnestness.

"Mother, you're crying. Why?" Tuuwee whispered in a weak and shaky voice. His eyes were cloudy, but his mother's relief was more than visible to him. "Your mother cries with happiness. I have my son back. You were gone from us for many days and nights." Tuuwee looked puzzled. He ran his tongue across his dry, chapped lips. "May I have a drink of water, Mother?" Tuuwee asked as he stared at the ceiling remembering the awful incident with the hyena and Ruuski's old and ugly face bending down upon him.

Puulu was on her feet in an instant. "Yes, yes of course. You must be terribly thirsty. I will awaken Ruuski at once."

"No, Mother!" Tuuwee said. "I can manage without Ruuski. Just bring me some water, please."

Puulu thought a second, smiled, then turned and walked toward the corner of the hut where a skin pouch filled with water hung against the wall.

The rain beat steadily against the hut, with the sounds of rushing winds and distant thunder echoing in the distance. Tuuwee had always been frightened of thunderstorms. It was the one childhood boogeyman he couldn't quite shake. But now, all of a sudden, he realized that he wasn't bothered in the least by the storms raging outside.

Tuuwee watched the soft flame from the candle. Each time the wind rushed and the rain pounded down upon the hut, the tiny dancing flame would shrink bringing the room to near darkness. This should have made him cringe, if not cover his head in dread.

Tuuwee remembered a wild and furious thunderstorm when he was a small boy. He had been frightened with his first encounter with lightning and had quickly left the confines of his parents' hut. He had raced some sixty yards through the pouring rain, lightning, and gusty winds to reach Zuuox. Just six years old, Tuuwee didn't bother to knock; he just burst into Zuuox's hut catching him and his wife bear-hugging in passionate intercourse.

Tuuwee stood there in the open doorway, wind and rain raging behind him, staring at Zuuox. Zuuox and his wife, panting and drenched in sweat, stared back at Tuuwee for a long moment.

Finally, Zuuox climbed from his bed, walked up to Tuuwee, and said in as patient a voice as he could muster, "You should be in your own hut."

"But I'm afraid!" Tuuwee responded.

"Then be afraid in your own hut," Zuuox replied as he put a gentle hand on the boy's shoulder and turned him around toward the open door. "Will you send me back out into the storm, Zuuox?" Tuuwee asked.

"You will only be in the storm for as long as it takes to get from here to your own hut," Zuuox said as he placed a hand on Tuuwee's back, "so run fast!"

Loud crashing sounds of thunder echoed in the heavens and rocked the earth below. Flashes of lightning streaked through the darkened sky. Tuuwee took a deep breath and, as the roll of thunder subsided, Zuuox gave him a gentle yet forceful push propelling him into the wind and rain. Tuuwee ran through the darkness as fast as he could. He managed to outrun the thunder and lightning, reaching his hut before another strike. But that night and during many other such thunderstorms, he slept beneath his bed.

Now, as Tuuwee lay on his back listening to the sound of rolling thunder explode over his head, he was unmoved and not the least bit afraid. He was amazed at his own calm behavior. He tried to rise up to meet the cup of water being offered him by his mother. But he discovered that his body was much too weak to obey his mind's command. Puulu had to sit on the edge of his bed and lift his head as she slowly fed him the cup.

"More," was Tuuwee's quick response before barely clearing his throat of the first swallow.

"My, how thirsty is my boy," Puulu said, jumping up to fetch more. Tuuwee was famished, but his lack of fluids was even more overwhelming. He wanted to tell his mother to just bring him the whole water pouch.

But he respected the fact that mothers were delicate creatures, and he was willing to tolerate her fragile handling.

While Puulu's back was turned, Tuuwee raised his hand to look at the damage the hyena had done, as well as Ruuski's handiwork in making the repairs. He turned his head away in disgust, letting his hand fall free. It landed on the edge of the bed a little too hard, and it exploded with pain. Shock waves of nausea and agony went through his body. He would have screamed had it not been for the fact that his mother was turning toward him with yet another cup of water. He forced himself to rise up and hurriedly take the cup from her before the need to scream overtook him. He brought the cup quickly to his trembling lips and gulped it down while, at the same time, swallowing his agony. Tuuwee did not want to see his mother cry anymore over his pain and grief.

"Your father will be pleased to know of your recovery," Puulu said as she pulled her stool close to the bed and sat down. She added, "And Euurus, the sweet girl. She has been worried sick about you and has been insisting on seeing you. But dread not. I fought off her pleas at every turn. And not once have her eyes seen you laying there on your back near death. No future bride should witness her husband-to-be in such a helpless and weak state. The prince on his sick bed shouldn't be seen by anyone. I made sure only Ruuski, Zuuox, Kuula, and Ruuski's young helper Cuunga were permitted in the room. That's Cuunga sleeping over there on the mat. Poor boy was so exhausted that he didn't have the will to go home to his own hut. Of course, Ruuski wouldn't have left this room for any reason until I finally insisted he go home and get some much-needed rest. Zuuox and Kuula are both sticking their heads in the door every hour on the hour to check on your progress."

Tuuwee came to a sitting position on the side of the bed and swung his feet to the floor. Blood rushed to his head as he fought against standing up. Puulu reached out for him as he wavered from side to side. But he quickly gathered himself and stood erect.

"I'm fine, Mother," he said shunning her helping hand. "Just let me be." Tuuwee wanted nothing more than to be left alone with his thoughts. He recalled fragmented memories of just before going to sleep and longed to revisit that frame of mind. But his mother's small talk about marriage to Euurus kept him from it. While the thought of Euurus was soothing to his soul, the idea of settling into a marriage and family was quite disturbing. Strange, because prior to Tuuwee's long sleep, marriage to Euurus was the largest upcoming event of his life—that and his engagement with the king's crown upon his father's death.

Tuuwee had, essentially, died for those four days, remembering no dreams, feeling only a sense of emptiness toward all his yesterdays and a curious new expectation toward his tomorrows. Marriage was the farthest thought from his mind, the least of his expectations. In fact, his mind was consumed with compelling thoughts of escape from his swampy prison, of returning to his true homeland of Cuuzanland.

First, Tuuwee wanted to escape his mother's babble and search out Zuuox to engage in some serious exchanges. But Puulu was in his ear and was continuing her dialogue. Painfully, he focused on her words.

"You don't look well, Tuuwee," she said with a concerned look. Tuuwee had lost nearly half of his body weight during his ordeal. "Maybe I should waken Ruuski?"

"Never mind Ruuski, Mother. I'm fine," Tuuwee said as he looked sideways at her. "And please, Mother, call me Cuuh!"

"What?!" Puulu asked, startled.

"Calling me Cuuh from now on will be sufficient."

"But your name is Tuuwee. I named you." Puulu leaned closer to her son and studied his face. "Are you all right?"

Tuuwee truly wanted to avoid a long discussion about his decision to change his name. He was feeling too physically drained. Suddenly, he realized how hungry he was! And food meant strength.

"Mother, I ask for nothing of great difficulty. Only to be called Cuuh and not Tuuwee. Please honor my wishes and call me Cuuh. Now may I eat something before my backbone and belly button become permanently glued together!" Tuuwee tried a smile, but his face only cracked a pitiful frown.

Puulu was not swayed by Tuuwee's dry sense of humor as she said, "My son, you went to sleep four days ago named Tuuwee. As far as I'm concerned, you are still Tuuwee and will remain so until the dirt is thrown on me in my grave!" Puulu's expression turned sad. "Why would you want to desecrate the name I gave you, a name with honor and dignity. No other name except the sun itself comes before the morning star."

"That's the whole point, Mother," Tuuwee said in a weak voice but still strong in conviction. "Why should I be second to anyone or anything when all that exists is one and the same?"

"Do you profess to be one with Cuuz who is the almighty?"

"Yes!" Tuuwee shot back.

"I see," Puulu answered, her intensity vanishing. She looked into his eyes and said, "I named you and I will address you as such—Tuuwee—in spite of whatever or whomever you think you are." Puulu paused and slowly got to her feet. "Now I will feed you as I've done all your life. That is, unless you possess the powers of a god and can fend for yourself right now?"

"Mother, you misunderstand my point," Tuuwee pleaded with a hangdog look upon his face. He just didn't have the energy or willpower to offer his mother an elaborate explanation.

"Perhaps I did misunderstand you, perhaps not. We are of two different generations. My generation respects everything as it is. Your generation questions everything as it is. But no matter," Puulu said pointedly, "you are my son, my one and only. And your name will always be Tuuwee. That is my final word on the matter!" Puulu stood with both hands on her hips glaring angrily at her son as he sat stunned on the side of his bed.

Tuuwee avoided his mother's eyes, afraid of what he might see there. Instead, he stared at the floor, utterly surprised by this kind of heated reaction. Tuuwee had never witnessed his mother's anger before, let alone experience her wrath.

"Do I make myself clear?" Puulu asked in a stern voice. "Yes, Mother." It was all Tuuwee could think to say, still unable to raise his eyes to meet hers. "And your name?" Puulu persisted.

In spite of his humiliation, Tuuwee willed up a measure of humor in a desperate attempt to lighten the tension. "Starving Tuuwee. Now can I eat?"

Puulu breathed a visible sigh of relief as she looked at Tuuwee with endearing eyes. Then she cupped his ears in her hands, leaned down, and kissed him on the forehead. "You sit tight and I'll fix you a meal." With that, she headed over to the kitchen area of the large hut. As she passed the front door, it opened slightly and Kuula's head peeked inside.

Seeing Tuuwee sitting up caused Kuula's eyes to widen with surprise and delight. "He's awakened!" Kuula shouted as he swung the door open wide. He started inside then suddenly stopped. "I must get Zuuox and Guumal and—"

"You will do no such thing!" Puulu snapped and turned on her heels. "I will not have a bunch of warriors trampling through my hut this day or any day. Besides, Tuuwee needs peace of mind and not a whole lot of excitement. So run and get Zuuox and inform the king of his son's recovery."

Kuula looked over at Tuuwee and, as difficult as it was, Tuuwee managed to make a funny face behind Puulu's back. Kuula smiled and said, "I'll be back in a heartbeat," and then bolted out the door.

Ten minutes later Kuula and Zuuox returned together. Zuuox looked pleased to see Tuuwee, but his demeanor seemed cautious in a reserved sort of way. He looked worried about something, which was not at all like the fearless Zuuox Tuuwee remembered before his long sleep.

"You gave us quite a scare, Little Eagle," Zuuox said after an embrace. Little Eagle was Zuuox's pet name for Tuuwee, and only he ever called him that.

Zuuox pulled up a stool and sat down in front of Tuuwee. Kuula was seated on the side of Tuuwee's bed. As Tuuwee held the plate of food in his lap, munching gingerly, Kuula helped himself to bits and morsels of meat, shoving them into his mouth when Puulu wasn't watching from her place in the kitchen.

"I remember nothing except . . ." Tuuwee paused and looked down at his sore left hand with the missing little finger. He kept his hand in his lap as if ashamed for anyone to see it.

"It's good you remember," Zuuox said with authority then added with a touch of humor. "You may manage to keep the other nine fingers if you remember!"

Tuuwee was just placing a piece of bread in his mouth with his good hand. He moved slowly and warily and felt even weaker than he looked. But he fought hard to appear strong before Zuuox and Kuula.

"I'm sure my father wishes I had lost my head!" Tuuwee said as he looked down into his plate of food. His stomach was so tight that he already felt full on only the few bites he had taken. Kuula, meanwhile, was fast emptying the plate. "Did it ever occur to you that you could be misunderstanding your father, the king?" Zuuox offered.

Tuuwee looked at him with surprise written across his face. "Zuuox, my father hates me and you know this. He hates you as well for pledging your allegiance to me while I was inside my mother's womb. I am still asleep, dreaming that you now take a different position!"

"You've never really known my position, Tuuwee. No one has," Zuuox said. Then he leaned forward and rested his elbows on his knees while looking into Tuuwee's eyes and adding, "I pledged my allegiance, and that of the other warriors, to the tribe as a whole. You are no more than the tribe. Your father, the king, is no more or no less than the tribe! When I did what I did at the border crossing on the morning of the exodus, I did it for the Cuuzan nation . . . both the homeland tribe and our beloved exiled clan. I didn't pledge my allegiance to you exclusively. My oath goes out to the tribe which includes everyone, including the king!"

Tuuwee looked shocked. Inside he was even more astonished by what he was hearing. Zuuox had always aligned himself with Tuuwee in all matters of dispute between him and King Muusamali. Even though Zuuox had never openly spoken out against King Muusamali, Tuuwee was of the opinion that Zuuox thought very little of him.

"Puulu, Tuuwee wants more meat," Kuula shouted. Uncomfortable with where the discussion was leading, Kuula grabbed the empty plate from Tuuwee's lap and rushed off toward the kitchen and Puulu.

"You've changed overnight, Zuuox," Tuuwee said as he looked at him with his head tilted slightly to the side. Zuuox sat straight up and said, "No, my prince. I haven't changed. You've grown in understanding with your age, and I'm here to help you get a grip on your new awareness. Your father, King Muusamali, has always cared about you. You're his eldest son and crown prince! Make no mistake about that!"

"Wait. Hold it," Tuuwee said as he raised his good hand while shaking his head. "Are we talking about the same person . . . my father?"

"Tuuwee, listen," Zuuox replied as he moved closer. "Someday you're destined to be king of the Cuuzan. It was always my greatest dream that you be king in the motherland. But it was merely a dream. I planted that dream in your head which may or may not have been the right thing to do. The gods alone will be the judge. What I forgot to do all these years was to instill in you a sense of duty toward our tribe—the tribe here in exile—and toward your exiled father, the king of the tribe!"

"I've heard enough," Tuuwee said as he slammed both hands to his ears. Momentarily forgetting his wound, he was rocked with another jolt of pain as he quickly brought his sore member to rest again in his lap.

Zuuox seemed totally oblivious to everything except his urgent speech as he pressed on. "Tuuwee, this is your home away from home. Respect it, honor your father, and strive to be a good king to our people in exile."

Tuuwee jumped to his feet. In his weakened condition, the blood rushed to his head, blinding him with an exploding bright light. His knees gave out instantly, but Zuuox managed to grab him before he hit the floor.

Zuuox gently laid him back on his bed. Puulu's aid Kuula, seeing what happened, rushed over to his side, and Zuuox slowly backed up to make way for them. Puulu sat on the edge of his bed as she put a hand on Tuuwee's brow. His eyes were wide open, and he stared at the ceiling avoiding everyone's gaze and saying nothing. He simply laid there motionless.

"He's fine," Puulu said. "Just weak and needs some rest," she added, getting up and turning on Zuuox and Kuula. "And to be left alone!" Puulu began pushing them both toward the door. "So you two make your presence known elsewhere!"

"I'll see you in a little while, Tuuwee," Kuula called out just before Puulu shoved him through the door.

Zuuox paused and looked Puulu squarely in the eyes. He had a strange sense of urgency about him, and Puulu detected it the moment he first entered the hut. "Puulu, listen. At first light tomorrow, I'll be leaving the village to go on a hunt with a party of warriors. I've managed to put the hunt off until Tuuwee recovered consciousness. While he still doesn't look too well, I can't put the hunt off any longer. Tell him for me that I wanted badly to take him but . . ." Zuuox paused as he looked at Tuuwee staring up into space. Finally he said, "I will make sure Kuula remains behind in the village. Call on him for anything you or Tuuwee need."

"I'll have my hands full trying to keep Kuula away from here," Puulu said with a smile. But Zuuox's face remained dead serious. "Good," Zuuox said, still looking at Tuuwee hoping he would glance his way. "The two of them, Tuuwee and Kuula, should always be together."

"Zuuox, is everything all right?" Puulu asked.

Zuuox finally looked at her as he forced a smile onto his lips. "With everything in the hands of the gods, why shouldn't everything be all right?"

"Well, you just seem a little—"

"The only son I've known is laying here in pain," Zuuox said, cutting her off. I'm feeling Tuuwee's pain. That's all."

"Well, by the time you return from the hunt, in three or four days, his pain will be no more. His mother will see to that."

Zuuox spoke no more. He glanced at Tuuwee one last time and then quickly slipped through the door.

The next day, Tuuwee was up and walking about. Kuula was in the hut with him almost every minute. The only time they were apart was when Tuuwee was sleeping or whenever Ruuski came around on his doctor visits three times a day. Whenever he came, Puulu would chase Kuula away to allow them privacy.

On the third day, King Muusamali came to the hut. When Puulu tried to excuse herself and Kuula from the room, Muusamali insisted they both stay. Even when Kuula offered the king a stool and everyone but Tuuwee tried to remain standing, Muusamali directed everyone to sit while he stood.

Puulu joined Tuuwee on the edge of the bed while Kuula sat on the stool. Muusamali stood before the three draped in magnificent leopard-skin coats and holding his white bone staff. He looked as dignified as any tribal king, but there was a touch of uneasiness about him. Tuuwee, as usual, didn't bother to look upon his father, so he was oblivious to the peculiarities about him.

Kuula was simply too busy trying not to appear awed by the king's presence in the room. He knew if he seemed too humbled by the experience, even though Muusamali was king, Tuuwee would tease him later.

Puulu was somewhat amused by Muusamali's nervous demeanor. Although she didn't know the exact cause, she entertained her own suspicions. It was her guess that Tuuwee was the cause of his nervousness. Puulu had known Muusamali most of her life, and she knew of no other man on earth who brought the shyness from him like Tuuwee did.

"Son," Muusamali began as if he were addressing an audience, which he was and which is why he most likely kept Puulu and Kuula from leaving. He didn't relish confronting Tuuwee one-on-one. "I realize you suffered some humiliation in failing to complete the ceremony the other night—" Muusamali was suddenly cut off as Tuuwee spoke up.

"But I did complete the ceremony, Father," Tuuwee said then added, "What more could you have wanted than to witness me fail so miserably. Perhaps see me killed?"

"Tuuwee!" Puulu said as she poked Tuuwee in the ribs with her elbow. She stared at her son in disbelief. She then looked at Muusamali with a pleading expression and said, "He's been through quite a lot, my husband. Don't take him seriously."

Kuula sat frozen stiff with fear, wishing he was someplace else.

Muusamali looked at Tuuwee first with an expression of anger and then a sudden change took place. A certain sympathetic look came to his piercing eyes. His voice was rather flat as he said, "Contrary to what you may think, my son, I am actually quite proud of your performance. I think you danced superbly." Muusamali paused switching his tall staff from side to side, finally placing it in front of him and returning his gaze to Tuuwee.

All the others' eyes were on Muusamali. Puulu looked at him with a measure of surprise mixed with admiration. Kuulu sat stunned by the whole tension-filled exchange.

Muusamali, leaning on his staff, continued, "I've witnessed many such dance routines. I taught you and have taught many others. But your moves are like none I've ever witnessed. In the end, you made the mistake of surrendering yourself to extremes. A man must know his limits and stay within their bounds, especially when dangers involved. Not doing so caused you to lose control." Muusamali paused and looked at his son with probing eyes. As he suspected, Tuuwee's expression changed from a look of defiance to one of longing. Tuuwee, Muusamali knew, had an addiction to knowledge. Tuuwee respected his father's knowledge as he did Zuuox's as well as the other village elders. And in spite of their strained father-son relationship, they did have an unusually strong teacher-pupil bond. It was that which held them when nothing else could.

"A mighty lion's strength comes from confrontation," Muusamali continued, holding Tuuwee's undivided attention as well as Puulu's and Kuula's. "So it should be with a mighty warrior. The more obstacles you confront and overcome, the stronger you become. The lion ignores pain. And the humiliation of losing a battle, or losing a prey, only serves to strengthen his resolve to win the next time, capture the next prey which crosses his path. A mighty warrior like a mighty lion is measured by the war scars about his body."

Tuuwee eyes instantly fell to Muusamali's leg where an old, deep, and ugly gash was still visible. It was the result of an enemy's spear taken during one of the Cuuzan-Kodok tribal wars in the homeland long before Tuuwee was born. Muusamali's tone suddenly changed as he shifted his staff again and held it with one hand at his right side. "Now you've been cooped up in here under your mother's wing since your confrontation with the hyena. This is not appropriate behavior for a future king." Muusamali's words, like his tone of voice, suddenly turned sharp and biting. Tuuwee appeared only slightly ruffled, unlike Puulu and Kuula, who were sitting on the edge of their seats.

"The tribal elders are worried. I expect you to get out and assert yourself. Show the people that you are a well-rooted oak tree. A strong wind may bend you, but you will not break."

With that, Muusamali turned on his heels and headed for the door. He stopped and looked back one more time and said, "Fuudambe, the father of your bride-to-be, expresses a worried concern that, perhaps, his choice of a son-in-law is a bad one. Fuudambe, like any father, wishes his daughter to bare him strong grandsons. But your actions the past few days worry him."

"Fuudambe's worry is groundless," Tuuwee shouted a little louder than necessary, then added, "I am no less a man now than I was before I lost my finger. And if Fuudambe wishes to withdraw his daughter's hand in marriage, then I am man enough to accept his decision, just as I am man enough to accept these nine fingers I have left."

Muusamali smiled, not outwardly, but inside. Then he turned and disappeared through the door.

Tuuwee decided to leave the confines of his hut. On the following morning before Kuula arrived for his daily visit, Tuuwee grabbed his trusty spear and headed out the door. Cuuzan males never leave home without their spears. It was like a third arm.

Tuuwee, with spear in hand, strolled along the narrow path leading from his doorstep to the main trail that ran past his hut. As he reached the main trail, he turned south and headed for the forest. His destination was to find some tribespeople and, as his father had suggested, to mingle!

As he traveled, he was flanked on his left by a long row of huts which stretched all the way to the forest. About fifteen huts in all. To the right was a cornfield covering some three acres. On the far side of the cornfield were even more huts. About twenty-five. Several outhouses were tucked off to the side.

Tuuwee found it unusually quiet and the huts looked deserted—on both sides of the cornfield. As he came to the end of the trail where the huts and cornfield ended, he reached a fork in the road. Several trails branched off from that point. Two ran deep into the forest's black wall in front of him. One was the back entrance to the village itself and led all the way to the outskirts of the Bomu Plains some thirty miles away. The other led to the freshwater lake, the gardens, and fruit orchards. The trail that turned right paralleled the cornfield and connected with the other paths which served the huts on the far side.

To the left, the trail led to the village square, which was located behind the row of fifteen huts he had just passed. To Tuuwee's left, a wall of trees separated the village square from the back portion of the long row of huts.

Directly on the other side of the wall of trees stood several VIP huts and other important buildings. The king's hut, as well as Ruuski's and few of the tribal elders', could be found here, along with the weapons storehouse, the tool shed, the hospital, and the hut which housed their dance costumes and sacrificial equipment.

Assuming that the majority of men-folk were still off on the hunt, Tuuwee decided to stroll down by the gardens where he was sure to find many of the women doing their chores. Whatever men remained behind would likely be found there, including Kuula.

Just as Tuuwee was about to get onto the trail leading to the gardens, he looked to his left and spotted a group of four boys playing on the path and heading his way. Among the group, whose ages ranged from seven to nine, was Guumal, Kuula's younger brother and Tuuwee's cousin. Upon seeing Tuuwee, the four boys rushed forward to greet him.

"Hello, Prince Tuuwee!" Guumal exclaimed as he pulled up to a stop, his friends coming to rest beside him.

"Guumal, you're my cousin. You don't have to address me as prince. I've told you many times—call me Tuuwee," Tuuwee said.

"Yeah—only we can call him prince," one of the other boys said to Guumal, speaking for the other two who stood silently at ease nodding their heads in agreement.

Tuuwee wanted to give the other boys the same message but noticed Guumal staring at his left hand. The scarred hand was no longer swollen and, although Tuuwee was right-handed, he carried his spear in his left—following Ruuski's advice to exercise and toughen his four remaining fingers.

Without warning, Tuuwee raised his left hand and stuck it squarely into Guumal's face. Surprisingly, Guumal wasn't frightened by the gruesome sight of the nubbed finger and didn't jump as Tuuwee had expected. In fact, the other three boys quickly stepped in closer, crawling over Guumal to get a better look.

"Wow. I bet that hurt!" one boy offered.

"Warriors don't feel pain, stupid," Guumal said with authority. Guumal was obviously the older of the three as evidenced by his size.

Tuuwee allowed his hand to rest again at his side. He looked at his little cousin with compassion. He was still amazed that the boys didn't cringe at the sight of his deformity. Tuuwee suddenly thought about his father's words. Then, without thinking further, Tuuwee found himself saying, "Warriors do feel pain." Glancing at each boy in turn, he continued, "But like the mighty lion, a mighty warrior ignores the pain. Furthermore, also like a mighty lion, a warrior is measured by the war scars about his body."

Guumal and his peers hung onto Tuuwee's every word. However, Tuuwee abruptly turned and walked off, leaving the four youngsters waiting for an encore that wasn't to come.

While Guumal's friends quickly conceded and headed off down the back trail toward the fruit orchards, Guumal remained standing at the crossroads watching Tuuwee as he headed for the gardens.

"Tuuwee, everyone is gathered in the square!" Guumal shouted after him. Tuuwee stopped, turned, and looked back as Guumal continued, "Didn't you know? The hunters have returned and, for some reason, they stopped at the king's hut."

This was news to Tuuwee. It was strange indeed that the hunters' return was kept so quiet. Usually the entire village would be bustling with activity and cheering the arrival of fresh meat. Tuuwee immediately changed trails and hurried around the bend toward the square.

The village square was a two-acre patch of barren land. The reddish-brown dirt which carpeted it was finely granulated and hardened from the villagers' bare feet trampling and dancing for two decades. The square was the front entrance to the village itself. It overlooked the Swamp Lake as the lake surrounded one-third of the western half of the island on which the village sat.

The village island was elevated well above the level of the surrounding Swamp Lake. One hundred yards of sloping hills separated the square from the lake's edge where the Cuuzan docked their canoes. Approaching the village on the lake by canoe, the villagers would harbor their boats and climb the gently sloping hill to its top and would then face the village square with its backdrop of huts horseshoeing the reddish dirt clearing before them.

The king's hut was the one stamped in the center foreground facing the dirt square. Flanking the king's hut, on both sides, were the other VIP huts. They circled the square and came back around the lake.

Beyond the king's hut, not visible from the lake because of the wall of trees, lay the remaining community of huts situated on the various roads and trails.

Tuuwee, as he made his way toward the village square, came from the back side of the VIP huts. As he rounded the bend and entered the reddish dirt square, he saw the crowd of warriors gathered in front of the king's hut. Everyone had sour and gloomy expressions stamped on their faces. The game they had killed and brought back lay on the ground before them unnoticed, it seemed, by the dozen or so women who stood quietly to the side. All that prized meat, wild boar, deer in abundance, just laying out in the sun untouched by the women was a clear indication to Tuuwee that something was seriously wrong.

Kuula was standing alongside his father Luuka and a few of the returning hunters. When he spotted Tuuwee coming their way, Kuula broke off from the others and turned to meet him.

"What's happening, Kuula?" Tuuwee asked. Kuula hesitated then said, "I can't get a straight answer from anyone, not even my own father."

Tuuwee looked over Kuula's shoulder and spotted Guuramus looking his way. But when Guuramus noticed Tuuwee looking at him, he quickly turned his gaze to one of the other warriors and engaged him in a conversation.

Tuuwee abruptly stepped around Kuula and walked toward Guuramus. He was Tuuwee's age and King Muusamali's choice to become commander of the warriors in the future. Tuuwee respected and trusted the young Guuramus, who was known for his bravery. However, Tuuwee's obvious choice for the commander appointment was, as everyone knew, Kuula.

"Something is wrong, Guuramus. What is it?" Tuuwee asked. Before answering, Guuramus looked around at several other warriors who were staring back at them. "You'd better go inside, Prince Tuuwee. The king and Suubala will be expecting you."

The king and Suubala? Where is Zuuox? Tuuwee thought to himself. But he sensed he wouldn't find out unless he went inside as Guuramus suggested.

Tuuwee turned and walked to the front door of the king's hut. He parked his spear in a rack designed for such purpose, opened the door, and stepped inside. A tall partition stood before him. To his right was the king's bed chamber. Without hesitation, Tuuwee turned left, took several steps down a narrow walkway, and turned inside a spacious room draped with colorful animal skins. Stuffed animal heads adorned the walls.

At the far end of the room sat King Muusamali upon his throne of plush fur. In front of Muusamali, just off to his side, stood Suubala. To his other side stood Ruuski and the other Huzza priest Muutus.

Tuuwee paused just long enough to see that Zuuox was not present. Then he marched down the center of the room, stopping only feet from Muusamali's footstool.

Muusamali was seated upright, leaning slightly forward with both elbows on the armrest. His hands were folded and his fingers locked together. He and his three closest and most trusted aides had obviously been engaged in serious talk before Tuuwee barged in. Yet no one seemed surprised to see him—only annoyed by his timing.

"Where is Zuuox?" Tuuwee asked. His eyes were centered on Suubala.

Suubala's eyes never once met Tuuwee's as he looked at the floor then slowly raised them to fix his sights on Muusamali without speaking.

Tuuwee followed Suubala's gaze and looked at his father. "Well?" he snapped.

Calmly Muusamali leaned back in his high-backed chair. Keeping his hands clamped together, he brought his fist up and rested his chin on them. His expression was intense, his eyes unwavering as he looked at Tuuwee and said, "Son, Zuuox met with a sudden death. He was struck and killed by a bolt of lightning during a thunderstorm."

"What?" Tuuwee shouted. A gut-wrenching pain was slowly building in his stomach. He turned toward Suubala. "Suubala, say it's not so!" he pleaded. But Suubala could neither answer him nor look his way.

"Suubala is deeply grieved by this whole incident," Muusamali spoke up. Suubala appeared distressed, in a strange kind of way. He looked visibly dependent upon Muusamali to speak for him, which Muusamali eagerly did. He continued by saying, "As difficult as it was, Suubala had to make the tough decision to bury Zuuox's body out on the plains rather than bring him here to the village. Apparently, the lightning burned most of his body, and it was wiser to place him in the ground immediately and allow the earth mother to consume him rather than allow his remains to rot while en route home."

Tuuwee was in a state of shock. Muusamali's words were like shooting arrows directed to his gut. He wanted to turn and run away, but he also felt an overpowering urge to attack. In the meantime, while his mind measured the unbearable, his pain worsened. Tuuwee dropped to his knees and buckled over. Then he began pounding the floor with his fist screaming, "No, no, no!" Over and over again he pounded with both his good hand and bad.

Finally, Ruuski went over to him, put and arm around his shoulders, and grabbed his left arm. Ruuski's concern was for Tuuwee's damaged left hand as Tuuwee appeared oblivious to the possibility of reinjury.

For a moment, Tuuwee wept in Ruuski's arms as the others in the room looked on in silence. The story seemed unbelievable to one part of Tuuwee's mind. But one of the strictest moral rules in Cuuzan society was that a warrior's word was sacred. To lie was a crime worse than adultery. So as far as Tuuwee was concerned, Zuuox died exactly as Suubala had described. But hearing the details from his father's lips instead of Suubala's sparked him to believe that Muusamali was relishing in Zuuox's demise.

As abruptly as he'd dropped to his knees, he scrambled to his feet once more, shaking Ruuski from his back as he came up.

Tuuwee stood in front of Muusamali with fire blazing in his eyes. He had the same look on his face as he did the night when he stood before Muusamali just after losing his finger to the hyena. "You're glad, aren't you?" he screamed at his father.

Muusamali sat motionless and silent, watching Tuuwee's every move with his hawklike eyes. "Admit it, Father. Zuuox's death is something you've wished for ever since he pledged allegiance to me in my mother's womb!" Tuuwee paused. Muusamali didn't move a muscle. Suubala, Ruuski, and Muutus also stood watching silently.

A look of desperation surfaced on Tuuwee's face as he searched the eyes of the others in the room looking for nothing in particular but hoping against hope for some kind of relief from his mental agony. Finally Tuuwee's gaze settled on Suubala as he said to his father, "Now I suppose you'll make him your chief warrior?" Tuuwee wouldn't even say Suubala's name. He just used his hate-filled eyes, eyes which Suubala still fought to avoid by staring at Muusamali.

Tribal history was being made this very moment, and the two tribal elders were carefully recording, in their heads, every word being spoken, every act being performed.

Muusamali was as cool and calm as an eagle perched on a limb high in the treetops. He watched Tuuwee closely and showed no sign of either anger or fear.

"When it's my turn to sit on that throne, I shall choose my own chief commander from the ranks of the warriors. And my choice shall undoubtedly be Kuula! Do you hear?" Tuuwee shouted, but still, Muusamali refused to speak.

The silent treatment Muusamali was displaying only exasperated Tuuwee and compounded his anguish to the point where he couldn't bear it any longer. Without another word, Tuuwee turned his back on his father and the others and stormed out of the room.

That night, there wasn't the usual roasting of the pigs and cheerful feast of thanksgiving for a successful hunt. Instead, Muusamali called the entire tribe together into the village square where he stood upon a high platform and made a public announcement. He informed the people of Zuuox's death and the circumstances surrounding it. Prior to King Muusamali's speech, none of the returning hunters were permitted to speak a word about Zuuox or his death. Muusamali had decreed that no none was ever to speak Zuuox's name again or discuss the incidents surrounding his death. He declared Zuuox's death a bad omen, and it should be wiped clean from everyone's mind and forgotten.

After King Muusamali's public address, a celebration of another kind commenced—a sort of "dance of death"—which was meant to ward off the evil spirits which had visited a member of the tribe. A number of dance groups, males and females, donned themselves in gory costumes and took turns on the dance floor. One group behind the other, they danced wildly from sundown to sun up the next day.

Tuuwee didn't attend the king's public address or the death ceremony afterward. He spent that night alone in his mother's hut. Even though he was informed of his father's gag order against speaking about Zuuox's demise, Tuuwee ignored it. He spoke of Zuuox as often as he wanted to over the course of the next few weeks. However, no one in the village was at liberty to listen except one person: Kuula.

Two weeks after Zuuox's death, Tuuwee went out from the village alone to perform a premarital duty-chore. On one of the dry islands not far from the village enclave, he found himself preparing for a wedding he neither wanted nor intended to attend in spite of the labor he was exerting toward that end. As was customary, the Cuuzan male went into the wilderness and, with only a single shovel-like instrument, dug a hole in the ground large enough for his wife and himself to mate. There they would live for seven days.

Once the six-foot-deep and eighteen-foot-wide love nest was completed, it was lined with animal skins and the floor cushioned with soft feathers and homemade blankets. The task of building the honeymoon lodge was meant to be a labor of love. The male received no greater joy than seeing the pleased and satisfied expression of his wife when she first set eyes on the cozy quarters, built especially to comfort and impress her. Sometimes the bride's parents would come and inspect the place where their virgin daughter was to be transformed into a full-blown woman. The parents expected to find a comfortable decorated underground shelter fit for a king and his queen. And so, the bridegroom would pour his heart, soul, and sweat into the task at hand.

Kuula was paying a surprise visit to the site Tuuwee had chosen to build his underground honeymoon den. It was actually the graveyard of honeymoon dens: a dry land enclave located a half-mile from the village. To reach it, you had to cross the lake portion of the swamp by boat.

The enclave totaled one square mile and was mostly a barren piece of grassy high ground. Persimmon trees in full spring bloom dotted the area as far as the eye could see. Scattered mounds of dirtlike giant molehills were everywhere, remnants of previous labors of love. Each honeymoon den, once used by a pair of newlyweds, was customarily stripped of its furs, feathers, and other decorations and refilled with dirt.

Kuula paddled his compact-size canoe slowly across Swamp Lake toward the banks of the honeymoon enclave. The lake's surface was blanketed with fallen leaves and thick, floating moss. Kuula's canoe sliced easily through the floating debris. But he had to take particular care to avoid ramming his canoe into the underwater tree roots scattered through the water. Huge marsh hibiscus trees littered the lake. The marsh hibiscus actually grew above the surface of the water, mounted on its fingerlike roots that ran amok beneath the surface. Kuula's skillful maneuvering brought him to the bank where Tuuwee's canoe was docked by the edge. Kuula climbed to shore, pulling his small boat behind him.

It was a late springtime evening, and the smell of blossoming wild chasa filled the air. The sun, as it sank behind the horizon, cast its long shadows which brought a chill sweeping off the lake. Kuula, naked but for his loincloth, reached down and removed a long spear from his canoe. He paused a moment with his spear dangling at his side and looked out over a field dotted in one direction with chasa trees and in the other a grassy marsh that met with the winding lake on the lower quarter of the enclave.

Kuula set out in the direction of the chasa trees where mounds of dirt were piled everywhere, between and beneath the trees. The Cuuzan had transplanted the thirty or so chasa trees which now dotted the field. They grew no more than seven feet tall and produced wide shady branches which blossomed into colored flowers speckled with glorious edible berries. In the late spring, the flowers gave off their sweet aroma just before yielding themselves into the berries of the season.

There was a certain tranquility about this area. It held no particular beauty but, like a graveyard, aroused the spirit in Kuula. It was not an eerie sense, but, rather, a feeling of eroticism swept over him as he thought about all the marriages which had been consummated upon the ground on which he walked. He stepped on overturned patches of dirt which he knew at once was a refilled den. He wondered with a smile which of the clan's females had left her virginity buried there.

Kuula wasn't married. He was once engaged to a beautiful girl named Bwayaka who died suddenly of swamp fever just before their wedding took place. Good luck and happy times were supposed to accompany a marriage engagement. Bwayaka's sudden death was considered an omen.

In spite of Kuula's macho, stallion popularity, eligible single maidens who would otherwise jump at the chance to marry him shied away from accepting his marriage proposals, their fears and superstitions raging foremost in their minds. Kuula found they quickly backed off when it appeared the relationship was growing more serious. Not that Kuula suffered from a lack of female intimacy. He was suspected of being the father of a couple of offspring, and he was but twenty years old.

Kuula headed toward a faint sound coming from the near distance. As he rounded a chasa tree, he caught sight of something flying out of a hole in the ground. Upon closer inspection, he realized it was dirt being shoveled out. The mouth of the hole was some ten feet in diameter. As he approached the edge, he was surprised to find Tuuwee lowered ten feet at the bottom of the cavity and boring down at an angle. What Tuuwee had dug was a far cry from meeting the worst standards of an underground den.

Kuula stood on the edge and silently watched Tuuwee for a moment as he worked with the small picklike instrument, breaking up the hard dirt. Then he threw down the pick, as though angry with it, and grabbed the shovel. Tuuwee began scooping up the loose dirt, tossing it over his shoulder and out of the hole at a frantic pace.

"Tuuwee," Kuula called out. Tuuwee stopped his work and looked up. He was sweating and panting. His eyes held a certain faraway look. "You dig as if you intend to bury a bride does not marry and mate with one. And she must be an elephant!" Kuula finished.

Tuuwee glanced around at his dirt-walled enclosure. He frowned as if he were viewing his surroundings for the first time.

"You've done three days' work in one. And by the look of this . . . this hole in the ground . . . you haven't really accomplished anything." Kuula said.

"Never mind that," Tuuwee said at last. He tossed the shovel up to Kuula followed by the pick. "Have you been giving serious thought to our discussion?" Tuuwee asked as Kuula reached down to give him a hand up, dropping to both knees.

"I've been giving it serious thought, yes," Kuula answered as he pulled Tuuwee into the light. "How were you planning to escape that elephant trap anyway?"

Tuuwee glanced back down inside the hole with wonder. He was surprised himself at how much digging he had done. He found he couldn't account for the time he had spent in accomplishing his work. He simply couldn't remember anything after the initial groundbreaking. Tuuwee turned to his friend and said, "I would have managed it just fine by myself." Tuuwee paused for just a moment and then began walking toward the nearby chasa tree where he had left his spear and provisions. Kuula turned and followed. Tuuwee added, "Just as I will manage a journey to the motherland alone if you don't quickly make up your mind about accompanying me."

"You know that I will never let you attempt such a journey alone," Kuula said, watching Tuuwee's movements as he grabbed for his waterskin pouch and sat down against the chasa tree. The sun was slipping away fast. The shadows had practically disappeared, and there was about thirty minutes of light left. "Your answer is yes. We depart from this swamp prison tomorrow."

"Tomorrow!" Kuula shot back. "But you spoke of waiting until the day before your wedding when you'd be expected to spend the entire day and night out here in the den alone. You know we'll need at least a day's head start. We don't want our absence discovered too quickly."

"I've already thought about that," Tuuwee said solemnly, still holding the waterskin in midair poised to take his fill. "The night I'm to spend alone is the night Euurus's parents may decide to come for their inspection. Besides, if your absence from the village is found out, my father will send his underlings straight out here to search for us both. No! I've figured a way in which we can guarantee an even greater head start than one night. And we can leave this godforsaken swamp a week earlier." Tuuwee finally brought the waterskin to his lips and took a drink. He realized that there was less water in the pouch than he brought with him. Suddenly he remembered he had drunk from the pouch twice before and even ate a snack while taking a break from his digging. It was strange, though, how his mind was only now remembering what he'd done. He looked over at the hole and was amazed at the amount of work he'd done with no recollection of his actions.

"Did you forget to boil your water again, Tuuwee?" Kuula asked as he studied Tuuwee's expression and watched as it went from one of high expectation to one of a flat masklike quality.

"No!" Tuuwee shot back.

Kuula said nothing. He just stared at him with a puzzled expression. Ever since Tuuwee had awakened from his long sleep, Kuula has found his temperament to be harsh. Tuuwee was always known for having a solemn streak in him. But he always managed to display a sense of humor even when being critical. Now, however, he seemed overly pragmatic with the one person for which he had always reserved his humorous better nature.

"Tonight, I will confront my father with a request to go hunt a mighty leopard on the Maradi Plains. That's a two-day trip," Tuuwee said as he stretched out a hand toward Kuula. Kuula caught hold and pulled him to his feet. "But you are days away from getting married." Kuula said. "This is no time to talk about hunting. And that's just what the king will say about such a crazy idea."

"Kuula!" Tuuwee's tone was one of surprise. "Where have you been, Cuuzan? It is customary that the bridegroom presents his bride with a gift. Remember?"

"A gift, yes, of flowers or feathers. Not the coat of a mighty leopard. Such gifts are meant to soften the hearts of fathers who stubbornly resist their daughter's marriage to you. You, however, are the crown prince. Any father in the village would freely give you his daughter's hand . . . anytime."

"But think about it, Kuula. What better way for a prince to prove his love to his bride than to present her with such a fabulous gift when it wasn't called for?"

"Your acceptance of her is proof enough," Kuula said, reaching down to grasp the pick and shovel. He handed Tuuwee the shovel.

"I'm just wasting my argument on you. I shall save it for my father," Tuuwee said, taking the shovel from him as he also grabbed his spear. He made ready to move out. Kuula stopped him, saying, "Euurus is a pretty girl. She can cook fairly well. Her teeth are all straight, I think. But she is no Bwayaka and not worth a mighty leopard's coat. Your father will tell you so himself. Just watch and see!"

"You watch your tongue, Cuuzan!" Tuuwee said as he swatted him lightly on the shoulder with his spear. "Euurus is a fine young woman, an outstanding cook, and she does have all her teeth as well as all her fingers." Tuuwee held his left hand up in the air, playfully revealing his four remaining fingers.

Kuula's face lit up with a wide grin. He was delighted that Tuuwee was being his old self once again even though the matter of discussion put a dull edge on the moment.

"If Euurus is such a living, breathing goddess, why don't you just stay here and marry her?" Kuula said falling in step. Tuuwee was leading the way as they headed to the Swamp Lake and their waiting boats. He turned to Kuula and said, "I will surely not stay here and marry her. But who's to say I will not someday return from Cuuzanland with an army of my uncle Nuumyu's warriors and claim Euurus from this exiled tribe of Cuuzan taking her back to the motherland with me? Her along with anyone else who might want to leave this place. I will rescue them as well."

Kuula was silent for a moment as he followed his cousin across the field. Tuuwee was filled with so many high expectations regarding what he perceived as his diving destiny. Kuula was not all that optimistic about his cousin's dream. However, he would never reveal his thoughts to Tuuwee. He kept his most profound opinions secret, especially those opposed to Tuuwee's. Kuula was indeed a part of Tuuwee, like a shadow's stubborn position behind its master. Never before had Tuuwee's persistence and yearning for adventure been so extreme.

"What makes you so sure that King Nuumyu will accept you? It is by his decree that we are forbidden to enter Cuuzanland," Kuula said as he thought about the do-or-die consequences of Tuuwee's wild idea. He tossed his shovel and spear into the boat harder than he might have, upset by the ultimatum Tuuwee had put before him: stay here in the swamp and live out life in boredom, or leave with Tuuwee and live it on the edge of uncertainty. Kuula would much rather stay where he was and enjoy the carefree life the swamp afforded him. But he knew he would stay only if Tuuwee stayed with him.

"Because blood is thicker than water," Tuuwee said as he frowned at the sight of Kuula treating the fragile lightweight canoe so roughly. Tuuwee took a half-step toward Kuula and continued in a soft, understanding voice, "It is my father's decree, Kuula, which is holding us all here as prisoners in this swamp, under the threat of death. This is the only land that will accept my father. He is the one forbidden from returning to Cuuzanland. Nothing is keeping us inside this prison except our own fears and superstitions about being fruit of a poisonous tree. My father is the tree and we his fruit. To return to the motherland is not to be killed and have our poisonous bodies set on fire. That is the superstitious deception my father wishes us to believe. It is only by the hand of the poisonous tree that we face death if we are caught trying to break away from its thorny branches. Well, I'm not afraid of my father any longer, Kuula, not after what Zuuox confided in me some months before his death. I'm not going to be swayed by superstitious deceptions my father has created in order to keep us prisoners in exile with him."

Tuuwee paused and took another step toward Kuula. His eyes were now pleading and matched the emotion of his voice. "Besides, Kuula, it was your father, Luuka, who taught us that nothing is forbidden to a man with a divine purpose. What could be more divine than a man on a quest to find his true, beloved homeland? To tread the same soil as his ancestors and on which they are buried? Their great tribal spirits embody the rocks and plains of the land. A man has the God-given right, Kuula, to live on the very land that gave birth to his blood. You know that as well as I. The swamp is not our home. We are prairie dwellers by nature. Kings of the grassland!

"Like the lion, we require space to freely roam in whatever direction we point our noses without having to go around a single obstacle. Tell me, Kuula, from your heart: Does this swamp make you feel as the lion? Or do you feel like a miserable old gator consigned to lying around day and night on the muddy banks of a filthy lake whose water is not fit to drink?"

Tuuwee didn't tell Kuula what secrets Zuuox confided in him. But as a result of those secrets, Tuuwee became convinced that his true destiny was to travel to the motherland. Zuuox revealed to him on his nineteenth birthday that his uncle King Nuumyu, the homeland king, had not fathered any male offspring prior to the exodus. And in the likely event that King Nuumyu still hadn't fathered any male children, then the eldest brother of the homeland king would succeed him to the throne. In the absence of the eldest brother, the eldest son of that brother would be next in line. Muusamali was King Nuumyu's eldest brother, and Tuuwee was Muusamali's eldest son.

Zuuox planted a map in Tuuwee's mind detailing the exact course to take to reach the homeland. Zuuox instructed him that he was like a migratory bird born abroad. If he followed the map, Tuuwee would reach Cuuzanland safely on the wings of the wind god Cuu-wa.

Without answering Tuuwee's last question, Kuula went about making awkward use of his hands, readjusting his spear inside the boat and first picking up then setting down the shovel. Kuula's mind was anguishing over being forced to do something he knew and felt was wrong. Yet to not go along with Tuuwee's plan would be an even greater wrong. Kuula was convinced that Tuuwee couldn't survive such a trip without him at his side. In fact, Kuula was obsessed with the belief that Tuuwee couldn't accomplish even the simplest of tasks unless he was there to help.

Kuula straightened up and faced Tuuwee, saying, "I remember when you were just five years old. You wanted to make your first spear out of teak wood," Kuula began with a calm voice. "Warriors made real weapons out of the teak's hardwood. Boys made their spears from the soft, keey tree which grew everywhere in the middle of the village. But you wanted to go into the forbidden belly of the swamp where only warriors dare go, to cut your teak."

"And you refused to come with me into the forbidden belly!" Tuuwee said.

"Yes, I did," answered Kuula in a thoughtful tone. "And for a whole day we searched for you. My heart suffered great agony during that time because I felt responsible. I was the oldest and I should have known you were just foolish enough to sneak off by yourself."

"I remember that glad smile on your face, Kuula, when I walked back into the village that morning, empty-handed but full of high spirits!"

"Just tell me!" Kuula said sternly. "Would you really try to go in search of Cuuzanland alone?"

Tuuwee didn't hesitate. "Yes, I would," he answered, then added, "Because it is my destiny. It is the destiny of both of us!"

Kuula nodded. He stepped over and put a hand on Tuuwee's shoulder. "Then, so be it. I cannot let you go alone," Kuula said, remembering the times long ago when he used to pat Tuuwee on top the head whenever Kuula would yield himself to one of Tuuwee's wild proposals. Now in keeping with the old habit, Kuula reached out and patted Tuuwee on the side of the head, saying, "Our destinies are one."

Tuuwee's expression remained stern as he met and held Kuula's eyes. He no longer resented the pat on the head as he once did when they were children. As a young man, Tuuwee learned to appreciate the pats from Kuula for what they were really worth, realizing that along with the touch also came Kuula's unwavering support and loyalty.

"You know what, Kuula?" Tuuwee said as they both tossed their canoes into the lake. Kuula kneeled on the bank's edge and while holding his canoe by a short rope, he paused and looked at Tuuwee. Tuuwee quickly climbed into his canoe and grabbed his paddle before continuing. He said, "Would you believe it if I told you that I never left the village that day you and the others went searching for me in the forbidden swamp?" With that, he laughed out loud and began paddling across the lake.

Kuula didn't budge for a moment. He didn't even think about leaping into his canoe and giving chase, as he knew Tuuwee expected. Under normal, playful circumstances, Kuula would have done just that. He and Tuuwee right now would have been paddling across the lake in high spirits, playing and laughing. But in Kuula's mind, these circumstances were far from normal. He was heavy-hearted by the fact he was likely crossing the lake for the final time. And suddenly, the floating debris carpeting the lake's surface could have easily been rose petals in his mind, the polluted lake a freshwater oasis, and the surrounding swamp a tropical jungle paradise. As his canoe moved past the old chasa tree which sat in the lake like a misplaced gravestone, Kuula looked at it with eyes filled with longing. It appeared to him to be like a magnificent waterfall which he would miss most of all.

The Cuuzan village sat a hundred yards off the lake's shore. It was partially engulfed by trees, but the open end faced the lake. Mud-brick huts shaped like tiny pyramids sprinkled the landscape. Many huts were also stamped inside the surrounding forest. Trails and paths skirted the forest leading from the village square to the doorsteps of each of the huts inside the backdrop of the forest. In dusk's twilight, cooking fires burned here and there in front of some huts and resembled glowing, grounded stars.

As Tuuwee approached the shore of the village looking into the mouth of the perfectly lined huts which horseshoed the square, he was looking at a setting that was pure utopian, as wonderful as any that possibly existed. But he was not really seeing the stark serenity which lay before him. Tonight, he was not interested in the carefree life. His mind was clouded with a deep-seated longing for another kind of life in a land which he'd never seen but often dreamt. It was a ruthless and violent land steeped in political upheaval and far removed from the simple tranquility upon which he now gazed. The land in his thoughts he knew not except for sketchy directions learned both directly and indirectly from listening to Zuuox and the other old warriors reminisce. They often talked about the motherland and their months of sojourning between it and their ultimate home here in the swamp.

Tuuwee climbed from his canoe and pulled it out of the water onto the bank. Several small boys came racing down the hill from the village square to the water's edge to greet him. He paused and looked back at Kuula slowly paddling his way to the shore. Tuuwee plainly sensed that Kuula's heart had grown roots in this swamp, and he yearned to stay. But he also reasoned that Kuula's heart would grow to forget this wet hole in the earth just as soon as he experienced a taste of adventure on the wide-open, dry plains and the tropical jungles outside the swamp.

Tuuwee, unlike Kuula, was always an avid listener to campfire storytellers— always taking in their tall tales. Thus, he considered himself to have a sampling of experiences from which to draw and a certain knowledge upon which to base his opinions on the outside world.

Kuula reached the shore close behind Tuuwee and climbed from his canoe to the bank. Like Tuuwee, Kuula was approached by a group of young boys offering to pull his boat from the water. The children were thrilled and were noisily chattering among themselves, bucking each other to give assistance to Kuula and Tuuwee, who were their two favorite idols among the ranks of young warriors in the village.

The boys exchanged hard blows as they vied for Tuuwee's and Kuula's shovels and waterskins. Their prized spears, however, the boys knew not to touch without permission. Kuula gave his spear to his little brother, Guumal, and Guumal proudly strutted up the hill toward the village square, spear in hand. The other boys followed behind, begging to have their turn at carrying this most prized possession.

Tuuwee was surrounded by the children as well, as he started up the hill. "Let me carry your spear, Prince Tuuwee. Let me! Let me!" a boy walking by Tuuwee cried over and over again. "Permit me! Permit me!" the others cried out.

Tuuwee noticed one boy who had the little finger of his left hand tied down with a strip of hide. Cuuzan boys customarily imitated their favorite young adult warrior by dressing their naked little bodies with certain beads and ornaments in the same fashion as their idol. Thus, Tuuwee was moved by this particular boy's extreme measure of imitation. So Tuuwee handed him his spear.

The boy clutched it against his chest with loving affection but also with a desperately tight grip and wary, watchful eyes. He was the smallest of the pack, and the others pawed at his treasure as they followed along behind Tuuwee.

As they approached, the square was all ablaze. A giant fire was burning in the center, and a host of other fires burned atop tall poles on the perimeter. Men and women milled casually about, largely concentrated near the storehouse where the dance costumes and other gala paraphernalia was stored.

Tonight, was the weekly social when the entire tribe gathered to teach the children dance and drum lessons.

Kuula bid Tuuwee farewell as he headed toward the trail leading to the back portion of the village where he shared a hut with his parents and little brother Guumal.

The mood throughout the village square was upbeat and festive. It was always like this whenever a social occasion arrived calling for music and dancing. Tuuwee met with smiling happy faces wherever he looked. He tried to put on a gay face himself, but considering the critical nature of his thoughts, he found it difficult to do so. And so he hurried toward his destination, anxious to confront his father King Muusamali with his request to leave the village tomorrow morning with Kuula to go on a leopard hunt.

King Muusamali's hut looked deserted as Tuuwee approached. The other VIP huts surrounding this end of the square showed signs of life by the lights glowing inside and the activity visible outside.

"The king is off visiting one of his wives, I suspect," a voice said. Tuuwee turned to meet Ruuski as the old Huzza priest stepped slowly up to him. Tuuwee's entourage of little people kept their distance as they went about their child's play making a point not to interrupt the two adults before them.

"I see," answered Tuuwee looking from Ruuski to Muusamali's hut then back again. "I'll return later." Tuuwee slowly backed up toward the trail which led to the community of huts in the back.

Ruuski stared at Tuuwee. His expression revealed his curiosity. But Tuuwee knew not to linger long. Otherwise he'd surely have to answer questions. So Tuuwee waved goodbye, turned, and hurried off into the darkness. The rambunctious children fell in step behind him.

At the crossroads, Tuuwee paused. He looked right, down the long row of huts toward his and Puulu's near the end of the trail. Like all the other huts before him, there was a light streaming from his window.

Tuuwee thought about going home, but the thought of Euurus kept weighing on his mind. She lived in a hut on the far side of the cornfield. Tuuwee looked across the field at the cluster of lighted huts in the distance. The sound of babies crying and wood being chopped could be heard coming from that direction.

During the late evening, warriors and elders relaxed with the children while the women of the tribe busied themselves preparing meals. The smell of roasted meat made Tuuwee's mouth water. Aside from the tiny snack at noontime, he hadn't eaten since early morning.

He remembered his last breakfast meal with fond delight. It was a meal which Euurus had prepared especially for him. As part of the Cuuzan courtship ritual, the bride-to-be would occasionally prepare a special feast for her future husband as a flirtatious, teasing kind of gesture. The man, however, was always kept in suspense as to when and how often this form of foreplay to marriage would occur. It was the male's duty to make himself available by showing up and lingering near the female's hut around mealtime each morning and evening. The female would remain hidden from view and, using only one hand, would place a platter of food outside the doorway, quickly shutting the door behind her. This benign gesture on the part of the bride-to-be was what the groom-to-be anxiously hoped for each time he showed up.

On the other hand, if the male were unlucky, the female would exit the hut empty-handed. More often than not, she would be accompanied by a sister or girlfriend. They would stand about casually talking in an aimless manner as if they didn't know the hungry man was posted nearby watching.

Euurus had broken the ice this morning by placing that first platter of food on her doorstep. Now Tuuwee remembered that breakfast platter and decided to pay her another visit with the hope she intended to present him with a dinner platter as well.

Tuuwee took the trail leading across the darkened cornfield toward the cluster of lighted huts and tiny fires in the distance. The frisky youngsters tagged along behind. This hut Euurus shared with her parents and young sister was one of several positioned in a row near a backdrop of thick brush and tall trees.

Tuuwee and his small band passed several other huts along the way. In front of one, a group of adult males sat lazing around a campfire passing the evening away watching a group of young boys playing war games. The boys were younger than the group following Tuuwee, and they waved little spears and shields at each other as the grown-up cheered them on.

As Tuuwee and the others approached, the young would-be warriors shifted their activity in his direction. They started swinging and stabbing at each other with renewed vigor in an effort to impress their prince. Tuuwee didn't give much notice to them—no more than he did to the older boys following him. To the adults, however, he waved as he passed.

Tuuwee walked another forty yards where he came alongside a wall of trees and tall grass. Euurus's hut was less than twenty yards away. Sitting at the edge of the wall of trees, Tuuwee could see the front entrance. He noticed there was no platter of food to be seen on the doorstep. There was, however, a light visible from the inside, but otherwise everything was completely quiet.

Tuuwee resolved to wait it out as he eased closer to the darkened forest to his left. He turned to the small boy holding his spear. The boy didn't hesitate turning it over to him at once. For the first time, Tuuwee showed some sensitivity as he patted the child on top of his head. He then began shooing the children away, keeping an always constant eye on Euurus's front door.

At first, the youngsters playfully resisted his efforts, so, finally, he began swatting a few rear ends with the butt of his spear. The boys quickly got the message and ran off, leaving Tuuwee smiling.

Tuuwee sat down at the edge of the forest in the darkness and watched. The cool chill of evening bit at his almost-naked body. An uneventful half-hour passed without any sign of Euurus. The interior of the hut was well lit, and Tuuwee knew if the front door cracked open, a stream of light would spill out into the darkness. So he waited and watched with anticipation, anticipation that was waning as the minutes passed. Surely Euurus must know he was here? Freezing his loincloth off and starving for a meal? he mused. Yet she refused to feed him or to make the customary appearance to tease him.

Disgusted, Tuuwee searched the ground for a rock. Finding one, he stepped out from the forest a small way and tossed it lightly at the hut. The rock struck the hut with only a slight thump. Moments later, the door opened and a stream of light filtered into the night. A silhouette of a female exited the front door and took three steps into the darkness. She peered into the night, and Tuuwee recognized the shapely figure to be Euurus.

He stood up and crept slowly toward the front of the hut. He was careful to remain low and on his tiptoes. Moving like a quiet cat, he crept closer and closer to Euurus, who had her back turned away from him.

Before she knew it, Tuuwee was on her as he touched her lightly on the shoulder. Startled, Euurus quickly turned to find him grinning in her face. "Tuuwee," she said in a loud whisper, grabbing her chest to silence the heart wildly beating beneath her breast.

Tuuwee stepped even closer and, as he gazed into her eyes, said, "Yes, it is I. Who else were you expecting?" He moved to plant a kiss on her thick, full lips which were slightly parted. Her eyes were closed slightly as though in some dream state. Then, suddenly without warning, she backed up.

"You aren't supposed to do this, Tuuwee," she said as she gave him a stern look. She was a pretty brown-complexioned woman with short tight hair. Her large dark eyes sparkled sweetly off the hut's reflected light. As Tuuwee held her in his sights, he was aroused by her smooth brown beauty standing against the backdrop of total blackness. He began to feel goosebumps just watching her. As Euurus looked back at him, she sensed the yearning in Tuuwee as he burned for her, and, on one hand, this excited her. But it also put her even more on guard as she said, "You're supposed to remain hidden, Tuuwee, until after I set the food tray on the doorstep and the—"

"What food tray?" Tuuwee said, taking very small steps toward her.

"Well, I would have, maybe, fixed one for you had I known you were here expecting it . . . just maybe!" she replied.

"It's not food I want," Tuuwee whispered. Then he reached out with his left hand and gently took hold of Euurus' right hand. He gave no thought to the fact he was handling her with his mutilated member. And she, seemingly, didn't notice or care. She allowed Tuuwee to slowly pull her toward him.

"Tuuwee, you're not following the rules of courtship," Euurus said as she came to rest in front of him. They were standing face-to-face now, just close enough that the nipples of her naked breast touched against Tuuwee's chest.

"If I played by the rules, I wouldn't be able to do this," Tuuwee said as his other hand, still gripping his spear, came up and around her. He moistened his lips and brought his mouth closer to hers. But Euurus ducked and spun around beneath him. All in one motion she wound up on his other side, watching him stumble forward. He added a step or two on purpose just to look more foolish than he actually was.

Euurus giggled. And as he watched her, he found her smile to be heartwarming. He was even more elated that he was the cause for her pleasure. For a long moment, they stood some five feet apart and simply stared at each other in silence. Euurus's smile was like beautiful music in motion, and as the music slowly disappeared, Tuuwee watched her pretty face. He felt her soft eyes caress him with such tender affection that he was left speechless in their wake.

Neither realized they had company until the door slammed shut. Euurus's father, mother, and sister were already out the door when Euurus turned around and Tuuwee looked over his shoulder to find they were being watched. Tuuwee raised his spear in greeting and said, "Good evening." "Good evening to you, Prince," Euurus's father, Fuudambe, said in reply.

The mother smiled and nodded as did the sister. "Come along, Euurus. The Samba will be starting shortly," her mother said.

"Let them court!" Fuudambe said to his wife. Then he turned and looked at Tuuwee with understanding and said, "Only the old and the very young arrive early to a Samba."

"I will be along shortly, Mother," Euurus said as Fuudambe shoved his wife along the trail and they disappeared into the night.

Euurus' sister lingered behind. She was a few years younger than her sister but was just as pretty and very high-spirited. "Well, I would have fixed you a meal if I'd have known you were here," she said as she mocked Euurus. Then she looked at Tuuwee and added, "Prince, a big platter of food has been waiting for you all evening inside—"

"Get out of here!" Euurus shouted as she motioned toward her sister. And the girl turned and ran off into the night after her parents.

"So you see, I did fix you a platter," Euurus said with a blush. Turning serious once more, she added, "But you were late. You're supposed to show up before the sun goes down, not after." She stepped over and stood before Tuuwee and said, "I hope when we're married you'll be on time for the evening meals like a 'good husband'?" She gently and playfully pinched Tuuwee's arm.

The mention of marriage suddenly put a chill on Tuuwee's mood. He turned and looked up into the sky. The stars were out in force, and a three-quarter moon hung in the midst of them.

Euurus eased up next to him and slipped an arm inside his and hugged it. "You want me to go inside and get the platter, Tuuwee? It's fish and potato cakes with your favorite cheese."

Tuuwee was hungry indeed. But his mind was urging him to satisfy another need: the need to level with Euurus and tell her the truth. "I don't want to eat right now. I want to tell you something," Tuuwee said as he looked into her pretty face. She snuggled up even closer to him and said in reply, "I bet I know what it is. You were away practically all day on Honeymoon Island, digging our love nest!"

Tuuwee thought about the digging he'd done and said in a weary voice, "You bet."

"You don't sound very happy about something which is supposed to be a labor of love," Euurus said.

"Euurus . . . we are not getting married," Tuuwee bolted out. "What?" Euurus said, frowning in surprise. "Not yet anyway," Tuuwee replied then added, "Not until I return from Cuuzanland."

"Cuuzanland?" she said loudly and Tuuwee moved quickly to quiet her as he put a hand to her lips. "Keep your voice down, Euurus. No one must know about this but you, Kuula, and me."

"Tuuwee, have you lost your senses?" Euurus asked as she strained to keep her tone to a whisper. You're breaking a sacred law by even thinking about the homeland. You'll be punished severely, Tuuwee. Please don't—"

"My minds made up, Euurus," he said. "Nothing you can say will change it. And no sacred law or curse is going to stop me." Euurus dropped her head and stared at the ground. "Then why did you start on the love nest? Why come here to court me if you know you're leaving?"

"I don't know why I went out there and began our love nest," Tuuwee said as he frowned and looked off. "Maybe a part of me wants to stay here and go through with the wedding. In fact, I know a part of me does. But another part desires something else. Something better for you and for our future children. These swamps are not the home of the Cuuzan. Our home is on the open plain. Cuuzanland! And I'm going to go there and make right all the wrongs my father committed which put us here in the swamps. When I'm king of Cuuzanland, I'm going to reverse the curse and rewrite the sacred laws. I'll bring you all home to the motherland. Then we'll marry. We'll have a real Cuuzan wedding on the soil of our ancestors."

Euurus stared at him with loving eyes and said, "Tuuwee, dreams are not always reachable. Some dreams are just meant to think about and wish for. To enjoy. Your dream of becoming king of Cuuzanland is just that kind: a wish, a thought to enjoy, and not a dream to pursue."

"That's where you're wrong, Euurus," Tuuwee said with total conviction. "And I will prove it!" With that, he turned and started off.

"But where are you going?" Euurus asked.

Tuuwee stopped and turned toward her once again, "I've told you enough already, Euurus. It is time for me to act. And I expect you to keep my secret. No one, and I mean no one, is to know about my plans." Tuuwee spotted the tears welling up in her eyes. He stepped over to her once more and put a hand to her face catching a tear as it ran down her cheek. "I shall return to get you. I promise." "Why did you bother to tell me? Why didn't you just go?" Euurus said with both sadness and anger.

"Because I trust you and I felt you should know," Tuuwee said as he gazed into her eyes. She looked at him as she wiped her own tears away and asked, "Why else did you divulge such a secret to me?"

Tuuwee pulled her in closer to himself even as she stepped closer to him. In a whisper he said to her, "Because I love and respect you."

Slowly Euurus moved her mouth closer to his waiting lips, "You really do, don't you?" she whispered. "Yes, I do." Tuuwee answered and they pressed their lips together and held each other tightly.

Tuuwee and Euurus kissed and hugged for some time. It was difficult for Tuuwee, as it would be for any young man driven to the point of sexual conquest, to withdraw at a moment of ecstasy. But Tuuwee did just that. He released her and abruptly walked away.

Euurus's trust and respect for Tuuwee, at that moment, reached new heights because she realized how difficult it must have been for him to back off . . . even before she herself found the strength to save herself from premarital transgression.

Tuuwee walked to another cluster of huts near the cornfield. His mission was to locate his father and talk with him in private. He was slightly dazed by the build-up of his sexual frustration, something Zuuox, his father, and Kuula told him would happen if he engaged in too much foreplay without release. They warned against it and now he understood why.

Tuuwee approached a group of huts and met some women just leaving the front door. Tuuwee's sights were set on one particular hut. He stood on the side of the trail and watched as the women approached. "Anyone seen my father?" he asked.

One woman quickly looked around at the group in her company and said, "Nuufy is not among us. So she's likely with her husband the king in her hut." Tuuwee thanked her and the women walked off toward the lights in the distance.

Tuuwee sat down beside the trail and waited as he kept his eyes fixed on Nuufy's hut. He didn't like the idea of crashing in on his father in this manner. But he knew if he didn't catch Muusamali before the king reached the Samba, he wouldn't get a chance to talk with him in private. The Samba, which was a high-spirited dance festival, usually left the men sexually intoxicated. Tuuwee knew his father would be off chasing another one of his wives, perhaps even Tuuwee's mother Puulu. So Tuuwee felt compelled to pursue his father this night—something he had never done before.

In a short while, King Muusamali finally left the hut with Nuufy close behind. Muusamali was carrying his customary walking staff, wearing his high-top headdress with the remainder of his body wrapped loosely in catskins.

"Father, I wish to talk with you in private. May I?" Tuuwee glanced at Nuufy and before answering, Muusamali also turned his head and looked at his youngest and most recent of brides. Nuufy got the message without another word being said. As she walked past Tuuwee, she gave him a curious expression. Tuuwee kept a straight face and avoided her gaze.

Tuuwee's and Muusamali's eyes met. "Is something wrong, Tuuwee?" Muusamali asked.

"No. Everything is fine," he began. "I seek your permission . . . to go on a leopard hunt. And I wish to do so without an escort party. Just Kuula and me."

Muusamali studied his son's face. Finally he said, "This is all rather sudden, isn't it?" Tuuwee searched for an answer and, just as he was about to deliver one, Muusamali interrupted him by touching his arm and saying, "Why don't we walk, and you talk?"

Tuuwee turned and fell in step beside him. Once again, Muusamali had managed to jar Tuuwee's self-control. It never failed whenever he was in his father's company—he was made to feel powerless.

"Father," Tuuwee began as he matched his father's long strides, "I've always wanted to test my hunting skills against a big cat. And not as a student in training. For once I'd like to go out on my own with just Kuula as my point man. The coat of a leopard would make a wonderful gift for my bride."

"I'm not sure you're ready to take on such a task," Muusamali said. "We mustn't forget the ritual dance ceremony in which you lost your poise, costing you a finger. Your dance was superb, but you weren't quite ready to perform solo. And yet I thrust you into the arena. I'd hate to make the same mistake twice by allowing you to hunt a leopard without a senior escort of some kind. You're not ready and you could very well lose your life."

"Then you could choose another one of your sons to become crown prince, Father," Tuuwee said as he stopped in his tracks. Muusamali, however, took three more long strides before coming to rest. He didn't bother to turn around. He simply stared straight ahead and remained chillingly silent.

Tuuwee quickly closed the gap between them as he continued in a loud voice, "You don't have to pretend that my living means more to you than my dying. My life is mine to throw away if I choose to do so. You, of all people, won't miss me any more than you miss my finger. Just give me your blessing so that I may go on a leopard hunt. That's all I ask of you."

Muusamali kept his eyes fixed on the burning torches in the distance. The sound of rhythm drums suddenly broke the tense silence and filled the night with sweet, soulful melodies. The pulsating medley of the drums in the night never failed to lift Muusamali's spirits. But at that moment, as he listened to the mournful drums, he only felt downtrodden. He was struggling to stay calm and to maintain a steady voice as he said, "There are many paths that lead to manhood, my son. As a father, it's my duty to set a course for you to follow as you journey toward maturity. And it's in accordance with the course my father set for me, and his father before him." Muusamali paused and trained his eyes on Tuuwee. Muusamali's stare was so intensely fixed that Tuuwee felt uneasy as he remembered that his father was known to express his anger with impulsive physical outbursts. "Go on your hunt!" Muusamali suddenly said, totally surprising Tuuwee. "And may you mature and reap the rewards you seek as you journey along the paths you choose." With that, Muusamali walked off alone.

"Tomorrow morning, Father," Tuuwee called after him. "I'll leave at first light tomorrow!"

Tuuwee watched his father's form slowly fade into the night without answering. Suddenly, he was left with an empty feeling inside. He realized that, once again, his father had managed to make him feel small. But this time, the feelings of mediocrity were short-lived. Tuuwee found comfort in knowing that this was a closing chapter in his life. From this moment on, he was free from his father's authority. Free from those nagging feelings of inferiority. Tuuwee, at that moment, resolved within himself that no other man would ever make him feel that way again.

The village square was brightly lit by a huge bonfire near the center and a host of burning torches mounted high in the air on poles. The night was alive with singing and dancing to the rhythm of the drums.

The evening's activities were broken into two main groups. Male drummers pounded away on several different types of instruments which echoed through the night, slicing the silence with a sweet surrender belonging strictly to a fragrant jungle evening. Not far away, the women danced. They were adorned with colorful gold beads and jewelry, and their flashy headdresses kicked up dust to the beat of the rumbling jungle drums. The other villagers, children too small to join in and adults too old to still participate, gathered around stomping their feet to the rhythm of the drums, bobbing their heads with the dancers.

The drummers, about twelve in all, were teenage boys—beginners in training. They were seated on the ground before their instruments, surrounded by warriors of the tribe along with several of the veteran musicians. The musicians were the coaches, while the warriors participated in a wild foot-stomping exhibition intended to encourage the young, novice would-be drummers.

One night each week, the adults got together with the boys and girls of the tribe to give them lessons in dance and drumming. It was most important to the Cuuzan that the young be taught harmony and instilled with a sense of group unity. Besides severe and rigorous manhood initiation rituals which all the boys had to face, some were chosen and groomed to become percussionists. These chosen boys, usually a dozen at a time, were taught the fine art of playing percussion instruments—bongo drums, conga drums, tambourines, and tom-toms. All combined, these instruments delivered a soulful melody which encouraged the body to move and sway.

The women stole the show with their graceful and enticing dance. They were teaching the young girls the art of "nukumanu," which is, in essence, body talk. Like the men's group, there were about seventy women gathered in an area some thirty yards away from their men. But it was the adult women who had center stage. They were teaching the girls, by example, a certain dance routine.

As the women performed their graceful number, the men couldn't help but stare at them with fascination. They cheered them on just as enthusiastically as they encouraged the young drummers. The kind of attention the warriors were showing the dancers never failed to ignite an uncontrollable passion in the women. It made them increase their effort and continue all evening to the dismay of the younger girls standing by and waiting their chance to practice.

Tuuwee fell in with the crowd of males. He worked his way over to Kuula, who was both listening to the drummer yet keeping an eye on the women dancers. He was so engrossed that he didn't immediately notice Tuuwee was beside him.

"Kuula!" Tuuwee called out over the noise and excitement.

Kuula turned and said, "Hello, Cuuzan!" All the while he kept his head bobbing and feet stomping to the sounds surrounding him.

"I have good news." Tuuwee announced loudly as he, too, began to bob and weave. But his movements were subdued in comparison to those of Kuula and the others.

"Oh?" Kuula answered, finally taking his eyes off the women to glance quickly Tuuwee's way. "Are you going to share with Kuula what a delicious treat you received from Euurus tonight?"

Tuuwee frowned and said, "Kuula . . . do you only think about food and women? There are other things in life more important, you know."

"Oh?" Kuula answered in an earnest tone. "Like what?"

Before answering, Tuuwee glanced around at the other warriors who were thoroughly absorbed in the invigorating music and dance. Satisfied that no one was paying any attention to their conversation, he yelled, "Freedom, you fool. Freedom!" Then, in a softer voice, he added, "I'm not so sure you are man enough to want freedom. You are not yet ready for such a giant step."

"I am man enough for anything," Kuula shot back.

"But are you ready?"

"I am ready!" Kuula shouted. "For what?" he quickly added.

Tuuwee moved in closer. "At first light tomorrow, we leave here for Cuuzanland!"

"Tomorrow?" Kuula asked in a voice so quiet and timid Tuuwee barely heard him.

"Yes, tomorrow." Tuuwee answered. "My father has granted me permission to go on a leopard hunt. And for you and only you to accompany me."

A few seconds elapsed as Kuula silently stared ahead contemplating what he had just been told. A perplexing look blemished his handsome face. Tuuwee leaned toward him and whispered, "Are you, or are you not, man enough to walk away from here Kuula—tomorrow?"

Kuula thought hard and fast, then gave the only answer he knew possible, "Yes, Cuuzan, I am ready."

As the evening wore on, the young apprentice dancers finally got their moment in the spotlight. This was, however, only after the adult females grew tired and weary. Tuuwee even got an opportunity to watch Euurus dance. During the closing minutes of this nightly extravaganza, everyone both young and old came together in the center of the square and danced, sang, and expressed their farewells for the night.

While the closing minutes of the nightly celebration was the ideal time for Tuuwee to approach Euurus, he decided not to do so instead preferring to simply watch her from a distance. As she went about her cordial mingling, she never once looked his way. As far as Tuuwee could tell from his distance, Euurus was ignoring him. But what he couldn't see through the dust and smoke across the torch-lit square filled with milling black bodies was Euurus's quiet search of the crowd often catching sight of Tuuwee and her quick glance the other way before he could catch her.

It was Tuuwee's mother, Puulu, who eventually approached her son and, throughout the remainder of the evening, stayed at his side the way in which a devoted mother or fiancée would do. He was unusually solemn tonight. Puulu detected it, but she was accustomed to her son's mood swings. And so, she did what she'd always done. She made herself available to Tuuwee, available for him to lean on should there be a need.

Tuuwee, as he sleepwalked through the crowd, was conducting a private struggle within. He was contemplating whether or not he should reveal his exile plans to his mother. Tuuwee, as well as all Cuuzan warriors, was taught that the ability to tell the truth was a true measure of manhood. A boy became a man when he could face it straight on and tell it without bending it one way or the other. His real struggle was what he knew would befall his mother if he told her everything. He had never before been faced with such a decision. His entire life, he never thought he would have to hurt her in such a way. Even if he didn't tell her, his failure to return home would have as harmful an impact as would the truth. Yet he didn't want to risk having his mother try to stop him. Indecision tore at his heart and was visible on his face.

"Tuuwee, you don't look well, my son." Puulu said as she and Tuuwee slowly walked among the ocean of bodies that had begun to drift toward a cluster of huts. Nearly everyone carried a small burning torch.

He turned to his mother and put a reassuring arm around her shoulder. "I'm fine, Mother," he said, trying to muster a smile. "I'm hungry for some of your good cooking. And until I fill my empty painful belly, I will be sick."

She took her son's explanation for the surface one that it was and said no more.

The dusty square had emptied out as several teenage boys went about their assigned task of putting out the pole fires. Tuuwee noticed his father standing outside his hut in the company of Suubala, as was usual. But Kuula's father, Luuka, was also among them. Tuuwee paid it little mind and walked on toward the huts in the back.

Upon reaching their hut, Puulu with smoking torch in hand, waved good night to their neighbors as Tuuwee took the moment to call after Kuula.

Kuula was walking up the trail just beyond in the company of several young men and women who lived in huts tucked away at the farthest end of the village.

"I will meet you here at first light tomorrow, Kuula!" Tuuwee yelled.

Kuula stopped, turned to face his friend, but did not answer. He studied Tuuwee for what seemed like an hour, but was in reality only seconds, before his female companion tugged on his arm and pulled him away.

"Kuula and I are going on a leopard hunt tomorrow, Mother," Tuuwee said as he stepped quickly around Puulu and into the darkened hut. She followed him inside, the burning torch in her hand illuminating the room and revealing cozy, spacious living quarters with two fur-lined beds resting against opposite walls. At the far end was a fireplace made of stone and a specially hardened mud.

Tuuwee headed straight for the fireplace where several pottery dishes filled to the brim with food had been placed.

"I've heard nothing about a leopard hunt tomorrow," Puulu said as she moved closer to where Tuuwee had set himself on a footstool before an idle fireplace. Tuuwee had stuffed his mouth with so much food, he had to busy himself chewing before he could answer her. Secretly he was glad. This gave him time to think.

Meanwhile, Puulu went about her task of placing firewood into the fireplace from the neatly stacked supply by the wall. Then she sat on a stool next to her son. She took the torch in her hand and held in steady on the wood. It caught, and she kept her eyes fixed on Tuuwee and he finally freed his tongue and began to speak.

"Father just tonight granted me permission, Mother." This was all he said before his hands were once again busy stuffing his mouth with nourishment.

"I see," said Puulu as she studied Tuuwee's face. "Strange that your father should allow just you and Kuula to go on a leopard hunt alone. If I'm not mistaken, a hunt for leopard will take you all the way to the Maradi Plains?"

Tuuwee, steadily chewing and swallowing, noticed that the fireplace was ablaze and fire was fast consuming the short-handled torch in his mother's outstretched hand. Alarmed, he reached and snatched the torch from her and quickly tossed it into the fire.

She turned to him with an embarrassed smile, one that matched the warm affectionate look in her eyes. Tuuwee, on the other hand, as he looked toward his mother, appeared troubled as if he had just eaten a bug. He calmly put his food down as he kept his gaze on the fire. How could he leave his dear, sweet mother behind . . . all alone? Without him, she had no one. Just a husband who shared her with three other wives. A husband who never visited and only required her to visit him once a month to share his bed. Suddenly, she looked so vulnerable and helpless in Tuuwee's eyes.

But he was under the spell of self-induced ambition. An ambition he had been nursing for far too long to control on just a whim. He had a purpose that was sweeping down a fast-moving river heading for a waiting ocean. He was helpless to stop himself from rushing onward toward his objective. That waiting ocean of ambition. Only a strong, solid outside influence could stop his flow. And she now sat before him—the one who could bottle his intentions. He would give her that chance, the chance to put a halt to his lifelong dream. He would be frank and straightforward.

"Mother, I am leaving here tomorrow and won't return for some time, if at all. I will hunt a leopard, true to my word to father. But return right away, I will not," Tuuwee said in a stern, even tone. He watched his mother and waited, expecting tears to rise up within her. He waited for her pleading words to overwhelm him. But surprisingly, none came from her.

Puulu turned toward Tuuwee and said, "Where will you go? Have you decided that?"

He was astonished! If his eyes hadn't been watching his mother's lips, he might not have believed his ears.

"Cuuzanland," Tuuwee heard himself say, just as surprised by his own reaction as he was by his mother's.

"Cuuzanland," Puulu echoed back, her expression not more or less grave than if she were inquiring about one of his daily activities. "Of course. Where else would you go?" she added, looking away for a moment and looking into the fire. Then, as if she was watching Tuuwee's reflection in the flames, she added, "Don't look so surprised, my son. Zuuox had prepared me for this day long before he died. Long ago, Zuuox convinced me that your destiny would someday lead you away from me. I knew in my heart that you would leave my life early. You left my womb early, and when your father tried to hand you over to me, you nearly leapt to your death trying to fight your way free of his grasp. I was tempted to give you a feisty name. A name like Fighting Fish, or Little Wild Legs!" Puulu allowed herself a smile only to let it slowly disappear before Tuuwee's eyes, as her expression once again turned serious.

"But Zuuox, chief among the warriors, had pledged the warrior's allegiance to you in my womb, making you an unborn king—in a sense, the warrior's king. However, only your father was the rightful king of the tribe. Zuuox's move put two kings in one tribe, one small and helpless and the other large and capable. As you were being snatched from my womb, I had a glimpse of Muusamali standing tall in the background. His eyes were bigger than I'd ever seen them. And I was reminded of a rising sun as it peaked over the horizon. Then, there you were! The sight of your beautiful shining body fighting in the midwife's hands reminded me of the morning star struggling each morning to stay in the sky only to be erased by the larger, more powerful sun." Puulu paused. Now, her once-dry eyes began to ware and soften. She fought desperately to hold back the building tears. Her voice was straining under the effort to stay calm. Finally, she said, "If your mind and heart are made up to leave here, then go with the knowledge that you at least have your mother's blessing. It means little since your father is adamantly opposed. But my blessing should allow you some measure of comfort and peace of mind. Go with that."

Tuuwee was uncertain about what to say. His mother's tears, which finally flooded her eyes and began to roll untouched down her cheeks, weren't helping his confused mind.

Tuuwee turned slowly to Puulu and said, "I intend to come back for you. You and Euurus. Once I get to Cuuzanland, I will convince my uncle, the great king, to give me an army of Cuuzan warriors and I will return and free you. You and anyone else who wishes to leave this watery hellhole. I am not just Tuuwee, the morning star, which is every day eaten up by the sun. The sun and the morning are both one and the same. And when I return, my father will accept this, or he will be made to accept it. Be glad for your son, for that day in which I will return."

Puulu was suddenly torn between sadness and pride for her only child. She knew that Tuuwee's leaving meant he was headed toward a dangerous and uncertain road whereby he would likely face a doomed awakening before his dreams come true. But there was untold courage in what he was contemplating. To attempt to pursue a dream of this magnitude was unheard of. Young Cuuzan warriors didn't develop ambitions beyond marriage, children, and honing their hunting and fighting skills. Some boys were bred to become chief warriors. Zuuox was the one responsible for Tuuwee's restless ambition! Zuuox had been King Nuumyu's personal valet and chief warrior. Ever since he was initiated into manhood, Zuuox knew what kings were made of. And ever since Tuuwee was old enough to walk, Zuuox put forth every possible effort to instill a king's heart into the small lad. Tuuwee's fertile mind was receptive to his teachings. Even though Muusamali's fatherly wisdom found prolific ground with Tuuwee, it was Zuuox's seeds of masculinity, courage, and virtue which seemed to blossom in his being. What Puulu saw in Tuuwee allowed her a degree of faith.

Puulu decided not to press her son any further. She realized she must allow him to leave under any terms he chose. In spite of the pain and anguish she felt at having to lose him, she knew it was best he leaves the tribe before he got any older and stronger, becoming too much of a threat to his father Muusamali.

"Just stay strong, do you hear?" Puulu said as she used the backs of both hands to angrily wipe the unwanted tears from her eyes. "You remember to pay timely homage to Cuuz and the Mane's. You are a Cuuzan warrior, and God and the great Mane's will be with you wherever you go, as long as you're a good warrior and remember to pay your respect as a regular offering."

"I will give timely sacrifice to Cuuz and the ancestors who dwell with him in heaven. This I promise you, Mother."

Tuuwee and Puulu fell silent. For a long, extended moment they stared into the other's face. Finally, as Tuuwee picked up some sticks and began tossing them into the dying flames, he said, "Mother, will you be all right here alone?"

"I am the king's first wife," Puulu responded. "Maybe not his favorite any longer since I've grown older and uglier. But by the grace of Cuuz, I will want for nothing as long as I live."

"You are the most beautiful woman alive," Tuuwee said with deep conviction. "My father is a fool if he thinks otherwise!"

"You flatter this tired thirty-nine-year-old hag," Puulu replied. Then quickly she placed a hand on Tuuwee's arm. "But don't let that stop you . . . Wa' Tuuwee . . ."

The saintly smile on Puulu's face as Tuuwee looked upon her nearly took his breath away. He couldn't speak for a long while as his eyes took in the last most heartwarming sight he would see for a long while to come.

"Mother, I don't want to leave you all alone," He finally said. Tuuwee's heart was wrenching. A part of him wanted desperately to break down and cry . . . to just let the tears of weakness that slowly crept into his unsuspecting eyes flow forth. But like a proud, conscientious warrior, he fought back this mark of frailty with all his power.

Puulu could plainly see what a difficult time her son was having, being forced to face the emotional consequences of a situation he had gravely underestimated. None of Tuuwee's life experiences had prepared him for a moment such as this.

"Don't worry about me, Wa' Tuuwee," Puulu said as she made a decision. "My being alone will be short-lived." She rose to her feet, and Tuuwee was bewildered by what she'd said. As he looked up at her from his place on the floor, his mouth opened slightly. She reached down, took his head into her hands and pulled him gently to her with his ear resting on her stomach.

"Say hello and goodbye to your little brother or sister. The great merciful Cuuz has blessed this old hag with a child . . . one to replace the man-child who will soon leave me."

Tuuwee's heart was so heavy. The mixed sentiments racing through his mind and heart were building toward an explosion. Tuuwee and Puulu held each other, their grasp growing tighter and tighter. Now, no amount of will-power or self-determination could hold back Tuuwee's tears. He wept with force, a force mingled with joy and overwhelming sadness. These tears he shed were the first he could remember . . . and would not be the last.

The old warrior was as quiet as a seasoned cat on the prowl. Suubala eased open the door and stepped stealthily inside. The room was partially dark, but daybreak was fast approaching. Of the two small cots in the room, one was empty, the other occupied by a soundly sleeping Tuuwee. Contrary to his norm, he was in a rocklike slumber. He should have heard Suubala's heavy, asthmatic breathing, which was the only noise the old giant made as he crept up to Tuuwee's bed side. Suubala dropped slowly to one knee, then leaned over Tuuwee's ear and screamed, "Wake up, Cuuzan!"

As he leapt upward at this unceremonious awakening, he would have hit his head on the ceiling had his bed been positioned toward the back of the hut. His eyes bulged with sudden fear and his hands raised to defend himself.

Suubala's eyes widened, and his grin glittered with childish amusement. His few remaining teeth were nothing more than rotten bits and pieces. He held Tuuwee's frozen eyes, grunting like an old hog each time he exhaled.

Tuuwee was angered by Suubala's practical joke and even more nauseated by the repulsive sight of this old warrior's grin. He looked away as he tried to shake off his jitters and settle his thoughts and nerves.

"Up at 'em, young son of the king. We have a long journey ahead," Suubala said as he rose, straightening his long body. Fully erect, his head nearly touched the ceiling.

It took a moment for Suubala's words to take hold. But when they finally did, Tuuwee asked, "What do you mean long journey? What journey?"

Suubala's grin turned into a smirk as he said, "Did you really think the king would permit you to go on a leopard hunt all by yourself? How foolish of you!"

Tuuwee was struck with the realization, and it hit him hard. His father had deceived him. Actually, Muusamali didn't state specifically that he was allowing Tuuwee to go alone with just Kuula. But Tuuwee felt he was deceived all the same, and this caused him great distress along with the anger he felt for his father.

"It is that time of the season when the killer cats are with new kittens. The nursing mothers are most dangerous at this time. So prepare yourself well. And be quick about it!" Suubala said and then backed up and disappeared out the door.

The mention of the word mother caused Tuuwee to look over at his own mother's empty bed. He ran the palm of his hand across his face. He did this hard and forcefully as if to rub off the effects of Suubala's words.

Tuuwee realized he had overslept; by how much he couldn't calculate from where he stood. So he headed out the door grabbing his spear and shield from their resting place against the inside wall. He noticed the knapsack hanging next to his spear. He grabbed it and looked inside and saw it was packed with dry meats, nuts, breads, and herbal medicines which he knew were antidotes for snake bites and other poisonous insects. Tuuwee silently praised his mother's foresight and thoughtfulness with a smile.

The sky was partially light and thick with morning rainclouds. The heavy smell of wet dirt filled the warm air. Tuuwee hurried toward a large wooden keg containing drinking water. It was equipped with an elaborate gutter system for collecting rainwater each time it fell. He leaned his spear and shield against the wooden support beam and, setting the knapsack to one side, he picked up a bowl-like piece of pottery. He pulled a small peg from the key as the water squirted forth in a thin, swift stream. He placed his bowl beneath the stream and filled it with water.

Plugging the hole, he placed the bowl over his head, tilted his head back, and positioned his face skyward. He recited his morning prayers to the Cuuzan chief deity.

Slowly Tuuwee tilted the bowl further, allowing the cool water to pour onto his face and over his upper body. Once the bowl was almost empty and his face drenched with liquid, he used his free hand to rub the sleep from his eyes and to wash his ears. Then he brought the bowl up to his lips again where he took in the remaining water. His jaws filled and he swished the water between his cheeks before spitting out the residue.

Tuuwee, at last, began to settle into that Cuuzan frame of mind where the Cuuzan believed that man and the earth are one and God being all. If he was appeased, then all the forces of nature were on Tuuwee's side. The pouring of the water over the body was symbolic of the earth receiving rain . . . that most mystifying and essential substance necessary for life and growth. Immediately, he felt a surge of energy sweep through his body. A feeling of confidence ran through him . . . as it always did when accompanied by the prayer ritual performed each morning.

Unbeknownst to Tuuwee, he was being watched the entire time he performed his prayers. And as he turned around, he received a sudden start. He found Kuula standing on the trail with his little brother Guumal at his side. Just behind them stood Suubala wearing his now-familiar grin.

Tuuwee stood frozen for a moment as he studied the situation. Kuula, as well as his little brother, wore knapsacks under their arms and, like Kuula, Guumal carried a smaller version of a spear and shield. Of course, Suubala was equipped with spear, shield, knapsack as well. In addition, he also carried a large net made of strong fiber folded tightly and compactly strapped to his back.

Tuuwee, for a brief moment, was furious and his anger was directed at his father for not only throwing Suubala into the mix . . . but also Guumal.

But then Tuuwee thought about what Zuuox would do if faced with a similar situation. All at once it hit him. A favorite saying of Zuuox's was "Obstacles are overcome by faith, patience, and a calm mind." Tuuwee found hope in these words, and he determined that if he remained strong and true to the principles Zuuox had taught him and followed his instructions on how to reach the motherland, then the wind god, Cuu-wa, would carry him on his mighty wings safely to Cuuzanland.

Tuuwee slipped his knapsack across his shoulder, grabbed his spear and shield, and headed out onto the trail.

Kuula was wearing a hang-dog expression and, as Tuuwee approached, Kuula cut his eyes toward Guumal. He then looked back at Tuuwee, shook his head sadly, and said, "My father insisted I bring Guumal along. I pled with him over and over not to burden us with babysitting on a leopard hunt. But you know how stubborn fathers can be." Kuula, without turning his head, shifted his eyes to the side, directing Tuuwee's attention to Suubala standing just over his shoulder.

"Our father is just as stubborn as you are wrong," Guumal said, turning to Kuula. Then he turned and fixed his eyes on Tuuwee. Guumal was nine years old, although his round face with small petite features made him look younger. This was why his father took every opportunity to thrust him into situations that would toughen him up.

"I am not a baby as my brother thinks. I am stronger than I look, and I am as brave as he is!" Guumal kicked Kuula lightly on the shin. Kuula frowned at his little brother but held his tongue.

Tuuwee smiled and put a hand on Guumal's shoulder and said, "I bet you're every bit the warrior your brother is." Then he looked at Kuula, whose face revealed surprise. "Remember our first leopard hunt, Kuula? We were considered babies ourselves. But we proved otherwise!"

Kuula was speechless as he stared at Tuuwee. Suubala, however, had grown impatient by the whole exchange and roared, "Enough talk! We have a long journey ahead of us and we've started late. Let's move out."

With that, Suubala turned and headed up the trail toward the back path leading out of the village and toward the Maradi Plains.

Tuuwee would take up the position directly behind Suubala, the senior of the group and designated leader. But Tuuwee would not be totally led by any man. He made that promise to himself last night when he and his father had their last meeting. Tuuwee's first move to establish this fact was his lingering far behind Suubala.

As Suubala walked the lead, Tuuwee paused in front of Zuuox's old hut, bringing Kuula and Guumal to rest with him. He was looking, one last time, at the place which held his fondest of memories, memories of his initiation from boyhood to manhood. Zuuox's hut had been Tuuwee's home away from home. His schoolhouse away from the traditional one in the center of the village square. Zuuox's home had been Tuuwee's playground. He and his little friends had come here to play their war games. It was Zuuox, above all others, whom Tuuwee most wanted to be like and yearned to impress with his child-man fighting and hunting skills.

Tuuwee couldn't resist the urge to stop and stare in wonder at the hut as it sat so tranquilly against the darkened backdrop of the forest. It looked almost eerie. He felt a cold chill race through his body as he thought about his dear friend and fatherly mentor. He sensed that if he went over to the hut, he might catch a glimpse of Zuuox's spirit—an apparition of sorts—from the past. Cuuzans believe that their spirit never dies. Once the fleshly body breathes its last breath, the spirit is freed for a time to roam and explore the earth before its eventual call to heaven, the other side, to the side of the great Cuuz. It's here that Cuuz will assign the spirit yet another body to fill and encompass only the spirits of moral human beings. Immoral souls, however, were whisked off to a place where they were judged then pardoned or punished by a curse.

During its free time of roaming, the spirit could embody any living being except that of another human. It was Cuuz and Cuuz alone who had the power to designate a spirit's next human embodiment. So while awaiting Cuuz's judgment, a spirit would often enter an animal whose characteristics were most like their own during their human existence.

So as Tuuwee watched Zuuox's old darkened and quiet hut, he grew convinced that his spirit was not present. It was Tuuwee's opinion that allowing for Zuuox's mighty attributes during his lifetime, his spirit would only embody the most free-willed and majestic of creatures. And there were none to be seen. However, the sound of something stirring in the brush behind Zuuox's hut could be heard. It could have easily been a stray goat or chicken, yet it caught Tuuwee's attention as well as Guumal's. "I heard it too, Prince Tuuwee. What do you think it is?"

Tuuwee allowed himself a small smile, but he kept it to himself. Cuuzan warriors took the business of schooling their young in the art of hunting and fighting quite seriously. "You will make an excellent hunter, Guumal. You are very alert. That's good," Tuuwee offered.

"Yes," Guumal answered standing tall and erect. "And when we face our leopard, will you permit me the first throw with my mighty spear?" Guumal held up his small, customized spear as he fell back into a throwing position.

Tuuwee remained quiet as he studied the boy's form. But Kuula stepped forward and abruptly wrestled the tiny spear from his brother's hands. "This is not enough weapon to kill a leopard," Kuula said in a stern voice. Guumal looked puzzled and then his face went flush with sadness.

Tuuwee studied Kuula for a moment. Then he looked down at Guumal and said, "Your duty will be to back us, Guumal. A leopard will not always be subdued with the first or second hit and sometimes not even with the third throw. That's where you may be needed. But remember to hold back until we call on you. Understand?"

"Yes," Guumal answered with renewed confidence, overcoming his momentary sadness. He turned to Kuula for his spear as Tuuwee headed up the trail. Kuula returned his own spear to Guumal—and kept Guumal's smaller one for himself. To his way of thinking, the whole purpose of bringing a boy along on a hunt was to familiarize him with the hunting process and to strengthen his young body. And the best way to strengthen the muscles in Guumal's boney little arms was for him to tote a big spear. Guumal's face lit up as he grasped the big spear in his little fist.

"Remember, little brother," Kuula said in a stern voice, "your place is in back of us whenever we face the leopard. In back and not in front!"

Guumal moved in place, sandwiched between Tuuwee and his brother. He was elated to be going on his first-ever live hunt. Unlike Tuuwee and Kuula, Guumal didn't consider the fact that he was leaving his family and village behind, never to see them again.

Kuula, as he brought up the rear, exhibited a certain hesitation and weakness with every step. He stared at each hut they passed along the way as if hoping the occupants would open their doors and allow him the opportunity to say a final goodbye. Occasionally, he would turn completely around and backpedal, staring at certain huts and noting sections of the village. As they came to the crossroads, Kuula looked down the trail leading to the central livestock corrals. There among the herd of animals stood his pride Brahma milk cow. He would miss that old cow as he would many other things of the village he was leaving behind.

The sun, though still hidden behind a thick wall of tall swamp trees, had already begun to blanket the sky with reflections of radiance. The morning star, as it hung poised in the heavens, was slowly growing weaker as it surrendered its tranquil sparkle to the streaming rays of the approaching dawn. The lingering presence of darkness was fast losing its grip on the forest floor with each passing minute, and the clamor of swamp creatures, preferring light to darkness, could be heard saluting the morn with joyful sounds of celebration as they greeted yet another day in the jungle.

When Tuuwee and the others finally caught up with Suubala, he was waiting for them in a clearing which overlooked the shrine of Cuu-ba, the god of hunting and war. The shrine consisted of seven giant-sized spears carved from the slender hardwood of the boora tree. These huge spears were mounted in the ground and towered twelve feet into the air. They were superbly sculptured and were arranged in a horseshoe fashion, flanking an even more imposing wooden likeness of the giant war shield. This giant oval-shaped shield was mounted upright in the ground, and in its center was a three-dimensional, life-sized sculpture of a lion's head.

Cuuzan warriors always stopped and prayed to the shrine of Cuu-ba before embarking on an important hunt, a hunt necessary to provide food for the tribe. A prayer for victory also went to Cuu-ba before going into battle with another tribe.

Suubala did not consider Tuuwee's leopard hunt of significant importance to bother Cuu-ba. Yet as Suubala watched Tuuwee and the others approach, he sensed that Tuuwee's intentions were to visit the shrine. So Suubala led the way as he left the trail and entered the clearing where the shrine sat against a backdrop of thick brush.

Traditionally, Suubala, being the senior leader of the small group, should have recited out loud a certain prayer asking Cuu-ba to grant them success in their hunt. But Suubala merely bowed his head and prayed in private. Guumal did what he saw Suubala do. Bowing his head, he too prayed silently.

Kuula quietly asked Cuu-ba to keep Guumal safe and out of harm's way. He also asked that he and Tuuwee be given the strength to reach their destination.

To Tuuwee, the shrine was more than a monument to Cuu-ba. It was one to Zuuox, since Zuuox was the shrine's engineer and builder. As young boys, Tuuwee and Kuula, under Zuuox' tutelage, had put some work into the sculpting as had Suubala and a few others. Tuuwee didn't bow his head in prayer. Instead he gazed upon the shrine of Cuu-ba lovingly. It was the last physical expression of Zuuox, the one man he loved more than his own father.

As he stared at the shrine, Tuuwee experienced that eerie chill race through his body once again. He strained his eyes and ears in an attempt to detect the slightest movement, some sign that Zuuox's spirit was present. He believed in his heart that Zuuox's spirit would visit him before it passed on from this early plain. The untimely and abrupt nature of his death only strengthened Tuuwee's faith that his spirit would linger for a time in a restless state of longing. Tuuwee searched the sky above trying to spot a hawk or an eagle soaring in the breeze, convinced that Zuuox's spirit would not embody any less majestic a creature than a hawk, an eagle, or perhaps a mighty leopard.

Moments later, Suubala, Tuuwee, Guumal, and Kuula, in that order, were on the trail again marching in single file toward the dense interior of the swamp. As they filed past the right shoulder of the gardens and fruit orchards, several women who were out doing their chores stopped to stare. A few waved, Puulu and Euurus among them.

Suubala and the others waved in return. Tuuwee, however, looked but did not raise his hand in greeting. He spotted Euurus and his mother standing together in the field and he stared at them long and hard. This could be the last time he'd see either of them. Euurus appeared to step forward as Puulu placed a gentle hand on her arm holding her back.

At his distance, Tuuwee couldn't see their tears. But they were there. Large tears fell from Euurus's eyes moistening her beautiful brown face. And Puulu, while she caught her tears in her fingers, wept as well as she watched her son walk out of her life.

Twenty miles outside the swamp region of the Sudd lay a patch of rocks and trees stamped in the middle of the hot dry Maradi Plains like an island in the center of an ocean. Its giant baobab trees made the tiny enclave a place of refuge for the desert animals to escape the hot, scorching sun. The nearest water hole, however, was located twenty-five miles across the Maradi inside yet another desert enclave, which was once an oasis, called Kinshasa.

It was late in the evening, that time of day when the big cats and other predatory hunters emerged from the shade where they spent their days resting and building up their appetites.

Tuuwee, Kuula, and Suubala were situated among the branches of a baobab tree about twenty feet above the ground. They were braced in the tree like three statues, their bodies camouflaged with leaves and twigs. They looked like natural extensions of the enormously fat branches of the baobab. With spears in hand, along with their giant net positioned at the ready, the Cuuzan hunters were poised to spring down from their perch the moment an unsuspecting prey walked near their grasp.

The bait for the prey was a young gazelle which was tied to the tree's base by a seven-foot-long rope. The gazelle was very much alive but completely exhausted, having waged a valiant fight since early morning against the bindings which now held it captive. Tuuwee had used the same surprise air ambush to entrap the gazelle as he was now using for his next prey. The young gazelle was so exhausted that it was now only able to struggle in spurts when it caught sight of its mother lingering off in the distance. The mother gazelle hadn't left the area since early morning when she and the other adults in her herd inadvertently led their babies into the Cuuzan trap. Instinctively, these small herds took the same narrow path each day, the path running beneath a certain baobab tree, as they ventured to and from their feeding ground.

In order for the Cuuzan to spring their trap on a big cat, such as a leopard, the elusive animals would have to be drawn to the appointed location by using live bait. Several leopards were known to roam the area, as well as prides of lions and bands of hyenas. The lion prides and hyenas were the only natural threat to the leopards, with the exception of man. Since the lions and hyenas favored the night to do their roaming and feeding, the leopards, which are natural loners, took quiet advantage of the cool evening hours just before dark to do their solitary searching.

It was imperative that Tuuwee, Kuula, and Suubala remain as quiet and still as the very branch on which they sat. Like praying mantises, they waited patiently without moving a muscle. For hours on end, they sat and watched every movement on the ground below.

In his role as student, Guumal was positioned atop another nearby tree, imitating exactly what he saw the others do. Since he was stationed a safe distance from them, he neither would be hurt nor would he foul things up by moving. From his vantage point, he had a view of the entire classroom. Not only could he observe every aspect of the lesson being taught, because of his position; he could also observe the mother gazelle and had the perfect opportunity to practice his own praying mantis stance.

Although Guumal was sternly cautioned not to participate in the event of the hunt, his urge to spring down on top of the mother gazelle like he'd seen the others do was an almost overpowering itch he wanted to scratch. He had perfect position on the gazelle. She stood frozen just beneath him, her ears pointed, her little white bobtail pointing straight up like the long, sharp horns of her head. As she peered over the rocky landscape in the direction of her helpless baby, she was paralyzed with fear and confusion, not knowing whether to run away or continue to slowly inch toward her entrapped young one in spite of the danger she sensed.

The fact that the ever-alert mother gazelle had no clue of Guumal's presence directly over her said volumes about Guumal's potential to become a great hunter. However, Guumal was exhibiting one critical flaw, a flaw that could cause him a grave injury, even death: forgetfulness! "You must have the poise and stamina of a praying mantis, unwavering even in the face of a storm. When the winds blow the prey within your reach, you must be ready to move with the quickness of a cobra and the strength of the lion." These words, oft spoken by Kuula, were words of wisdom passed down from one generation of Cuuzan to the next, and they were branded into Guumal's heart and soul. But his mind failed to remember and heed the final warning: "But never, ever pounce down upon a horned animal."

The gazelle had two fourteen-inch-long vertical horns positioned on its head like two sharp daggers. But Guumal couldn't see beyond his own runaway imagination. He was caught up with thoughts of how he would be praised by his peers back home if he single-handedly brought down a full-grown gazelle. At that instant, had not the mother gazelle suddenly spun on her heels and dashed off, Guumal's temptation might have driven him to leap to his death.

The leopard which had suddenly appeared and spooked the gazelle must have weighed more than three hundred pounds. The golden spotted beast burst forth from the cover of trees some two hundred yards away. A heart-throbbing hush fell over the entire area. As the hungry killing machine raced it way across the clearing, it kept its spotted head crouched low to the ground. All the while, its deadly gaze remained squarely fixed on the baby gazelle which was now on its feet, kicking and pulling against the rope which bound it to the tree.

In this harsh environment where food was scarce, survival for the leopard depended upon its swiftness, strength, and brute force. The mighty leopard wasted little time closing in on its next meal.

Suddenly, out of nowhere, the mother gazelle reappeared! Courageously, she raced into the arena and darted directly into the path of the charging leopard. At the risk of losing her own life, the mother gazelle was determined to distract the leopard and save her helpless baby. However, the leopard was an old and seasoned hunter, knowing full well the value to a quick kill and an easy meal compared to a fight which would cause it to expend energy and sustain injury. The leopard completely ignored the mother gazelle. With a single-minded effort and chilling determination, the deadly cat drove on toward its intended prey, picking up speed as it flew over the rocky terrain as though it were gliding on air.

Suubala and Kuula held the rope net at the ready. They were positioned on separate branches about four yards apart. Facing each other, they gripped the ends of the outstretched net as it hovered in the air about eighteen inches from the baby gazelle's head.

The unsuspecting leopard was expected to rush its prey and pounced on the baby gazelle, just as he was showing he would do. Thus done, Suubala and Kuula would simultaneously drop to the ground and blanket and surround the leopard and baby gazelle beneath the strong rope netting. At that point, Tuuwee would leap down from his perch into the fray and commence stabbing the leopard with his spear until it was dead.

A surge of intensity seemed to radiate from tree to tree as the leopard grew near and the three Cuuzan hunters sat at the ready. Their hearts were pounding with fear, anxiety, and the excitement of the hunt. Suubala and Kuula eyed each other with a mutual expression of readiness. It was a look of confidence in each other and in themselves knowing they were on the threshold of victory.

Very carefully, Suubala and Kuula rolled their eyes up to meet Tuuwee. Tuuwee was positioned on an even higher branch several feet above the outstretched net. Oddly, however, Tuuwee failed to acknowledge their stares. By virtue of Tuuwee's central role in what was a team effort to effect a very dangerous operation, he should have naturally been attuned to both Suubala and Kuula. Without a doubt, there should have been at least a moment of recognition wherein they conveyed to each other their mutual sense of readiness.

But Tuuwee's attention was fixed on the charging leopard as it raced in to make its kill on what it perceived as easy pickings.

Tuuwee hadn't moved a muscle in hours. His body was paralyzed, and his mind refused to focus on the task at hand. Instead, he stared at the charging leopard and marveled at its beauty and proud, graceful movements. His mind drifted back in time to when he was a young boy attending war games ceremonies as part of his schooling. He and several of his young peers were required to watch and study two opposing teams of elder warriors as they performed mock combat tactics in the middle of the clearing. As the two teams of spear-toting combatants charged toward each other, Tuuwee would always keep his eyes fixed on one warrior in particular—the leader of the pack. Tuuwee's hero and mentor, Zuuox! Tuuwee was mesmerized by Zuuox's physical grace. Zuuox would exhibit such strength and power as he fearlessly rushed into battle with his opponent.

Now, Tuuwee found himself equally captivated at the sight of the leopard less than twenty yards away, racing in to meet certain death. Suddenly it swept over him, and Tuuwee realized why his body was paralyzed and why his heart would never allow him to force a spear into the heart of this particular leopard.

Without warning, Tuuwee leaned forward, letting his stiffened body slip from the branch and fall right into the center of the outstretched net.

Suubala and Kuula, still tightly gripping the ends of the net, were suddenly pulled from their branches and went tumbling to the ground behind Tuuwee.

The leopard came to a halt as three bodies came crashing out of nowhere landing on top of his intended meal. The leopard took several quick steps backward as it eyed this potential threat. Not liking what it saw, it slowly turned and moved back in the direction from which it came. As it made its retreat, the leopard would occasionally stop and look back at its hijacked prey and the gang of robbers who stole it. This wasn't the first time, nor would it be the last, that the "lone hunter" would be outnumbered and robbed of his food. The land was harsh, and sometimes numbers counted more than individual strength. As the big cat slowly strolled away, he left the impression that while he was heavy-hearted over his current loss, he was not defeated. The leopard retained his health, vigor, and pride allowing him to hunt other prey on other days, and that was almost worth losing this meal to the three bumbling stalkers.

The next day, the Cuuzan hunters embarked on their ten-hour journey across the hot, dry grassland of the Maradi Plains in search of Runyum Lake, inside the Kinshasa region of West Central Africa. Looking out over the Maradi and its vast emptiness, they saw that it almost looked as though it were smoldering on the brink of bursting into flames. Waves of heat danced in the air in all directions. Off in the far distance, small separate herds of antelopes and zebras could be seen lazily mixing with the heat waves as though they were up to their necks swimming in a sea of heat and humidity.

The Cuuzan hunters were crossing this sea of heat waves at a hurried pace before the hot sun, and their thirst took its toll. Suubala headed up the march walking with a slight limp, a result of his fall from the tree. Nevertheless, he took long, giant strides as if to push the younger Cuuzans beyond their endurance.

However, Tuuwee, Kuula, and Guumal were holding their own as they followed their high-stepping leader in single file. Although Tuuwee could easily, at any point, close the wide gap of thirty yards between them, he chose not to do so, preferring instead to set his own pace for the others to follow his lead.

In spite of their thick and woolly hair serving as natural sunscreens, the hot midday sun was nevertheless like a fiery hallo hanging over them, and the course, dry earth beneath their bare feet was much like hot coals. Occasionally during the march, Kuula would look over his shoulder to evaluate Guumal's progress and condition, as Guumal brought up the rear about ten yards behind.

They were without the excess baggage of their giant net and sleeping gear, having left them for their return to the tree-laden rock island. Each was carrying only their spear, shield, and empty waterskin. Tuuwee, of course, also carried his pouch of first-aid concoctions. Guumal was toting his spear held high and with a firm grip. As far as Kuula was concerned, this was a good sign showing Guumal's energy level was not slipping.

Kuula noticed Tuuwee looking in his direction. Tuuwee was staring past him and looking back toward Guumal. When their eyes at last met, they both smiled acknowledging their mutual satisfaction for the littlest member of the group.

As Tuuwee turned, he was forced to rest his eyes once more on Suubala who marched ahead as if going to a fire. Tuuwee's lightheartedness turned suddenly heavy as he remembered the night before when the four sat around the campfire sharing the spoils of their kill: roasted young gazelle. Suubala did some roasting of his own as he spit fire at Tuuwee, openly ridiculing him for ruining the leopard hunt. Suubala's fiery response to Tuuwee's claim that he accidentally slipped off the branch and fell into the net was one of scorn and disdain, claiming Tuuwee was an example of Zuuox's bad tutoring.

His remarks about Zuuox greatly offended Tuuwee, but he was careful not to arouse Suubala's ever-growing wrath. Suubala alone held the authority to call off the leopard hunt and direct everyone homeward. If that were to happen so early in the hunt while they were still so far away from the Forbidden Zone, it could eliminate Tuuwee's chance for escape.

As it was, Tuuwee's unplanned and somewhat reckless behavior created a rather ideal situation. After losing the leopard, Suubala reasoned that some time must elapse before once again drawing the leopard back to the area; the only area in the Maradi, where the baobab trees were found and, thus, the only place where an ambush would be successful.

Suubala had decided the group would make the one-day trek across the Maradi Plains to the Runyum Lake to fill their waterskins as opposed to the day and a half it would take to return to the Sudd Swamp region. Somewhere on the far side of Kinshasa, beyond Runyum Lake, lay the land indigenous to the Cuuzan. This was Tuuwee's secret destination. If he was going to succeed in slipping away from Suubala, he was headed in a most opportunistic and convenient direction.

Kuula attested to this fact as he hurried his pace and pulled alongside Tuuwee. "Did you ever dream we would venture this far west, my cousin?" Kuula said in a whisper even though Suubala was far from earshot. Kuula was breathing heavily, but his long stride matched Tuuwee's step-for-step.

"No," Tuuwee answered without taking his penetrating gaze from Suubala. "And won't Suubala be sorry for his dumb decision to take us to Kinshasa."

"But once we reach Kinshasa, we'll be at the border of the land of damnation. We could easily slip away and enter before he could catch us. There'll be no need to drug him." Kuula's voice had a touch of urgency to it, knowing the unstableness of the sleeping concoction in question.

"Don't worry, Kuula," Tuuwee answered casually. "I only speak in terms of Suubala returning home without us and having to explain why he broke tribal law by visiting Kinshasa without a full party of warriors. We both know he is violating the law just to anger me and make this leopard hunt a nightmare. But little does his empty brain know he is doing me a favor and setting himself up for a great embarrassment."

"So," Kuula said as he turned and studied Tuuwee's face, "you did leap into our net on purpose, knowing our waterskins were low and we'd have to leave the area for a time. Tell me, what made you think Suubala would choose Lake Runyum over going back to the swamps for water?"

A grin crossed Tuuwee's face. "You give me more credit than I deserve, Kuula. My allowing the leopard to escape had nothing to do with this fortunate turn of events. My actions were purely unselfish. In fact, crucial is what they were." Tuuwee paused as his dusty and wind-dried face became solemn. "That leopard held the spirit of Zuuox," he said with total conviction.

"Ahh, I see!" answered Kuula, but his expression remained skeptical. Not having had the mystical training of a Huzza doctor as had Tuuwee, Kuula was less informed and indoctrinated in the religion's realm of Cuuzan tradition. "But Tuuwee," Kuula finally added, "do you think that Zuuox would fall for such a trap if indeed that leopard housed his wise spirit? Why, it was Zuuox who taught us every aspect of the tree ambush."

Tuuwee stopped in his tracks so suddenly that Kuula had taken two additional steps before noticing and turning toward him, Tuuwee's eyes were sparkling as he was lost in thought and stared past Kuula. For a moment, he seemed lost in the distance, riding the dancing heat waves.

Suddenly, a strange smile creased Tuuwee's lips. Kuula watched cautiously at first, remembering that one of the first symptoms of heat stroke was madness.

"You are right, Kuula!" Tuuwee said with a hint of excitement to his voice. "Had that mighty beast housed Zuuox's spirit, we would never have come so close to capturing it." "No," Kuula agreed, equally as excited with his own assessment of the situation.

"But I was so sure because of the leopard's awesome beauty and magnificent stride as it ran across that field. How blind I've been." "Yes, how foolishly blind you were indeed." Kuula agreed matter-of-factly after a moment's thought.

Tuuwee began to smile all over again, and as Kuula looked at him, he noticed the wide grin on his dusty face, realized the humor, and smiled in return.

By the time Guumal reached them, Tuuwee and Kuula were bursting with laughter and doing all but rolling on the ground. As he pulled to their side, Guumal didn't know what to think. But his sore, hot feet and dry, thirsty tongue didn't leave him in the mood to join in.

"You two are foolishly wasting energy," Guumal snapped and stepped around his comrades to follow Suubala, who was widening the gap between them. This display of maturity, coming from the little one who was supposed to be their protégé, quickly brought them to their senses. They turned and raced past Guumal. Tuuwee grunted as he passed and Kuula went a step further. Reaching down, he scooped up a fistful of sand and tossed it at his little brother's feet as he stepped around him to take his rightful place in the march.

Entering the Kinshasa jungle from the Maradi desert was like leaving hell's kitchen and walking into hell's backyard. It had once been a jungle paradise with thick foliage and vegetation, exotic plants, and giant trees towering toward the sky and canvassing the green forest floor. Now, it was an open wasteland of hills and valleys, ravaged to the core from overuse and an abnormal twist from Mother Nature. Sand brought in by devastating windstorms covered the entire western landscape. For miles, the corpses of fallen trees littered the remaining slopes and valleys and rotting stumps dotted the hillsides like ugly sores covering the earth. Through the early years, herds of elephants toppled most of the giant trees to feed from their top leaves.

But Mother Nature and the elephants weren't the only destroyers of Kinshasa, which means "garden of the gods." Forced migration of native tribes running from the peak onslaught of European invaders and slave hunters swept unchecked through Kinshasa like swarms of human locust.

Migrating from as far away as the tip of Southern Africa, fleeing with just the bare necessities for survival, these wandering and often-starving desperados had to cross some of the cruelest and harshest land in Africa on their way to some imaginary safe-haven homeland, far from the reach of slave hunters. These once civilized and productive people were forced to an extreme level of savagery in their quest to survive. And survive they did, as they used and abused every resource in their wake.

The ravaged and scourged condition of the garden of the gods was small evidence of how these migrating nomads grew to forsake all respect for the one thing that all African peoples worshipped and most revered: the earth!

For Suubala, the devastated condition of Kinshasa was a sight that always brought sadness to his heart. Having been one of the original members of the Cuuzan exiles as they sojourned here some twenty years prior, he remembered when Kinshasa lived up to its most noble name. Now, it was merely a jungle skeleton with one remaining natural treasure: a large lake which served as a watering hole for the local desperadoes . . . both human and animal. This was where only the strong and quick of feet were allowed to get in and out in one piece.

Suubala pulled up and stopped on a small, grassy slope overlooking the Runyum Lake. It was late in the afternoon and, strangely enough, the lake banks were deserted. Considering the fact that this was the usual time when the animals visited the lake, Suubala was suspicious of the lack of activity.

As the sound of quickening footsteps came up behind Suubala, he didn't let it faze him. He kept both his eyes and attention fixed on the jungle surrounding the lake. The calmness of the lake was a tempting sight, and Suubala's mouth watered. But his eyes and ears kept scanning the forest before him.

Tuuwee came up from behind. He stopped and stood quietly at Suubala's side and followed his stare. His eyes lit up at the sight of the still, blue water.

As Kuula reached them, he too twitched with excitement at what he saw. The lake was just too inviting. And before Suubala could react to stop them, Tuuwee first and then Kuula bolted down the hill toward the welcoming waters of the waiting lake.

As Guumal approached Suubala, he spotted the lake and immediately set off to join the others. But Suubala's big meaty hand sprung out and caught him by the arm, nearly snatching him off his feet.

Tuuwee and Kuula threw down their burdens as they raced toward the water's edge. As Tuuwee drew to the shoreline, he stripped off his medicine pouch and let it fall freely to the ground. Without losing a step, he jumped into the water feet first. And Kuula joined him, just a step behind.

The lake was deepest at this northern end, but gradually it went from its highest ten-foot depth to a mere inch on the muddy southern end. Tuuwee and Kuula remained submerged for a time, then one behind the other, they bounced to the surface faces beaming with jubilant relief.

Kicking their feet and using their arms to stay afloat, they drank their fill and splashed about as if they didn't have a care in the world, completely engrossed and enjoying the cooling comfort.

Tuuwee called out to Kuula and told him to watch as he imitated a jumping fish. Kuula pulled up short as he paddled his feet and arms to remain in one spot. Kuula was all eyes as he anxiously watched and waited. Like a heavy rock, Tuuwee suddenly sank out of sight. Moments later, he burst to the surface pushing himself high in the air as if he were trying to touch the sky above. The entire upper half of his body cleared the water as he arched his back and rolled forward into a perfect nosedive. As his head, arms, shoulders, and midsection sank out of sight, his feet came bottoms up and into the air before they, too, dipped beneath the surface.

Just as his feet were about to disappear, Tuuwee kicked the surface causing and instantaneous explosion of water to shoot forward and smack Kuula in the face. Kuula rubbed his startled eyes with the palm of his hand and, at the same time, snorted loudly in frustration, angry with himself for not seeing Tuuwee's practical joke in the making. Kuula then did a nosedive of his own as he went in hot pursuit of his friend. Thirty seconds later, they both broke the surface locked in a wrestling tug-of-war, gasping for air and laughing.

What had just amounted to several minutes of clean fun suddenly took on the image of an eternity of grave misbehavior. Tuuwee and Kuula looked up and noticed Suubala standing on the lake bank glaring down at them with eyes filled with rage. Guumal was standing quietly wide-eyed at his side. Guumal was less concerned with Tuuwee and Kuula than he was with the inviting water flowing before him, beckoning him to come and drink. But Guumal knew he dare not touch it until Suubala had given his permission to do so. In spite of Tuuwee's and Kuula's strange disregard for Suubala's official position with the group, Guumal knew his place and knew that his future indoctrination into manhood depended upon his behavior while in the company of esteemed elder warriors such as Suubala.

Kuula was visibly worried as he nervously shifted his eyes from Tuuwee to Suubala and then back again. The tension was steadily building as the awkward silence hung heavily over the lake like the quiet before the storm. Little was it noticed that Tuuwee's dogpaddling in the water was slowly carrying him closer and closer to the bank.

Tuuwee got within ten feet of where Suubala stood and stared up at him. Suubala looked down his nose at Tuuwee then Tuuwee lowered his gaze and fixed it on Suubala's feet. A childish smirk creased Tuuwee's lips as he boldly drew back his arms and pushed them forward, letting the palm of his hand scrape the surface of the water sending a well-directed stream flying through the air and drenching Suubala's bare, crusty feet.

Suubala looked down at his wet feet. Rage and disbelief were the first emotions to surface on his face. Then a profound transformation occurred before everyone's startled eyes. Suubala's weather-beaten and war-scarred face cracked into a full-blown, toothless grin. He shouted out a Cuuzan celebration cry and leapt off the bank. In midair, he locked his long arms around his knees and hit the water like a giant boulder, sending a tidal wave through the lake which rocked Tuuwee and Kuula. An explosive torrent flew into the air, finding Guumal's small body and showering him like spring rain. Guumal shook off the shower, laid down his spear, drank his fill, and joined in the splashing and dunking.

Some twenty minutes passed before Tuuwee began to tire of the water. He swam slowly toward a section of the bank some ten yards down from where they had first entered. Kuula noticed Tuuwee's departure, and he did a nosedive and swam beneath the surface toward Tuuwee.

Suubala and Guumal were in the shallow end of the lake, digging through the mud for crawfish. As they found them, they would break off the tail and peel off the scales then rinse the meat and toss it in their mouth. One after the other they scooped up the live crawfish and ate them, repeating this pattern over and over again.

Tuuwee reached the bank first. Pulling himself out of the water, he turned and sat down on the edge of the bank, letting his feet still dangle in the water. Finally, Kuula's head popped up directly by Tuuwee's feet. Slowly, Kuula climbed up the bank and sat next to his cousin. They both appeared to share the same train of thought as they silently sat staring across the lake at Suubala's and Guumal's mud-search for crawfish.

"No better time will present itself than now," Tuuwee said softly, keeping his eyes pinned on Suubala. "He will not follow us into Tabooland."

"How can you be sure of that?" Kuula asked. "If he is angry enough, he will do anything! He is Suubala, the 'Raging Elephant'—remember?" Tuuwee thought for a while then answered, "Even an elephant—with a brain as small as an elephant's—will not lead his young over a cliff. To lead Guumal into the land of Taboo would amount to Suubala placing a curse on Guumal. He will not do that and neither will he leave Guumal alone on this lake in order to come after us."

Kuula paused a second then asked, "And in case Suubala does the unexpected and comes after us?"

"I will not jeopardize Guumal's safety," Tuuwee said solemnly. Then he turned and met Kuula's eyes. "I will be the first to allow Suubala to capture me. The moment I see Suubala cross into the land of Taboo, with or without Guumal, my quest for freedom comes to an end."

A tiny smile crossed Kuula's handsome face. He stood up and extended a hand down to Tuuwee. Tuuwee grabbed it and climbed easily to his feet. "We'll fill our skins and be gone!" Kuula said.

But as they turned, they met a sight that froze them in their tracks. Six heavily armed warriors stood on the slope about a hundred yards away. They were spread out wide, and each held their shields and spears at the ready, poised to charge.

"You see them?" Kuula asked under his breath. "Yes," Tuuwee whispered. "Cowardly Foliose! They will not allow us to reach our weapons if they can help it. We must not waste a moment, my cousin. I am ready. Are you?"

"Let's go!"

With that, Tuuwee and Kuula made a desperate dash toward their spears laying on the ground midway between them and the Foliose warriors. Without hesitation, the six Foliose raced forward waving their spears and yelling their war cry.

It was a race that could determine the outcome even before the fight had begun. The capture or disarming of an opponent of his weapons meant automatic surrender or the risk of being seriously hurt or killed. The loser, in any event, would have to stand disgraced before the messenger gods for whom Kinshasa derived its name. According to Kinshasa tradition, which all the local tribes consented, when Kinshasa was a paradise, it was occupied by indigenous tribes of "flower children" who paid homage to the gods with offerings of fruit and freshwater. These messenger gods used to visit as they traveled to and from their missions on earth. As time passed, humans misused and abused the lake and destroyed the vegetation to the point where the lake and the surrounding forest was no longer fit to quench the gods' thirst and feed their hungry bellies.

The land was overrun and now ruled by several warrior tribes who collectively forged their own methods of appeasing the angry gods for destroying their paradise. These local tribes of warriors felt obligated to provide the messenger deities with sporting amusement by turning Kinshasa into a blood arena. Whenever these locals crossed paths with each other or any other tribes on the lake, they would engage in fierce battle. These violent scrimmages were a matter of territorial rule. Rarely fatal, but always bloody. The combatants fought hard and vigorously with whatever kind of weapon available until one or the other backed down. The victors were assured good blessings from the gods.

Usually, if one side outnumbered the other, that became a quick determining factor as to which side would back down first. But as Tuuwee and Kuula raced to put weapons in their hands, backing down was the least of their thoughts. Being Cuuzan warriors, they were not local combatants and did not fight according to any rules of engagement except their own.

Tuuwee's eyes were locked on his spear laying on the ground fifteen yards away. Although he saw the Foliose warrior charging toward him, he ignored the threat and lunged forward. Tuuwee was in midair diving for his spear when the young Foliose raced in and jabbed Tuuwee in the left shoulder with the point of his outstretched spear. The warrior yanked the spear back as Tuuwee followed through with his diving grab, hitting the ground hard on his belly. He grunted loudly from the impact and pain but kept both his arms outstretched, his hand reaching desperately for the spear now inches from his fingers. Finally, he grasped his hard-earned prize!

As he squeezed the hard, sturdy spear, a surge of energy swept through his body. He scrambled to his feet as the second Foliose stepped in and jabbed at him with his spear. But Tuuwee turned, spinning his own spear as he came around, striking the Foliose's spear just before it caught him in the ribs. Without missing a step, Tuuwee leveled his spear and drove the point of it toward the Foliose's midsection. But the young Foliose was quick and brought up his shield to cover his heart.

Tuuwee's spear caught the shield. As he yanked it back, the first Foliose stepped up and drove his spear toward Tuuwee's back. Tuuwee sensed it was coming and threw himself to one side, dodging the straight-on impact. But by this time, the second warrior had position on Tuuwee and a clear shot at his unprotected kidneys. Either a bad aim or a sense of compassion caused the Foliose to drive the point into Tuuwee's buttocks.

Tuuwee felt the impact as the point penetrated his skin, but he fought to ignore the pain as he swung his own spear in a roundhouse motion, gripping it tightly with both hands with all the might he could muster. The quickness of his move caught the first Foliose with his shield down and flat-footed. The sharp point of Tuuwee's spear, as it sliced through the air at eye level, caught the Foliose across the face. Blood gushed forward from his cheek and the bridge of his nose. The warrior dropped his spear and shield and buried his face in his trembling hands, screaming in pain.

A third Foliose armed with spear and shield ran up to join the fray. But as he examined his comrade's bleeding face wound, the young warrior, no older than sixteen, thought twice about rushing Tuuwee. Tuuwee wanted badly to get a shield in his hands, and the wounded Foliose's shield was laying directly in front of him.

Tuuwee detected the fear in the young Foliose's eyes, and he capitalized on it by displaying an act of ferocious, bold aggression. Clenching his teeth and growling like a mad dog, Tuuwee made vicious slashing movements with his spear aimed at the head and eyes of the Foliose warriors. The wounded warrior turned and quickly walked away while the other two reluctantly stood their ground. Backing up only slightly, the two-armed warriors kept their eyes pinned on Tuuwee as if they were sizing him up for an offensive attack. All the while, Tuuwee inched his way toward the shield laying on the ground at their feet.

Kuula had managed to grab his spear and shield from the ground and rose up just in time to catch two spear-toting Foliose rushing in on him. Using his shield to ward off one attacker who was jabbing at him, he dropped to one knee just as the second warrior charged, spear aimed at his upper body.

As Kuula ducked, the warrior's momentum carried him forward, causing him to step into Kuula's elbow as Kuula drove it up between the warrior's legs, crushing his genitals. The warrior bucked over and screamed in pain. Kuula sprang to his feet thrusting his spear toward the other warrior as he rose up. But the point of the spear met the warrior's shield. And in like manner, the warrior jabbed at Kuula only to have the point of his spear blocked by Kuula's shield.

Meanwhile, the second warrior, recovering all too quickly from the blow to his groin, surprised Kuula with a piercing blow to his back, as the point of his spear drove two inches into Kuula's flesh. The shock and pain caused him to lean over to one side, locking his elbow against the right of his rib cage. He dropped his shield just enough so that the other warrior standing in front was able to thrust his spear over the top of his shield, driving the point into Kuula's left shoulder.

The pain was excruciating, rendering his left shoulder useless. No longer could he hold the shield to block any further attacks. The warrior in front of him and the one at his rear were already taking deadly aim . . . simultaneously drawing their spears back about to deliver their final blow to the helpless Kuula.

At that instant, a rumbling noise broke out as a charging Suubala came thundering toward them, shouting a Cuuzan war cry and waving an enormous tree branch high over his head. Kuula's would-be attackers turned. The nearest warrior met the full brunt of Suubala's downswing, as the heavy branch crashed down upon his head and buckled him to his knees.

The sight of Suubala gave Kuula new life. Enough strength returned to his left arm that he managed to raise his shield. And to the amazement of the Foliose warrior before him, Kuula launched an offensive of his own! He charged the warrior, and the two engaged in a duel of spear versus shield.

Suubala was in a mad rage. He turned on his heels, once again positioned the tree branch over his head, and went in motion once more, as he raced toward two other Foliose who were coming against Tuuwee a short distance away. For a man the size of a small elephant, Suubala moved with the speed of a cheetah. Seeing Suubala charging toward them like an angry bull paralyzed the young Foliose. Before they could gather their wits, Suubala was upon them. His feet never missed a step; neither did he slow his momentum as he raced in swinging the tree branch with deadly velocity never before witnessed by those watching. The young warrior barely had time to brace himself behind his shield. With his spear at the ready by his side, he waited with clenched teeth. Suubala delivered a mighty blow! As the branch struck the shield, Suubala exhaled with a loud, chilling yell. The shear force behind the swing knocked the warrior from his feet and sent the broken shield flying through the air.

The other Foliose was visibly intimidated and fearful of his life. He might have turned and ran had it not been for his fallen comrade laying dazed at his feet and helpless to defend himself. The young warrior managed to keep his cool as he spotted an opening. He quickly stepped toward Suubala to take his best shot. He jabbed at him with his long spear just as Suubala made his move toward him. The point of the Foliose's spear punctured a small hole in Suubala's left side. He looked down and saw that blood was beginning to slowly trickle from the wound. The anger that was stamped on Suubala's face suddenly intensified into a twisted look of unbridled fury!

In desperation, the Foliose yelled frantically for his fallen friend to get up . . . and get up quickly. Tuuwee seized the opportunity to retrieve a shield for himself. As he scooped it from the ground, he didn't think twice about which way he was headed. He rushed toward Kuula, who was wounded and on the verge of being overwhelmed by his Foliose opponent. If not for Guumal being at his brother's side pestering the Foliose with his miniature spear, racing in and out with his quick feet taking jabs at the Foliose's backside, Kuula would have likely been overpowered long ago.

As Tuuwee hastened his approach, he yelled for Guumal to back off and stay out of his way. The Foliose who obviously held back from harming a child as young as Guumal didn't hesitate to turn and meet Tuuwee head on with all the force and might he could muster. Their shields and spears clashed loudly as they engaged in their battle to maim or kill. Ordinarily, when it came to these skirmishes on the lake, local combatants like the Foliose did not fight with a "kill or be killed" attitude. However, the Cuuzan were fighting with a certain desperation which quickly made the Foliose realize these foreigners were on a "do or die" mission.

Suubala raised the tree branch high over his head and lunged at the Foliose warrior who had wounded him. Suubala called on all the strength in his massive body as he brought the branch down in a lethal chopping motion, aiming straight for the top of the warrior's head. Terror filled the Foliose's face, and the fear all but paralyzed him as he somehow ducked and sidestepped the blow at the last minute. As the huge branch missed the warrior by inches, it slammed to the ground so hard it broke in three pieces, leaving Suubala holding a mere stub.

In spite of Suubala coming up short on weapons, the young Foliose—still armed to the teeth—made it obvious he wanted nothing more to do with the raging Cuuzan giant. The warrior raced over to where his dazed comrade was slowly dragging himself up from the ground. Using his shield, he gave his comrade a heave-ho in the back and once again urged him to run.

Suubala's rage, however, was focused on one particular Foliose—the warrior who had made him bleed. He charged the Foliose with the stub of the tree branch. The warrior was either amazed at Suubala's courage or spooked by his madness. In any case, he turned and ran toward the last of his friends who was being double-teamed by Tuuwee and Kuula.

Although Kuula's wound-weakened condition made him a small factor, together with Tuuwee they had the Foliose backpedaling, fighting desperately for his very life. When the warrior spotted the other last remaining Foliose running away from Suubala at full stride, he took that as his cue to pack it in and retreat as well. Turning his back on Tuuwee and Kuula, the warrior made a mad dash for the nearby hillside.

Tuuwee didn't bother to go after him. But Suubala was clearly unsatisfied with such an empty victory. Suubala wanted blood-for-blood revenge and, thus, he kept up the chase following the Foliose warriors as they reached the top of the hill and ran down the far side.

Guumal didn't intend to miss any of the action as he broke out running behind Suubala, waving his little spear in the air and yelling the Cuuzan victory cry to cheer Suubala on.

Kuula had flopped down on the ground, seated upright with his chin to his chest and spear and shield in hand. Tuuwee rushed over and dragged Kuula to his feet. They were both blood covered from their stab wounds. The hole in Kuula's shoulder was bleeding the most. "This is our chance, Kuula. We can reach Tabooland before Suubala's return!" Tuuwee said as he wrapped an arm around his cousin's waist and led him toward the spot along the lake where they had thrown their waterskins and first-aid pouch.

Kuula was silent, his left arm hung limp at his side. No longer strong enough to grip his shield, he slowly let it drop to the ground but kept a firm hold on the spear in his right hand.

Tuuwee didn't want to accept how badly Kuula was injured. But as he heard Kuula's shield fall to the dirt, he looked over at his bleeding shoulder and was forced to face the facts. "I think it's wise if we abandon the quest for now," Tuuwee said and began to carefully lower Kuula to the ground. Suddenly, Kuula's legs stiffened, and he pushed Tuuwee off.

"Go," Kuula demanded, "or take me with you. But do not let me stop you from seeking your destiny!" Tuuwee looked deep into Kuula's eyes and saw a certain strength, a magnificent resolve. "I can't leave without you." Tuuwee told him.

"Then it's settled," Kuula stated. Then, glancing at his wounded shoulder, he added, "Besides, you can better tend to this shoulder than Suubala."

Tuuwee said no more as he quickly broke a long piece of strap from one of the skin pouches and tied a temporary tourniquet around Kuula's shoulder to stop the bleeding. Then he directed him to head south along the lake toward a patch of woods in the distance. Without a word, Kuula followed Tuuwee's instructions, walking hurriedly with his head held high. He stumbled slightly, and Tuuwee watched him with an uneasy heart.

Tuuwee gathered up the empty waterskins and filled them with water. He then grabbed his medicine pouch and pulled out a large leaf which had been cured in an antibiotic sap. Then, he took a pouch filled with a powder concoction from the leather bag and raced over to the edge of the lake where Suubala's weapons and gear were lying on the ground. There, on top of Suubala's war shield, Tuuwee laid out the rubbery leaf and then poured a portion of the powder from the pouch onto the leaf. Tuuwee was sure that Suubala knew how to administer the antibiotic treatment to his own hip wound.

Finally, Tuuwee gathered up his weapons and two waterskins and took one last look toward the empty hill where Suubala and Guumal had disappeared. Then he quickly turned and ran down to the side of the lake to catch up with Kuula.

Suubala reached the top of the hill first. Soon after, Guumal climbed up and stood quietly by his side. From their vantage point, they could view the entire lake and its surrounding dry grassy shore, stretching out for several acres to the left, right, and beyond. The grounds were deserted. On the far side of the lake loomed a patch of barren trees and a few small hills, at which point twenty miles onward lay the Bomu Desert. Farther south, about a three-day journey, Cuuzanland could be found.

Where the skeleton forest came up to meet the lake on the far side, is the place where King Muusamali and the ruling counsel of tribal elders deemed the "Forbidden Zone"—Tabooland as it was formally referred to among the Cuuzan. Any Cuuzan exile who set foot inside its boundaries was doomed to a life of suffering and bad luck. And if they entered it for the purpose of escaping punishment for a crime committed against the king or against the tribe, sudden death would surely strike. King Muusamali and his Huzza priest cursed this southern end of Kinshasa immediately upon entering it from the Bomu grassland twenty years before. Placing a curse on this entire region south of Kinshasa was another shrewd move on Muusamali's part. He was placing an invisible barrier between Cuuzanland and his tribe of exiles.

Suubala stood silently with a hand resting on Guumal's shoulder, staring directly at that patch of trees which came up to meet the lake on the far shore, about three hundred yards south. Directly in his sight, as if he instinctively knew where to set his gaze, he could see a lone figure hurrying down the side of a rocky slope.

Guumal followed Suubala's stare and flinched at the sight of the figure who was obviously Tuuwee, hurrying along. Suubala slowly tightened his grip on Guumal's shoulder as the figure drew up to the side of another, and the two quickly greeted each other. The second was Kuula. And together, the two ducked out of sight beneath the trees.

It was the third night after Tuuwee's and Kuula's flight into the Forbidden Zone. They found a secluded clearing stamped in the brush at the base of a rocky hill about a quarter mile west of the lake.

They were laying on the ground in front of a small fire. Tuuwee was propped up against a tree stump as Kuula lay sleeping at his side. With one hand resting on Kuula's shoulder, Tuuwee gripped his spear in the other and listened to the sound of the night creatures stirring in the surrounding darkness. The laughing cry of the hyenas and the chilling roar of the male lions proclaiming supremacy over their territory could be heard in the distance.

Kuula's shoulder wound was quite serious. Tuuwee's herbal medicines controlled the bleeding and infection, but he'd lost a lot of blood. It was essential he remain as quiet as possible. However, keeping Kuula calm was a difficult task because of Tuuwee's own weakened state and Kuula's violent thrashing in his sleep.

Tuuwee's medicine supply was fast running out, and the complex herbal ingredients were a hard find in this region of Kinshasa. Tuuwee was exhausted from his own loss of blood and lack of sleep. He had been forced to stay awake during the night to keep the campfire burning. Fire was the only thing the lions and hyenas feared. As long as it burned, these deadly hunters of the night would keep their distance.

During the daylight hours, Tuuwee searched and scrounged for firewood and made exhausting trips to and from the lake for water, all the while nursing his wounds. On only two occasions during daylight hours was he able to take a short nap. But it was an anxious rest; he dare not succumb to full sleep.

Tuuwee's health was rapidly failing him, and he knew it. His faith in Cuuz and the other four lesser deities was starting to wane. He'd been taught, and it was instilled in him, the belief that a brave warrior who conducted himself like a man in all his dealings was assured good blessings from the gods during times such as these. He considered both Kuula and himself to be good warriors and brave men. They had fought valiantly against the Foliose and had sent them running. They were obedient in their use and care of the earth. What more could the gods want? Why weren't they intervening to ease this suffering? Why was the smell of death so strong in Tuuwee's nose?

Perhaps he needed to appease the gods with a sacrifice? Surely a fat blood offering would entice the gods to keep death away from their servants. How could Tuuwee manage to perform the sacrificial ritual if the gods would not grant him the strength to do so?

As Tuuwee lay next to Kuula, he leaned more heavily on his cousin's limp body. While he imagined his weight was an uncomfortable burden, he was helpless to sit up or to flex a muscle. And so there he stayed as if sleeping yet fully conscious, pondering their fate.

The pain in his shoulder throbbed, but the questions swirling through his mind were even more agonizing. Where was the unconditional, unrelenting compassion from Cuuz, the almighty supreme god? He had been taught that Cuuz didn't demand blood for favors like the lesser deities. How much more truth was there to Zuuox's deprogramming propaganda than his father's initial brainwashing doctrine?

Tuuwee realized he and Kuula were dying. It was just as the Muusamali curse had promised to anyone violating tribal law and entering the Forbidden Zone. On the other hand, Zuuox had spent many hours prior to his mysterious death educating Tuuwee about the falsehoods surrounding the curse, as well as Muusamali's absurd flight into self-exile.

As Tuuwee stared sleepy-eyed into the slowly dying flames, he realized the fire would soon be out. It needed fuel quickly, but the only wood he had was his spear, and he would rather face death a hundred times than to use it for kindling. Ordinarily, by the time the fire had grown this low, Tuuwee would have already made his wood run. But now he sat and merely looked at the flames about to burn themselves out. His desire to outlive their warmth was also growing dim as he slumped further over Kuula's body. One tiny flame remained as Tuuwee's hand touched Kuula's chest . . . and he failed to find a heartbeat. Hope was gone, and he realized he no longer wanted to outlive the blaze. He wept and, slowly, he surrendered himself. His eyes closed for what he thought would be the final time.

When Tuuwee awakened, it was late afternoon the day after he had passed out. He wasn't consciously aware of time and only barely aware he was still alive. He forced his thoughts to return to the events of the previous day. He tried to rise to his feet but felt something touching his shoulder, forcing him down flat on his back. Suddenly, his shoulder exploded in pain. He remembered.

Hyenas were attacking, and he began fighting them off. He yelled for Kuula to get up and run, knowing he was helpless to do anything for either of them. The hyenas, however, were too strong, and soon they had their sharp teeth in his shoulder. One of the beasts, in a cold act of cruelty, licked Tuuwee's forehead with a cold, wet tongue while others held him down. Still, he couldn't stand and finally relinquished himself to the hands of his captors and fell into oblivion once more.

Night came and went before Tuuwee awakened the second time. It was a warm, breezy morning. The sky was clear, and the sun was already halfway up the horizon. Its rays, however, were obscured by a makeshift umbrella of twigs and branches hovering over Tuuwee's head. When he was first able to pry his eyes open, his first impression was that this canopy contraption was something falling down upon him. As he raised up to avoid the impact, the pain shot through his shoulder like a dagger. He grimaced and grabbed for it with his right hand and was startled to find his left arm was in a sling and heavily bandaged with soft cloth.

Tuuwee looked around and was surprised to see that the fire he remembered as dying was now alive and burning brightly. Beneath its flames was a pot suspended over a wooden rock. He turned to look for Kuula and spied him only a few feet away propped up on his back beneath a warm blanket.

"So far so good," Tuuwee heard Kuula say in a weak voice. Tuuwee was thrilled to be alive, overshadowed only by the sight and sound of his dear friend and cousin. "The gods are good" is all Tuuwee could say, his eyes scanning his surroundings suspiciously.

"The gods are little people: four women and one old man," Kuula said with a touch of humor as he struggled to raise himself a little higher against the supporting tree stump. "Two old ones who tend to us, while two younger girls and the old man standoff in the distance watching."

Tuuwee had his own ideas about who the old man and his companions might be but, for the moment, kept his thoughts to himself. He was trying to cut through his mind's murky fog and grasp the totality of the situation, all the while his body betraying his good intentions. He was weak and his thirst for cool water crowded his consciousness. He looked around and his eyes quickly fell on his water bag which was within easy reach. It was a painful, one-handed ordeal, but he managed to grab hold and turn it up to his mouth, satisfying his longing.

Tuuwee found a chunk of bread and some dry meat, wolfed them down, and followed it with a swig of water. Almost instantly, he felt better. He then laid back and stared at the blueness of the sky, imagining Zuuox sitting among the gods urging them to grant free favor to him and Kuula in their hour of need. True to their benevolent nature, they seemed like they were delivering.

Tuuwee was convinced, now more than ever, that Zuuox's teachings were more authentic than Muusamali's superstitious indoctrinations. If ever there was a curse of death on Kuula and him for crossing the Forbidden Zone, the gods had no intention of letting them die. He remembered Zuuox's promise as if he spoke the words yesterday: "Like the migratory bird, born abroad, you will safely reach the motherland on the mighty wings of the wind god Cuu-wa only if you keep the faith and follow my instructions."

Tuuwee felt ashamed that he allowed his faith in the five deities to waver the other night. But as he stared into the heavens, he swore to the sun that he would never doubt the gods again and assured Zuuox's spirit that he would abide his instructions to the letter.

The afternoon slipped quietly into a cloudy evening. As the hot sun made its slow descent, a cool breeze swept over Kuula. The smell of rain was in the air. Tuuwee had drifted off to sleep only to be awakened by the sound of female voices. He didn't bother to sit up; rather, he watched them from his place lying on his back.

One old woman busied herself stacking wood and piling logs in the fireplace beneath a pot of boiling water. She was a small, neat woman and was partially naked. What few pieces of clothing she had draped over her were a striped green and black color which blended with the surrounding wilderness in wonderful camouflage. The other woman was tending to Kuula's wounds while he watched in silence.

The two women talked to each other in their native tongue, ignoring Tuuwee's and Kuula's presence. They spoke a pygmy dialect which Tuuwee couldn't understand but with which he was familiar. He'd often heard his mother and the other older women in the Cuuzan village speak to each other in this strange tongue.

Tuuwee laid perfectly still, not wanting to disturb their conversation, watching in silence, occasionally glancing toward Kuula.

Finally, the second old woman came over to Tuuwee with her medicine bag in hand. Still deeply engrossed in chitchat with her friend, she kneeled over him and began unwrapping his bandages. He stared into her eyes as she went about her nursing chores, but she seemed oblivious to his gaze. Not once did she smile or acknowledge him, choosing instead to tend his wounds and continue her conversation.

The women washed both Kuula's and Tuuwee's wounds with hot water, covered them with medicine, then rewrapped them with fresh cloth. Just before standing up, the woman attending Tuuwee touched him suddenly on the forehead, allowing her tiny fingers to run across the knotted scar tissue which ran from hairline to hairline like rows of tiny beads surgically embedded beneath the skin. The scars, which stretched evenly across his forehead, were the tribal markings of the Cuuzan. He laid still and accepted her touch where no one had dared touch him since the day the painful procedure was first done.

Muusamali had performed the bloody initiation rite on Tuuwee using a sharp instrument resembling a fishhook. One by one, inserting the hook just beneath skin and twisting it, a total of five beadlike knots were carried in a straight row across the forehead of the young Cuuzan boy. Each knot represented one of the five forces of nature: the earth, wind, fire, water, and the sun. Likewise, they also represented the five gods who controlled those forces and whom the Cuuzan worshipped and relied upon for blessings and goodwill.

The woman's actions caused Tuuwee to reminisce about that painful ordeal some years earlier. After the initiation ceremony in which several young boys were ritually operated on, Tuuwee retired to his mother's hut. As he lay on is bed, forehead swollen and burning with pain, his mother came and sat by his side. She applied soothing cream to her fingers and gently smoothed it across his brow. Tuuwee remembered how much better this made him feel, and while watching the old woman touching him now, he once again recalled his mother's loving voice as she told him "Now, my little eagle, you will always be a Cuuzan, and you will always know it. No matter how far from the nest you fly, you will always be a Cuuzan."

"I placed more medicine and a clean cloth in your pouch," the old lady said, snapping Tuuwee back to the present. Suddenly, she changed her language and was speaking broken Cuuzan. Tuuwee easily followed her every word. She eyed him as if she expected him to be surprised, but his expression remained fixed as he stared at her without speaking. "Be sure to keep the medicine leaves moist, and the cloths clean," she warned as she prepared to leave. She stopped, however, and added, "Gain your strength quickly then leave quickly for your destination. This land is swarming with bandits." With that, the old one turned, and she and her companion started off, leaving Tuuwee and Kuula ample provisions for survival, including a small goat tied to a nearby tree whose sack was fat with milk.

"Thank you," Tuuwee called out. But his voice was a mere whisper, and he realized the woman hadn't heard a word. So he spoke louder, this time almost yelling. "Thank you, Gatooma women. Thank you dearly!"

The women both stopped and looked back, surprised that Tuuwee had called them by their tribal name. For the first time they smiled, looked at each other, and smiled again as they walked off.

As Tuuwee watched them leave, he spotted an old man standing all alone on the far ground. As the women approached him, the three of them headed off together into the woods.

"Gatooma, Gatooma," Kuula mumbled to himself. "I've heard of them from somewhere. But where?"

"This was once their homeland," Tuuwee said. "It was before outsiders destroyed it and forced them back into hiding. Our tribe once lived among the Gatooma when we were tiny children."

"Now I remember where I heard their tongue. My mother spoke that giber when she talked about certain food and medicines," Kuula said as he attempted to sit up. But his face grimaced with pain, and he eased back down. He was still too weak and in too much pain to move.

Tuuwee watched him, his concern rising. "Take it easy, Cuuzan, and let your strength build up."

"If you say so," Kuula said, letting out a sigh of release. "But I'm ready to pack up and shove out the moment you are."

Tuuwee stared at Kuula from the corner of his eye. "I understand, friend," Tuuwee answered. He turned, searching for his trusty spear, and found it laying on the ground within easy reach. Tuuwee praised the Gatooma women. Allowing his gaze to fan over the campsite, he saw evidence of the Gatooma's concern for them everywhere he looked. There were the makeshift canvasses hanging over both their heads to block the penetrating sun, a hole dug in the ground where they'd concealed food, the goat tied to the post with her milk sack bulging, and the burning fire with the large stack of logs piled neatly to one side.

Tuuwee felt truly blessed as he lay back down. Eyeing the fat goat, he made a mental note that as soon as his health permitted, he would present the gods with a live sacrificial offering of gratitude.

As darkness crept over them, bringing with it a cool breeze, Tuuwee fixed his eyes on the burning fire as if it had a life of its own. Obviously, the women had provided them with the best wood in the forest. And again, Tuuwee reveled in the thought of the kindly old women. He gripped his spear with confidence that the night was under his command.

Tuuwee spoke softly to Kuula, "I will take the first watch, Cuuzan." But Kuula lay silent, sleeping soundly under his blanket with his spear laying across his chest. The sight of Kuula's peace gave Tuuwee yet another reason to praise the Gatooma.

Three days later, they were both up and walking. They shared the duties of gathering wood and cautiously going to the lake to fetch the water. Going to the lake was a dangerous task which they attempted only at night under cover of darkness. They feared being spotted by the Foliose warriors whom they spotted visiting the lake once each evening. From their hidden vantage point among the trees west of the lake, they watched as other bands of warriors also refresh themselves at the lake. On two occasions they witnessed the Foliose, who took claim as the dominant tribe in the region, engage these other warriors in combat. But not once did these skirmishes result in injury nearly as severe as that sustained during the fight between the Cuuzan and the Foliose.

Tuuwee and Kuula realized that they could have avoided their injuries had they played by the rules of engagement governing "mock battles."

However, Cuuzan warriors were accustomed to fighting mock battles only among themselves for ceremonial and training purposes. Tuuwee and Kuula were taught that to draw a weapon on another armed warrior outside the tribal family was to kill that warrior or face the likelihood of being killed themselves. While they did learn a vital lesson while watching these nonlethal skirmishes on the lake, it didn't change their outlook or change what would be their conditioned response were they ever to be confronted with such circumstances again.

Tuuwee's arm was finally free from its sling, but Kuula chose to stabilize his shoulder by keeping his arm tied to his chest. Their little campsite, which was tucked away inside a nest of tall brush at the base of a rocky cliff, was far enough from the main trail that they were undetected. They could sit and watch the westbound traffic going to and from the lake without fear of being spotted. Because of the confidence they had in their hideaway, they did not rush to leave the area as the women had warned, choosing instead to thoroughly nurse their wounds and rest for the long trek ahead.

Tuuwee and Kuula were completely surprised one morning by a visit from an old man. As they were just about to switch their lookout shift, Kuula was preparing to bed down after a half-night's watch, and Tuuwee was just awakening and getting to his feet. The old man walked right into their camp unnoticed.

"You must leave right away," the voice said. Tuuwee spun around with his spear in hand as Kuula scrambled frantically to get his footing, only to fall down grabbing his tender shoulder.

The old man watched without flinching as Tuuwee leveled the point of his spear at the old man's heart. The old man spoke with the same broken Cuuzan tongue as did the two women. He calmly explained to them that a large party of slave hunters was on the lake at that very moment, refreshing themselves and their camels. Judging by the small number of prisoners they had in chains thus far, they obviously hadn't reached their quota and possibly would comb Kinshasa in search of more black flesh.

Within a short time, Tuuwee and Kuula had gathered up everything needed for the long, two-day journey across the Bomu grasslands. The old man didn't move an inch since he first arrived. He quietly stood his ground and watched Tuuwee and Kuula as they finalized their departure by double-checking each other's carrying bags, waterskins, spears, and shields.

In as humble a fashion as Tuuwee could muster, he slowly approached the old man. As he stood before him, Tuuwee's 6'3" tall, muscular frame towered over the old Gatooma pygmy like an anteater over an ant. Yet the old man, who carried no weapon except for his bamboo blowgun, maintained an air of confidence as if he were protected by unseen forces, which perhaps he was. His face was wrinkled and sad.

"Will you be safe from these slave hunters?" Tuuwee asked as he looked down tenderly at the old man feeling rather awkward.

"Yes," the Gatooma answered. Then, in a reluctant way, he added, "We have hiding places where we retreat. They're secret locations, known only to my people, which is why our Council of Elders won't permit me to take you there."

Tuuwee remembered being told stories about how these Gatooma pygmies could disappear off the face of the land without a trace and remain hidden for months. But if ever discovered and cornered, they were fierce fighters and very effective in the use of shooting poison darts. Many of the Cuuzan recipes for extracting poisons from certain plants, animals, and insects had come to them from the Gatooma pygmies.

"I understand," Tuuwee said. "Besides, we are anxious to embark on our journey to Cuuzanland."

The old man's face turned to one pondering a deep question. He looked more closely at Tuuwee, then he stared over at Kuula, who was standing quietly off to the side holding the goat by its rope.

"That is no longer the name of your homeland," the old man finally said. Then he added, "You have never been to your homeland, which means you are of the Muusamali clan. Correct?"

"Yes," Tuuwee answered. "Muusamali is my father and Kuula's uncle." Tuuwee pointed at Kuula, who politely nodded his head in their direction. The old man's sad, wrinkled face cracked into what resembled a smile. He looked at Kuula and then back to Tuuwee. "Morning Star!" the old man said, but the words came out in his own native tongue.

Tuuwee frowned and said, "My name is Tuuwee." But the old man brushed his words off as his face tightened once more and his eyes turned cold. "We must leave now," the old man announced and abruptly turned and headed off.

"Gatooma, wait!" Tuuwee called out. But the old man kept walking. "You must leave," he yelled back, while his steps took him further away. "Tell me one thing," Tuuwee called, taking two steps forward then stopping. "What godforsaken name has taken the place of Cuuzanland? And are we traveling in the right direction?"

"Young man," the old Gatooma said as he stepped forward and turned, "I swore an oath to your father, and I am bound by my word. I saved you from early death. I owe you nothing more, Tuuwee, son of Muusamali."

With that, the old man turned and started off.

Tuuwee was left pondering the question, Why? Why would his uncle King Nuumyu change the name of the motherland? Also, it struck him just how far-reaching his father's power and influence were!

He watched silently as the old man's tiny frame grew smaller and smaller and finally disappeared. Tuuwee wasn't the least bit discouraged by the old man's sudden change of attitude or what he had told him. He was that much more driven to reach the homeland. And it was his homeland . . . no matter what name it was called.

Tuuwee and Kuula, with the goat in tow, set out through the jungle traveling southwest as Zuuox had instructed. Before the sun set, they had cleared the skeleton jungle and found themselves at the Bomu frontier. They stopped and stared in awe at the immense openness that stood before them. There wasn't a tree or animal in sight, just a boundless ocean of grass. All their lives they had been confined to the dense Sudd swampland and the neighboring Maradi Plains, which had an abundance of trees and roaming herds of animals. Never had their eyes seen such a vast, wide-open, and empty expanse of land.

With the shadowy skeleton forest looming behind them and with darkness settling down around them, bringing with it an eerie breeze off the Bomu, a chilling sense swept through their spirits that they'd reached the end of the world.

Kuula's once-sleepy eyes were now wide with a dreadful wonder as he stared at the sight before him. Tuuwee was a little more subdued but no less troubled by what he saw. Realizing that darkness was swiftly closing in, Tuuwee began to quickly think. His thoughts turned toward the two mountain peaks which Zuuox had told him to look for once he reached this point on the Bomu frontier. But the horizon was already too dark for him to spot such a place. By not having this all-important reference to chart their course, it would be foolish of them to venture out into the Bomu. Tuuwee could only pray that the two mountains, which Zuuox called Twin Peaks, would be there in the morning.

"We'd better make camp here for the night and start fresh at first light," Tuuwee said. This brought an instant sigh of relief from Kuula. But his words betrayed his expression. "Now or later. It matters none to me."

Pulling the goat along, Kuula turned and followed Tuuwee back into the wooded enclave. They ventured some thirty yards off the trail and set up their camp in a tiny grove. Total darkness soon fell upon them, and with the night came the familiar roar of the male lions thundering in the near distance. The roar was so overbearing that it drowned out all other night noises and stilled the darkness for some moments after it had ceased.

At long last, Kuula was making ready to take his turn at sleep while Tuuwee tended to a small fire supposedly preparing for his lookout duty. But in the spur of the moment, he suggested that they pay homage to the gods for their kind, kind blessings thus far and to ask for continued safe journey across the Bomu.

Although Kuula was bone-tired and sleepy, he nevertheless dreaded the thought of having to cross the Bomu the next morning. Therefore, he welcomed the idea of appeasing the gods with a blood offering before venturing out into what seemed like stepping off the ends of the earth.

Kuula eagerly pitched in and helped Tuuwee prepare his ritual altar to the gods. They constructed a four-foot table from sticks and branches. Without all the usual ceremonial fanfare of dancing and staging his fake hypnosis trick, Tuuwee tranquilized the goat by "enema injecting" the potent sleeping concoction.

They built a total of five small fires which they arranged in a circle around Tuuwee and the altar, the altar holding the paralyzed goat. Each of the burning fires represented one of the fire gods.

Tuuwee was on his knees before the altar. He gripped a stone knife with his good hand. With his head tilted back, he gazed upward toward the star-filled sky and mumbled the sacred words to an ancient Cuuzan prayer. As he prayed, he would periodically bow down before the altar allowing his forehead to touch the ground for several minutes before straightening up and continuing to address the stars above.

Not far to his rear, Kuula sat on the ground with legs crossed beneath him. It was his duty to keep the fires burning, as he fought to keep his sleepy eyes open. His head would nod until his chin met his chest, and he would snap back awake.

The small goat only weighed seventy-five pounds—not much of a prize to satisfy the appetite of all the gods. But Tuuwee figured that Kuula's injuries and his own were reason enough for the gods to take exception and accept what small offerings they could muster.

Tuuwee's first prayer went out to Cuuz, the almighty god of gods. Then, one by one, he recited a shorter prayer to each of the four remaining deities who governed the affairs of the almighty. "Beloved Cuu-ott, mighty god of the earth, grant us your blessing in our quest to reach the motherland. Accept this small gift of our respect and gratitude." Tuuwee laid hands on the goat to emphasize his gift. The goat was breathing steadily, its eyes open, yet the concoction had rendered it powerless to move.

Tuuwee closed his eyes and bowed again, this time allowing himself to lay flat on his face as he kissed the earth god Cuu-ott. For several minutes he remained in this prostrated position. Then he raised his head and recited a similar prayer to the wind god, Cuu-wa. This time, he humbled himself by opening his arms and gazing up at the blackened sky. He felt a slight breeze sweep across his face, and he considered this a positive sign that Cuu-wa was pleased with his offering.

After several more minutes of holding his position, Tuuwee turned his thoughts toward Cuu-el, the god of fire. By chance, he opened his eyes and looked toward the fires but noticed that each of the five in number had burned out. Not a single fire remained alive! Tuuwee turned and saw Kuula sitting upright with his chin resting on his chest, fast asleep.

Tuuwee's first thought was to grab his spear. But before he could rise to his feet, a huge male lion sprang toward them out of the darkness. In an instant, the ferocious big cat was upon him. Had he risen to his feet, he may have become the lion's target. Instead, the four-hundred-pound, full-maned lion rushed the altar. As it snatched the goat into its powerful jaws, it pounced on Tuuwee, knocking him hard on the back like a rag doll.

As abruptly as it appeared, the big cat quickly vanished back into the darkness. Tuuwee was dazed and hurting but was very much aware that another fire had to be built, and quickly so. Rambling to his feet, Tuuwee rushed over to one of the smoldering piles of hot ash. He grabbed a red-hot stick and quickly used it to ignite some dry grass.

Kuula was finally on his feet gripping his spear. Immediately he knew the mistake he'd made and the danger he'd placed them in. He danced around in circles jabbering continuously into the surrounding darkness in a desperate effort to keep further attackers at bay.

"I'm sorry, Tuuwee. I'm sorry!" Kuula was pleading as he kept his feet and spear in motion.

"Never mind. Just keep screaming and keep up the movements," Tuuwee yelled as he managed to turn a spark into a tiny flame.

Kuula did his best to comply, jabbing with his spear and yelling the Cuuzan war cry.

In minutes, Tuuwee had a fire burning. Shortly he and Kuula were settled down again. Kuula was lying on his blanket in front of the fire, and Tuuwee sat squatting on his heels staring into the darkness, spear resting on his lap. "Perhaps I wouldn't have fallen asleep had you put on one of your soul-stirring dance routines," Kuula said in a sleepy voice.

Tuuwee was engrossed in his own thoughts and didn't reply for a moment. Finally, he cut his eyes Kuula's way and said, "Well, I'm not dancing now,

Cuuzan, so go to sleep. We have a long journey ahead of us." But Kuula was already asleep, even before Tuuwee had finished speaking. Tuuwee smiled at his friend. It was a pleasurable emotion but short-lived and not likely to be experienced again anytime soon.

The Bomu grassland didn't prove to be as terrible as they had first imagined. Once they set out crossing the open grassland, they immediately discovered many signs indicating that others had crossed this way before. Footprints, wagon tracks, and debris littered the way and could be seen no matter which way they looked.

They began their trek at dawn, walking into the sun and keeping just to the outside of the far right Twin Peak which loomed on the horizon. It occurred to Tuuwee that, as he charted their course by the distant peak, the wagon tracks, and footprints seemed to be heading in the same direction.

By high noon, walking at an average pace with two short breaks, Tuuwee and Kuula reached the Bomu Canyon, just like Zuuox had predicted. The canyon was some three hundred yards wide and stretched for miles to the north and south.

Tuuwee encountered a much-used road that ran along the shoulder of the canyon. As he looked across the mouth of the steep cliff, he noticed another road carved into the grass which also ran along the edge of the cliff on the same side.

Slowly, they crossed the road and carefully approached the steep rocky cliffs. They peered over the edge into the mouth of the canyon and were awed by the sight of such a long, massive hole in the center of the earth. Kuula's mouth hung open in amazement.

Zuuox had spent time describing these landmarks to Tuuwee so he was a little more prepared to handle his emotions. What really struck his interest, as he stood at the cliff's edge, were a pair of black eagles in flight soaring 150 feet above the canyon floor. Tuuwee marveled at being able to see these magnificent birds in flight at eye level.

Kuula stood two steps farther back from the edge. He leaned forward to get a better look into the canyon and whispered, "What god could have dug such a hole as this, Tuuwee? And why?"

Tuuwee couldn't take his eyes off the eagles, not even for a moment. Finally, when they had taken their leave, he looked down into the mouth of the canyon and answered, "None other than Cuuz, the almighty. And who knows what goes on here when mortal eyes are not watching?"

Tuuwee's voice echoed off the canyon walls and back again. It was such a strange sound to Kuula's ears that it prompted him to step even closer to the cliff's edge. "Ah," Kuula yelled and, smiling, listened to his voice come back to him.

"Come, we must keep moving," Tuuwee said and he set out to the road on the right heading south. Somewhere up ahead, the deep canyon floor would eventually come up to meet the Bomu Plains once again. Tuuwee knew if he followed Zuuox's instructions they should expect to reach the canyon's end before nightfall. It was there he was told to wait until the next dawn, when the sun would rise in the east. They should travel against it and head west. Before the sun set that day, they would be in Cuuzanland.

Tuuwee walked at a hurried pace with Kuula in step behind. Tuuwee was anxious to reach the canyon's end, knowing that the next morning they would embark upon the last leg of their journey home.

They traveled several miles before stopping to rest. Tuuwee was seated on the ground among a bed of rocks and trees about twenty yards off the path opposite the canyon. The biggest boulder provided some small refuge from the hot sun as he relaxed in the cool shade watching Kuula. Kuula seemed fascinated with the canyon, and he chose to sit out in the sun and pitch rocks into the canyon's mouth just to hear their echo effect upon landing.

Tuuwee was feeling especially at ease with himself and his newfound freedom. The pain had finally left his shoulder wound, and the last time he checked Kuula's progress, he too was healing quickly. He somehow felt that the gods were showing them their favor, in spite of his failure to pull off the last sacrifice with the goat, and the fact that he was zero for two in his attempts at conducting the ritual from start to finish. He nevertheless felt confident that he would eventually succeed. Once he reached the motherland, he told himself, his luck would change. He promised himself that he would conduct the finest sacrificial offering the gods had ever witnessed!

With the thought of reaching home racing through his mind, Tuuwee became restless. He stood up and started to gather his possessions. As he was finishing the task at hand, he looked up and spotted a cloud of dust on the move, coming down the road in their direction. "Avoid all contact with strangers." Tuuwee remembered Zuuox's warning all too clearly. "See and hear everything in your path. But at all cost, avoid being seen or heard yourself." Zuuox's words haunted him.

Tuuwee dropped to a squat as he spoke in a loud whisper to Kuula, "Do not make any sudden move." The urgency in his voice was apparent, causing Kuula to freeze. "There are strangers approaching on the far side," Tuuwee whispered. "Lay back and crawl this way," he added as he slowly maneuvered himself out of sight toward the blindside of the rock pile.

Kuula looked and made his own assessment of the situation. An army of black bodies was, indeed, marching toward them up the opposite shoulder of the canyon. Ever so slowly, Kuula leaned down until his back rested on the ground. Then, he rolled over on his stomach and crawled across the road toward the rock pile where Tuuwee had been waiting. Once there, he discovered Tuuwee had moved. Kuula crawled around to the backside of the rock pile and there found Tuuwee squatting against a cluster of smaller rocks. Tuuwee didn't say a word, only stared at Kuula as if he had just seen a ghost.

Immediately, Kuula saw the reason for Tuuwee's strange behavior. At Tuuwee's feet, he saw dozens of scorpions, a few of which were already making their way up his leg. Tuuwee hadn't yet been stung because of his quick thinking and presence of mind. He'd remained perfectly quiet and still. He knew these creatures, who relied so heavily on their precious venom for survival, were not quick to waste it needlessly. As long as he remained still, he was under little threat.

Kuula's first reaction, however, was to swat a scorpion off Tuuwee's knee. In a lightning quick backhand motion, he sent it flying through the air. "Kuula, no!" Tuuwee hissed between clenched teeth. Kuula managed to restrain himself, but it was a very difficult assignment for him to stand idly by and watch as these deadly scorpions crawl over his cousin's body uncontested.

"Give them time to find their way, and they will leave me. Fight them and I'm dead," Tuuwee whispered.

As they played this lethal watch-and-wait game with, the rattling sound of scores of leg irons filled the air. The sound of clanging, dragging chains was foreign to Tuuwee and Kuula. They'd never heard such noise before. It was taking all Tuuwee's strength and willpower to ignore the scorpions and remain quiet. Yet he wanted to see where this new sound was coming from.

From their vantage point behind the rocks, they could peer through the cracks and view the far side of the canyon. They saw twenty-five or thirty naked black men and women marching in single file with their legs in shackles. One long chain was attached to each of their necks, binding them all together and forming a string of human misery. Three camels and their riders, wearing Arab turbans on their heads, led the march.

As the procession of shining black bodies reached the point directly across from where Tuuwee and Kuula were hiding, the camel riders stopped bringing the entire chain gang to a halt.

Kuula held his breath as he noticed the riders staring across the canyon, apparently looking at the very spot where they were hidden. Tuuwee closed his eyes and prayed.

Kuula looked beyond and saw three more riders approaching from the rear of the procession. They stopped and began talking with the others at the front. Soon two men on foot carrying bullwhips marched up and joined the camel riders. All of them were staring at the rock pile hiding spot.

"They've spotted us, Tuuwee. What can we do?" Kuula said nervously. "Stay still," Tuuwee hissed back. Sweat was running from his brow as a scorpion now stood on the very center of his chest. Two others kept moving over his body in a seemingly endless search for some unknown. Tuuwee knew the danger was when they stopped moving, and his heart raced with dread.

The Arab slave hunters definitely were interested in the spot where the two were hiding. Tuuwee and Kuula new very well the fate of those who crossed paths with the slave hunters. They were subject to being seized by force and thrown into chains. And these Arab slavers apparently thought their greedy eyes had spotted human prey across the road. As the slavers stared in their direction, their senses alerted them to the smell of fear among the rock pile. But too deep and too wide of a canyon stood between hunter and prey. While their camels were fast, quick, and sure of foot and could track down a man in mere minutes, they either decided to spare their precious camels, or these merchants of misery considered themselves already fat enough with human booty.

As the first three camel riders started off once more, the sound of cracking whips again shattered the tense silence. The long line of shiny black bodies responded, and the rattling of chains was, somehow, a welcomed sound to Tuuwee and Kuula. The last two riders remained behind for a long, agonizing moment. They kept their gaze pinned on the rock pile while the noisy chain gang filed past. Then, with their eyes still focused on the hiding place, they kicked their camels, headed out, and fell in line behind the others.

As the threat from across the canyon departed, and the sound of chains faded in the distance, all but one of the scorpions had left Tuuwee's body. And he was the granddaddy of them all. Tuuwee was growing more fearful but not so much of this scorpion explorer as he was of Kuula's impatience. Kuula stared at the invader with tense restlessness. "I can get him, Tuuwee. Just let me try it!" Kuula said eagerly. But before Tuuwee could answer, the old scorpion found his own way down and abruptly dropped to the ground.

Tuuwee gave a sigh of relief, while Kuula stared angrily after the scorpion, wanting to chase it down and stomp the life from it! But he knew that to kill the creature now, when it was no longer any threat, would be wrong.

Tuuwee's focus was on the slave hunters as he recalled points along the canyon. There were spots, not far from where they were, that were capable of crossing. If the camel riders were desperate enough, Tuuwee feared they could reach one of the crossings and, in a short while, double back and be upon them again with little notice.

Tuuwee went to stand up and, at the same time, reached for his spear lying on the ground next to his carrying bag. Unbeknownst to him, a scorpion was partially trapped beneath the bag's edge and, when he'd reached for his spear, he touched the bag and freed the angry, frightened creature. He never saw the scorpion but felt the painful stinger strike his hand. Just after it struck, it raced away between two rocks. Tuuwee rushed his hand to his mouth and, in a desperate effort, tried to suck the poison from his veins.

Kuula saw the entire incident and immediately went into motion. He grabbed the strap on the water bag and quickly tied it around Tuuwee's arm. Grabbing his stone knife, he then took Tuuwee's hand into his and cut a half-inch gash where the scorpion had left its mark. Tuuwee's face grimaced in pain, but he held still while his friend continued his efforts to keep the poison from spreading throughout his bloodstream. Kuula put his mouth over Tuuwee's wound and began sucking the blood and the poison from his system. As he spit the waste on the ground, he repeated the procedure over and over again.

Meanwhile, Tuuwee gently eased himself to a sitting position, conscious of the fact that he must not allow himself to become excited, causing his heart to race. He sat with his eyes shut and his body prone. His fate was up to Kuula. He felt a sense of calm spread through him, knowing he was in good hands.

Sometime later, a strange noise reached Kuula, and it continued to grow louder and louder. He knew it was coming up from the right shoulder of the canyon, the road they had taken to get where they were now. And where, Kuula wished to God, they could be anyplace else.

Two hours had elapsed since Tuuwee's battle with the scorpions. He was zapped of all his strength and energy to the point of being unable to move. Sweat was pouring from his body, and he was mumbling unrecognizable prayers to the gods. Kuula was helpless to do any more. In addition to sucking the poison from Tuuwee's wound, he'd fed him a gummy concoction, claiming to be a venom antidote, which he'd gotten from the medicine bag. Finally, he'd forced their very last drop of water down Tuuwee's throat.

Now, with the sound of footsteps approaching, they were at the mercy of the gods. Kuula gripped his spear with both hands in preparation to meet the worst the gods might allow. Suddenly, the footsteps were upon them.

The sight Kuula saw first, as he peered from his rocky lookout, was two men on foot walking past the rock pile. He then spied a covered wagon driven by a team of oxen with two black male occupants. Quickly, it had rolled on past. Soon, more men along with several women on foot appeared and then disappeared as they filed past the rock pile without glancing Kuula's way.

Kuula raised his head just enough to peer over the rocks and down to the road. He saw three more wagons approaching in single file, with people walking along at the sides and to the front.

These men and women, dressed in trousers and dresses, looked friendly enough, Kuula thought. However, they were all armed with rifles, but Kuula had no idea these were deadly weapons.

As the last wagon slowly approached, Kuula looked once more at Tuuwee, who appeared lifeless if not for the sweat streaming from his pores. "Better we be conquered by men than by insects, my cousin," Kuula whispered.

Slowly he stood up and, without further hesitation, stepped around the bed of rocks into plain view for all to see.

Tuuwee awakened to find himself laying in the back of a covered wagon, moving slowly along the rough road. He was laying on his back on bales of soft cloth. His nakedness was covered with a white cakelike cream which gave off a sweet, pleasing smell. Tuuwee felt weak and thirsty. His head was throbbing in pain like someone had struck him with their club. Trying to think didn't help the pain in the least.

Tuuwee realized, with much delight, that he was still alive. But until he knew Kuula's fate, he could not bring himself to rejoice. As he raised his aching head and scanned the wagon, his eyes found the perfect painkiller for his aching head. Kuula was seated at the open, rear end of the wagon with his back to him. His legs dangled over the side.

Tuuwee was speechless for a moment and couldn't do anything but silently watch and revel in the sight. Through the open canvass, he peered past Kuula and out to the welcoming sunlight. He could make out faint images of people on the ground walking beside the wagon. They all appeared to be women, and this was suddenly confirmed when he heard Kuula speak. The voices responding to him from the ground were unmistakably female giggles.

"Cuuz is merciful," Tuuwee uttered to himself as he eased his head back down to rest. But his voice was heard not only by Kuula but also by the other two occupants of the wagon. The driver and the passenger who sat on a seat just above Tuuwee's head turned and stared down at him.

"Ah, our sleeping guest has finally decided to join the waking world!" It was the passenger speaking. His coal-black face was heavily wrapped in an Arabian scarf, and Tuuwee found it hard to see anything except his teeth and the whites of his eyes.

The driver's complexion was just as dark, but his face was mostly hidden inside his colorful scarf. Tuuwee looked at the driver's broad smile, which revealed a peculiar mixture of sparkling gold teeth and black rotten stumps.

"I trust you are hungry as a young lion and as thirsty as the desert sands?" the man in the passenger seat added.

Tuuwee held his tongue and allowed his eyes to probe the two dark faces that had gently spoken but had the look of unyielding toughness.

Just then Kuula crawled up beside Tuuwee and placed a hand on his shoulder. As he looked down at his cousin, their eyes met. And in that silent way, it spoke of two old buddies meeting after a long separation.

"Food, young Kuula Cuuzan?" The man in the passenger seat roared as if he were speaking across a banquet table. "And freshwater, all your cousin may drink I give you permission to give." The driver nodded his head in approval but kept his attention focused on the road ahead. The wagon clattered along slowly behind the two men on foot carrying rifles.

"You were in bad shape young, Tuuwee Cuuzan," the man in the passenger seat was saying. He was speaking Bantu, which was a universal dialect and incorporated many of the Central African languages, including Cuuzan. "Your cousin saved your life. He bled and sweat enough of the poison from you before it overwhelmed your system. Your sweat medicine is good medicine indeed! That cream on your body now will further draw the scorpion's death from you. Relax and your strength and good health will return. Just like the calm after the storm! You are in the good hands of Ali Hakim Nadir and company. We're traveling merchants and hunters from the fabulous city of Ty of the Sudan. A guest of Ali is under the protection and care of Allah, the benevolent, the merciful."

Kuula moved around the wagon as if it had been his home all his life. He was totally at ease with Ali and accepted his hospitality with a childlike vigor. Wearing a wide grin, Kuula began shoving a barrage of sweet cakes and meats into Tuuwee's hands. What Tuuwee couldn't hold in his hands, Kuula laid on his chest. And rather than allow Tuuwee to set any food down, he fed water into his mouth from the waterskin. Tuuwee's hands and mouth stayed full, and Kuula kept close vigil making sure he ate and drank until his stomach was close to bursting.

Ali Hakim Nadir and his traveling merchants and caravans were on their way to Shacuwa, the fortified capital city of Kongolia, to buy, sell, and trade goods in the marketplace called Keetuu. It was the largest, busiest outdoor emporium east of Timbuktu and sat smack in the middle of what was once Cuuzanland.

Tuuwee and Kuula were told by Ali that Cuuzanland no longer existed but that their tribal people were still very much rooted in the land. They were also told that their uncle, King Nuumyu, was now referred to as "emperor."

King Nuumyu went on to attend the emergency summit conference of local chieftains on the appointed day following Muusamali's infamous exodus into obscure self-exile nineteen years ago.

The conference became a renowned event known as the "Shacuwa," meaning the assembly of the seven kings. The assembly was attended by King Ditiro of the Ikeele, King Mobutu of the Manono, King Mbogeni of the Kodok, King Mwanza of the Warri, King Sani of the Bakuwa, King Kweisi of the Owada and, of course, King Nuumyu of the Cuuzan.

The seven patriarchs agreed without argument that divided they would surely fall—one by one—into the hands of the invading European imperialists. Only by standing strong and together was there any hope of surviving to remain a free and sovereign people.

A series of Shacuwas were conducted over a very short period of time. Time was of the essence, as war drums sounded throughout the countryside signaling impending attacks from the great white human sharks sweeping through the land. These sharks had already conquered and enslaved countless other tribes and would stop at nothing until all were theirs.

A federation uniting the seven tribes was quickly established. King Nuumyu was the orchestrator and driving force behind the assembly and was soon appointed "Ghabasa," the king of kings. Soon, his organizing genius and military brilliance shone like a mighty guiding light, and he was elevated to the office of emperor. As a result of this promotion, King Nuumyu's seat on the Imperial Council became vacant.

In his new office, King Nuumyu's political skills were quickly put to the test. With little opposition, he managed to not only fill the empty council seat with a native Cuuzan, but the appointee was also his younger brother Duugawdu. Duugawdu, at the age of only thirty-three, was also the reigning prince of the Cuuzan tribe.

The combined tribal homelands of the seven federation members were vast and expansive. Each of the homelands contained valuable agricultural and mining resources, and the farmlands were abundant. The precious mineral-rich regions were all united and tilled under one economic system of production and distribution. Each of the seven member tribes were warrior clans. A few were long-standing and bitter enemies of the others; however, old tribal hatreds were put aside, and a strongly disciplined and determined military allegiance was established.

With two-thirds of the unified homelands surrounded by desert on one side and mountains on the other, it was difficult for invading armies to attack the heart of their unified front. The desert was a hot hell for the cold-weather Europeans. Also, a well-armed and organized group of Moors dwelled along the desert stretch along their boundaries. The Moors maintained a key trade route and desert waystation for Muslim traders, and they forbid non-Muslims to tread on their desert domain, most especially the Europeans.

The mountain region was the home of the Ikeele and contained vast resources of untapped diamond deposits. The Ikeele were strategically dug-in and well-situated. With the backing of the others in the federation, the Ikeele Mountains were impregnable.

Reason then led the federation to believe the only other feasible point of entry into their unified homeland was through the valley region once known as "Wagandu Valley." To strengthen and secure this weak area, the Shacuwa patriarchs (the seven kings) and their united army of warriors were forced to take on the very image of the imperialist army they were preparing to fight. Several small village tribes who were militarily weak and vulnerable to attack occupied strategically vital territory in and around the Wagandu Valley. However, the chiefs of these tribes had refused to take part in the Shacuwa.

By their refusal, the Shacuwa patriarchs declared them a threat to the security of the unified homeland, and they were forcibly brought into the federation to prevent the true imperialists from overrunning the land. Thus, it was hoped the European invaders would be stopped from gaining the perfect position from which to launch attacks on the unified front.

Although these valley tribes were forced to join the federation, they were nevertheless permitted to retain their sovereignty and maintain a portion of their farmlands. However, the majority of the land was converted into buffer zones—"fort cities"—and was occupied around the clock by federation warriors. After the first bloodbath of fighting in Wagandu Valley, its name changed overnight and became permanently known as "Puma (Blood) Valley." King Nuumyu and the other Shacuwa patriarchs built a strong federation of the seven united kingdoms which they named "Kongolia," meaning "empire of the kings."

Keepers of tribal history recount the story that one year after the famous "assembly of the seven kings," a horrendous war took place. Two battles raged in the Puma Valley over an eighteen-month period as the seven kings and their united warriors fearlessly fought to defend the homelands against the ruthless European invaders.

The first ploy the white imperialists used to gain entry into the mineral rich Kongolia territory was nonviolent and came in the form of a peaceful business proposition. An Ikeele native named Mokoena ventured from the homeland several years before the Shacuwa was formed and took with him a pouch of diamonds. Mokoena was ambitious and left his mountain home to seek a better life through education. He found what he was looking for in Europe but lost much of his identity in the process. Even before tribal markings became unpopular among member tribes of the Kongolian Federation, Mokoena abandoned the practice when he reached Europe by cutting off his reddish dreadlocks. The mark of the Ikeele was dyeing their hair red at birth and wearing dreadlocks all through life.

An educated and immaculately dressed Mokoena eventually returned home. With him, he brought a small group of white businessmen, colleagues who specialized in mining engineering. Their interest, of course, was the diamond-rich deposits in the Ikeele Mountains.

Mokoena's plan was to introduce his white associates to his tribal chief to strike up a mining deal. He believed this would make his backwoods tribespeople instant millionaires and would turn their primitive mountain homeland into a fabulous city. However, by the time he returned home, the Ikeele Mountains had already been incorporated into the Kongolian Empire. Mokoena was stunned by the hostile, almost paranoid tension which hung throughout the land.

The people of the Kongolia were thoroughly warned about black spies and undercover mercenaries coming disguised as merchant businessmen and traders. Parents taught their young, and drums and word-of-mouth carried the message that any and all contact with the white man or his black agents was strictly prohibited. Like great white hungry sharks, once inside the land they would devour everything precious and enslave the people without conscience.

Mokoena and his white colleagues were rudely turned away and returned to Europe. While they came to no physical harm, they manufactured lies to the contrary. Their false accounts of being beaten and tortured sparked a public outcry of rage from their European counterparts, just as they'd planned.

With public sentiment fired up in favor of retribution, the capitalist rulers of the diamond trade went right to work convincing the European governmental forces that they were justified in taking military action against the black racist outlaws of Kongolia. These same rulers financed what was deemed a "crusade" to civilize a renegade heathen regime.

The first Puma Valley battle was the bloodiest. A mixed army of European troops and black mercenary soldiers poured forth into the valley with guns and cannons blazing only to meet with fierce and determined resistance on the part of the brave spear wielding Kongolian fighters. The fighting raged for an entire day, ceasing only when the curtain of darkness fell upon the corpse-littered arena, forcing the battered European invaders to retreat.

Both the Europeans and Kongolians suffered heavy losses with prisoners being captured and held by both sides. The lure of the diamond mines. blind fury, and the uncontrollable urge to enact revenge, coupled with the fact that failure to conquer the heathens would mean disgrace when they returned home, drove the European generals to launch a foolish, all-out, second attack the very next day. Surprisingly, they were halted in their tracks by a fearless army of fresh fighters whom Emperor Nuumyu had held in reserve. Waves and waves of black warriors stormed up the valley straight toward the advancing invaders. Their only weapons were spears and shields, bows and arrows, and blowguns with poison darts. The courageous Kongolian warriors met with a hail of bullets and shots from cannons. Dozens upon dozens fell dead or wounded. Yet none who remained on their feet wavered one step in their head-first counterattack.

The relentless aggressiveness of the Kongolian's defensive stand threw the European invaders into a confused and panicked frenzy. The white troops and the half-hearted black mercenaries found themselves overwhelmed as the black Kongolian warriors, yelling battle cries, rushed their ranks like a swarm of army ants assaulting a bee's honeycomb.

Forced to engage in hand-to-hand combat, the invaders immediately began dropping like flies. Soon, but not soon enough, the retreat was sounded, and the beaten and battered invaders turn and fled, leaving behind their weapons of war. Cannons, hastily discarded rifles, and ammunition littered the valley's floor.

The European generals had had enough. They pulled their wounded and humiliated troops as far away from the battlefield as they could. They had been outnumbered and ill-prepared from the start. It was no fault of the field generals that the strength and fearless resolve of the Kongolians was so underestimated.

The generals dreaded having to send word home relating their failure and the number of lives it cost. They did, however, delay dispatching the bad news to Europe until they could free their captured comrades from the clutches of the murdering, savage infidels.

Emperor Nuumyu and his Imperial Council of Kings agreed to a prisoner exchange. However, the emperor stalled for some weeks to allow his commanders time enough to work with the white prisoners, forcing them to divulge the secrets of operating the weapons they'd confiscated from their battle.

At the appointed time, when the Kongolians were prepared and ready, they made the prisoner exchange. All went well. The freed Europeans and black mercenaries informed their field generals who, in turn, told their masters in Europe that the heathen Kongolians were now in possession of six cannons, some eighty rifles, ample ammunition, and sufficient know-how to use these deadly equalizers.

The Europeans had already lost 109 white soldiers and an untold number of black mercenaries. With the Kongolians now in possession of the arms of war, it was obvious to the European powers that any further gung-ho attack would result in the loss of many more white lives than had been taken in the first assault.

The capitalist "shot callers" based in Europe were forced to rethink their strategy. After much debate and shrewd planning, some eighteen months later, they financed a second crusade. This second barrage had three times the number of governmental troops and black mercenaries as the first. This time, the crusade was deemed "a goodwill mission to tame the infidels through intimidation and persuasion."

In conjunction with certain Christian leaders, several priests and their attendants were sent to accompany the one thousand reinforcement troops to Africa. They landed on the west coast where, in the city of Benin, the white priests solicited the services of several African priests who spoke Bantu.

The Kongolian conflict was just one of many wars of conquest and plunder being waged all over the African continent. European and Asian invaders raced against each other in greedy pursuit to conquer the land, steal its valuable minerals, and enslave black flesh.

The Christian church at Benin was just another European outpost in disguise. It was sponsored by the expansionist-minded capitalists and protected by the government's troops. On the one hand, the white and black priests were pawns but, on the other hand, genuine men of God. Throughout Africa, Christian priests were symbols of peace and love. Wherever and whenever a truce between warring parties was possible, the Benin church would gladly dispatch its robed peace brokers to the war zone.

The death toll from the first European-Kongolian encounter was staggering. One look at the might and size of the European reinforcements convinced the priests of Benin that the rebellious young Kongolian Empire was on the verge of massacre. Only God could prevent the slaughter. And being God's human representatives on earth, the white and black priests of Benin rose to the challenge.

Once the armed crusaders and their priestly peacekeepers reached a point several hundred yards from the Puma Valley, they set up a huge military camp. The troops went about making a lot of noise and put on a spectacular show of force as they assembled themselves and their arsenal of weapons in an obvious attack mode.

Only 75 of the 200 cannons they'd brought with them were real. The rest were merely dummies, but they were all positioned and aimed toward the Kongolian forces who had quickly gathered and formed a defensive front to protect their homeland.

Morning arrived, but the sun didn't shine with its usual brilliance. Thick clouds filled the skies warning of the coming rain. On the ground, a tense quietness cautioned of a different storm brewing between two armies squared off on a wide-open battlefield. The combined forces of the European troops and black mercenary soldiers were three times greater than those of the Kongolian warriors.

Just when it was certain that the mighty European armies were about to charge the Kongolian's front line, five priests wearing long white robes and riding donkeys suddenly appeared, moving into the center of this would-be battlefield. A fifteen-foot-tall wooden cross was planted in the ground, a large tent pitched, and the five priests (three white and two black) settled in for what became the famous sit-in demonstration which halted the Europeans from launching their dreaded second invasion.

The momentous "sit-in" also spun the shrewd progressive web of deception which first snared the hearts and minds of the common people, then moved to certain members of the ruling class, and finally seized upon and finally controlled the valuable land. It became apparent to the Kongolians that the European priests possessed some form of magical powers that kept their war-hungry countrymen in check. As long as the white priests remained on the scene, peace reigned between the black and white armies.

Within a year's time, a fully operational mission sprang up on the very spot where the five priests had pitched their tent and planted the wooden cross. Black Africans from towns and villages outside the Kongolian capital city flocked to it in droves when word spread about the priests' magic black bags which were said to contain strange magic potions. The European medicines were thought to be far superior to the traditional village medicines because of their mysterious painkilling powers and fast-healing properties.

Besides the free medical treatment offered to anyone who walked, crawled, or was carried into the mission hospital, food, clothing, and spiritual needs were also met. While they were not permitted inside the fortified capital city, it wasn't long before the white priests were allowed to venture freely in and out of the villages and townships. Eventually, other satellite missions were established throughout the rural territory surrounding the capital city.

In due time, white business merchants drifted in, bringing with them provocative goods of the kind never before seen in this part of the world. Retail stores and trading posts began to spring up in the larger cities. The store's shelves were stocked with the finest European wines, foods, spices, garments, and other household merchandise. Of course, there was also a plentiful supply of firearms, swords, tools, and a host of adult toys.

As expected, the lure of the retail stores and their rare, enchanting merchandise flushed out the black aristocratic ruling class who lived inside the fortified walls of the capital city. What the white priests and their mission did for the poor villagers and townspeople, the white merchants and their retail stores did for the rich Kongolians.

By creating a need and supplying the demand, the white imperialists succeeded in gaining a foothold into the rural countryside. Their next ongoing objective was to place themselves in a position to manipulate the Kongolian political machinery by gaining entrance to the capital city itself.

The ceasefire that the five priests brokered lasted more than fifteen years. The only exception to the peace, which was so welcomed over the homelands, was a homegrown separatist group of war veterans who adamantly opposed the existing constitutional laws which indefinitely bound all seven member tribes to the Kongolian Empire. The law read, in part, "No tribe or tribes shall ever secede from the union of tribes which is Kongolia. As long as one member tribe exists, it shall be, in whole and in part, Kongolia."

The objective of the underground revolutionary group known as the Puma Dorrs (Blood Brothers) was to force the Kongolian government to change that old law and allow independence to any member tribe who wished to break with the empire. The Puma Dorrs were financed and backed by Asian imperialist forces who themselves were vying with the European imperialists for access to the Ikeele diamond mines.

Since the Kongolian government refused to recognize the Puma Dorrs as a legitimate political party, the Puma Dorrs and their secret supporters felt justified in their aim to overthrow the government by any means necessary.

They were heavily armed, well organized, and very active in violent guerilla campaigns against the government.

Emperor Nuumyu and his Imperial Council took perfect advantage of the fifteen-year ceasefire with the Europeans. They promoted the building of the Kongolian Empire on a grand scale. A mixed economy of mining and agriculture flourished as the Kongolian borders opened up, and traders and traveling merchants of African descent poured in and out the year round.

Elaborate irrigation systems were developed. Dams were built and towns sprang up. Roads were constructed which connected all the outer provinces with the main border town of Bawku. Bawku, in turn, was the gateway into the walled capital city, which was named Shacuwa, after the famous gathering of the seven kings.

Shacuwa became a large trade center and mecca. It was the grandest marketplace east of Timbuktu where traders came to buy and sell goods from as far away as the southern tip of Africa, north from the Mediterranean Sea, and from the horn of East Africa. The Kongolian Empire was well on its way to becoming a great empire of states. But besides the rebel Puma Dorrs nettling the government with its hit-and-run strikes against economic and military institutions, there was also serious internal quarreling among certain high-ranking members of the Imperial Council and the emperor himself. The conflict surrounded the constitutional ban prohibiting the government from establishing official accords with whites.

The emperor's brother, Duugawdu, was the highest-ranking council member in favor of establishing an economic treaty with Europe. He alone was responsible for creating the first reform bill ever to challenge the constitution and the emperor's authority.

A thirst for knowledge and power and a craving to experience the mysterious world outside Africa drove Duugawdu to break with old-line thinking and ignore certain basic ancestral warnings which he deemed superstitious. He had long been engaged in low-profile associations with the white priests.

Recently, the priests had introduced him to a shady European diplomat who claimed to hold the title of ambassador.

The white ambassador played to all of Duugawdu's political ambitions, as well as to his personal struggle to stamp out the dreaded Puma Dorrs. The ambassador promised that, given an opportunity, he could make one of Duugawdu's fondest dreams a reality—that of instilling foreign affairs studies into the Kongolian educational system by establishing a university. Duugawdu believed this university would give young Kongolians a window to the outside world.

That same outside world had an uncontrollable appetite for gold and diamonds. This demand for the precious stones presented the Kongolians with an opportunity to catapult their economy into riches beyond imagination. The ambassador and his countrymen were offering Duugawdu all the latest in high-tech mining equipment to extract these valuable minerals, as well as the ready cash to begin buying every speck of gold and each tiny diamond found.

The ambassador also claimed to have the perfect remedy to rid Kongolia of the Puma Dorrs and any other antigovernment element that threatened to overthrow the emperor. But the ambassador's ideas were extreme and so unconventional and grotesque in nature that Duugawdu knew he would have to first become emperor himself before he could suggest such a solution to the Puma Dorr problem.

Duugawdu was on one of his rare visits to the emperor's chambers. Emperor Nuumyu's old age and failing health kept him confined to his royal bed twenty-four hours a day. While he considered them treacherous and a betrayal of the people, he didn't have the strength to publicly oppose Duugawdu's reform bills. But the old emperor still retained controlling influence over four of the council members, each of whom were old hard-liners like himself. Duugawdu only came to the emperor when he wished to convince him to use his influence over these four old conservative guardians of the constitution.

This day, Duugawdu was in the emperor's chambers to confront his brother about an obscure and long-forgotten episode in Cuuzan history which had suddenly risen from the grave with crucial implications. However, his original intentions got sidetracked, and the discussion fell on other antagonistic subjects.

"These Europeans are a meaningful source of aid, information about the outside world, and a great comfort to our people. Can't you see them for what they are truly worth?" Duugawdu was saying to Emperor Nuumyu as the old king of the Cuuzan lay in bed and propped himself up against a mountain of plush pillows. Nuumyu's hair was snow white, as were his thick, bushy eyebrows which were frowning above a pair of dark, piercing eyes which tore through Duugawdu like daggers.

Duugawdu was on his feet pacing the floor, both hands behind his back. Being of tall frame and broad shoulders, he moved with a graceful air of dignity. Even at age fifty-three, his back was straight, and he moved with vibrant ease. Looking at him, Nuumyu was reminded of himself some sixteen years earlier when he was his age. But Duugawdu's patriotism and political views of late were like foul breath to Nuumyu.

It pained the old emperor to have to sit and listen to his brother's pro-white rhetoric. Nonetheless, with a fiery stare, he listened all the same while Duugawdu continued. "The Europeans possess certain hidden knowledge and secretly learned skills which have already proven beneficial to scores of our citizens, those who suffer illnesses which our very best Huzza could not cure. The Europeans' medicines, as well as their modern farming and mining technologies, could speed the future growth of our young nation threefold if we were to establish an economic treaty with them. A young nation aspiring to be a great empire needs advanced technologies like a budding flower needs the rays of the sun. If only you would meet with the Christian priests and white merchants, you would be convinced, as I am, of their sincerity and their true worth to our people and our land."

The old emperor's voice was weak, and he spoke as though it pained him. But his steely eyes were firm and penetrating. He chose his words carefully and slowly like the prudent and cautious man he had always been in life.

"Why do you persist in coming to me expressing these twisted views? To see if my mind has fallen into decay as has my body? Or do you just feel a need to spew forth that foul rubbish from your system because its stench is driving you mad? Spare me, my foolish brainwashed brother. I'm a man already dying, and I don't wish to speed up the process by listening to your poisonous views. I wish only to rest in peace for the short time I have left."

Duugawdu ceased his pacing and faced the emperor. He opened his hands in a pleading gesture and said, "But that is exactly why I persist in my efforts—to make you see the light, my dear emperor and beloved brother. So that you will not only rest easier, but live longer. The priests have assured me that their medicine is capable of curing your illness. You can, indeed, have your health restored if you'd rid yourself of this hate and superstitious fear you have toward the white man. It's hate and fear that's keeping you physically ill, and it's also keeping our people down as a nation. The almighty Cuuz has blessed us by sending the white man into our midst. If you'd only embrace this fact, conditions for you and our people would instantly improve!"

"God has cursed us," Nuumyu shot back with a renewed touch of vigor to his voice. "Cuuz has cursed me and this empire with the likes of you. A treacherous thorn in the lion's paw is what you are! If you are not careful in your dealings with those European devils, you alone could bring down what hundreds of our brave warriors have died to build. The nerve of you!" Nuumyu paused and looked up as if to make his next point to the gods sitting in heaven. "My own brother would dare come and ask me to put my life in the hands of my sworn enemy. Why, that is worse than treason! If I could get up from this bed, I would stomp the life from your brainwashed body. You are on the verge of destroying Kongolia, and I am standing in your way. Is that it?"

"Nonsense!" Duugawdu said as he began pacing once more. He made a point to utilize more of the spacious room to avoid coming too close to his hostile brother's bed. A threat from Nuumyu, even an old and sickly Nuumyu on his death bed, was more than a little disturbing to this younger brother. "My association with the white priests will guarantee a permanent peace between Kongolia and all the European kingdoms."

He continued, "With due respect to the brave warriors who died during the historic Puma wars, the focus now should be on the future as we try to prevent another war with the European powers. Consider who our real enemies are for a moment, my emperor." Duugawdu stood partly in the shadows, next to the window overlooking the sun-filled courtyard. His voice dropped to a quiet, low pitch. "The Arabians are threatening our northern border towns. Slowly, but continually, their numbers are building in that region. Ask yourself, my brother, why the Arab military build-up unless they intend to invade?"

Duugawdu remained insistent, saying, "We know for certain that the Arabs are financing the Puma Dorrs with arms and are providing them with guerilla training in order to stage these ongoing forays against our economic interest. These Puma Dorrs are growing stronger and stronger with Arab assistance. An immediate alliance with the Europeans is not only essential to our peace and prosperity now, but to the very future and survival of our nation. Listen to me, my emperor, those two battles against the Europeans in the Puma Valley were mere exercises compared to what we will face if the Arab powers decide to launch a full-scale invasion."

Duugawdu persisted in making his argument, saying, "There are no more mighty black tribes of warriors willing to team up with us for another "Shacuwa." They are all either allied with the Europeans or with the Arabs. Kongolia stands alone. Our gold and diamond mines, along with our fighting warriors, the European's guns, ammunition and military backing, would bind us together into a powerful economic-military force which will be able to wipe out every one of our enemies—overnight! We could become a great empire. No army on earth would be able to defeat our mixed black and white forces.

"The only obstacles that stand in the way of Kongolia's greatness are the fears and superstitions that some of our leaders have toward the white powers that be. But take heed, my brother, if we don't quickly form a union with one or the other of the foreign powers, then eventually one of them, or both, will sweep us away!"

In the back of his mind, Nuumyu knew that most of his younger brother's message rang true. African drums and traveling merchants carried the same revelation that—one by one—countless African tribes were slowly being conquered by unstoppable bands of Asian and European forces. And that, before long, the entire African continent would be under the yoke of foreign power. But Nuumyu was in a stubborn state of denial, powerless to do anything about the situation. The old emperor's bitter frustration made him lash out at the messenger who dared bring him the message in person.

"I've heard enough," Nuumyu said with a look of defeat on his weathered and wrinkled face. However, his voice was considerably steady, and his penetrating eyes never lost their fix as he added, "You found your way into my chambers without my summoning you. Don't make me have to tell you to leave."

With no hesitation, Duugawdu started for the door. But it was just a gesture of respect, a ploy to put the emperor at his ease. Duugawdu had no intentions of leaving just yet. "My emperor and dear brother, grant me just a moment to ask you to clear my thoughts on a certain matter. What can you tell me about the Muusamali exodus which I don't already know?"

The question caught Nuumyu by surprise and visibly so, as his head of bushy white hair titled further back on his neck allowing him to glare down his nose at Duugawdu. "Why do you ask about the exodus?" he questioned.

"Why shouldn't I inquire about such an historic event shrouded in so much mystery and not a few lies too, I suspect?" Duugawdu answered as he took several steps toward his brother. He clamped his hands behind his back in that confident pose which suggested much about how he felt at the moment.

"What you already know about our brother's self-exile is sufficient enough for you to maintain your dubious personal affairs and, regrettably so, the affairs of the Kongolia government. You don't have to overly concern yourself with that part of Cuuzan history," Nuumyu replied.

"It must have been painful for you to see your favorite brother turn coward and run out on you with a number of the tribe?" Duugawdu asked in a searching manner.

Nuumyu suddenly began to feel trapped—trapped in a lie that had caused him great personal pain ever since Muusamali's exile. Now, after all these years of internal suffering and with just a short time left to live himself, he was finding it unbearable to allow the great lie to outlive him. Yet, still, it was hard for the old emperor to confide in his rebellious younger brother.

"You went away to Timbuktu to attend the university there. The Puma War had been fought and won before you returned home. So how can you call our brother Muusamali a coward?" Nuumyu said with little conviction.

"You ordered me to go to Timbuktu—remember?" Duugawdu said with a frown. "It was your insistence that I go away and obtain a military education so that I could return and educate our warriors to a superior method of fighting. And had you not insisted that I also take a curriculum in business and agriculture, I might have arrived back home in time to be at your side before the war started."

For the first time, Nuumyu's eyes dropped, and he almost looked beaten. Slowly he raised his head, and his steady stare once again found Duugawdu. "I'm inclined not to believe you really wanted to stay and fight. But I wholeheartedly believe that Muusamali wished that he could have been a part of the fight to defend the homeland."

"You are being very evasive, my emperor. And rather unfair to me in regard to my character," Duugawdu said as he looked his older brother squarely in the eye.

Nuumyu returned the stare without blinking and coldly said, "As I told you before, you invited yourself in here. Feel free to leave—immediately!"

Once again, Duugawdu faked a motion, as if he were heading for the door—but quickly turned back and faced his brother. "With all due respect to your highness," he began with a solemn tone, "and the almighty Cuuz is my witness, I pray every day for your longevity. But in all reality—and you yourself taught me to always confront reality head on—the regretful day will eventually arrive when you, my emperor and dear brother, will pass on from this earthly world. And I will become emperor of Kongolia. It's only right that you share the whole truth with me. I don't really believe in my heart that our brother, Muusamali, was a coward who just ran to avoid fighting. I demand to know the truth about him and that exiled clan of our people!"

Nuumyu fell quiet as though in a trance. For a long moment, he stared at one of his elaborately carved oakwood bedposts situated at his feet. Each of the carved posts depicted giraffes as they held up the massive bed on all four corners. Their long necks stretched upward toward the ceiling and were taller than Duugawdu's 6'4" frame.

It was with deep regret that Nuumyu reminded himself that Duugawdu was his brother and next in line to succeed him on the emperor's throne because Nuumyu had failed to produce any male offspring. Ordinarily, it would have been Muusamali who would have been the heir apparent by virtue of the fact that he was the older brother, having a few years on Duugawdu. But Muusamali was absent and, for the sake of making sure the crown remained within the royal family bloodline, the old emperor and king of the Cuuzan was forced to submit to the will of the one brother he deemed his enemy.

Finally, Nuumyu looked at his younger brother and said, almost in a whisper, "The exodus, indeed, was not what it seemed at the time. It was a well-thought-out secret plan to take a small portion of the tribe and relocate them somewhere far away from the homeland for safekeeping. It had to look like an act of cowardice on our brother's part so that no one in the tribe would be tempted to follow. Only a chosen few—those whom I picked—were ordered to go into exile with Muusamali. It was decreed that whomever was chosen to leave with Muusamali, was never to return or be admitted back into the homeland. And if anyone else other than those whom I chose decided to follow, they would to be stoned to death.

"I foresaw the possibility of the white invaders killing off our people down to the last tiny child, as they were known to do to other tribes who refused to surrender. If we were to be annihilated, there would still be a clan of Cuuzan existing elsewhere. But I had a deep faith that we would survive in the face of an onslaught from the white devils from Europe. So I and the better portion of our tribe remained, fought, and won!"

Nuumyu paused, took a hard look at his younger brother, and continued. "But have we really won?" his voice taking on a sharper, deeper tone. "Or did the white devils silence their guns and cannons because they found a more ingenious and less violent way of pushing forward in their greedy quest to conquer our people and steal our land?"

"I can see in you, my bewitched brother, the hand of the white man at work. Through you, he is carrying out his plan to defeat us. The same thing happened during the Puma War when our warriors were bewitched by the mysterious powers of the Europeans' guns and cannons. Those so-called 'magic fire sticks' which spit out instant death, terrified many of our warriors to death. If not for our quick thinking upon capturing the white soldiers and forcing them to reveal the secrets of how to use their fire sticks, we might have been defeated.

"But learning the secrets of their tricks and having a number of their own weapons in our hands turned the tide of the war and forced the whites to retreat and stay in their place. But alas, not for long. The white man has proved to be as clever in mind as he is vicious in spirt and in battle.

"Realizing they could no longer beat us with the magic of their fire sticks, they sent in priests wearing robes and carrying their god on a wooden stick to do the job that the white soldiers failed to do. That job was to conquer our people and seize our land! And you, my foolish brother, are the white man's tool. You allow yourself to be bewitched by these robed priests just as they did to our warriors with their fire sticks during the Puma War. Our nation is doomed.

"Thank the almighty Cuuz for the exodus! That so-called appalling episode in our history which disgraced my brother's good name and never allowed me a day's peace. The exodus has indeed lived up to its true intent and purpose. Somewhere, far away from our polluted homeland, lives another pure race of Cuuzan exiles, free from the white devils and free from your black devil heart and white tongue!"

Duugawdu looked at his brother with a mix of admiration, pity, and resentment. The old emperor suddenly looked worn and haggard after his verbal marathon. It had been the most talking Nuumyu had done in some time.

Although Duugawdu was bitter over much of what Nuumyu had said, he was however glad to learn the truth which he had so long suspected. Something sinister lurked beneath Duugawdu's calm demeanor as he said, "So you sent the exiles away as a means of preserving a part of the tribe! How wise and practical of you, my emperor and brother. I've always admired your practicality. Certainly, no other mass migration was attempted after that ill-fated exodus. Grand move, my brother, grand move!"

Duugawdu stepped closer to Nuumyu's bedside. He thought to reach out and touch the old, wrinkled hand which lay across Nuumyu's lap but, at the last moment, thought better of it. "Rest yourself. I will leave you now. I've learned all I need to know about our brave and loyal brother."

As Duugawdu turned and headed for the door, and this time sincerely and hurriedly so, Nuumyu stopped him when he asked, "Tell me this before you leave. Why this sudden interest in the exodus? Make it brief. I'm still paining at the sight of you."

Duugawdu let a tiny smile crease the corner of his thick purple lips. Then a look of urgency swept over his face. "It's nothing really. A couple refugees from some swamp tribe attempted to sneak across our eastern border saying they were Cuuzan exiles returning from the exodus. But then, you know we get this rush of foreigners each year around this time. They will say anything to gain entry into our land. These two swampers I speak of didn't even know that the exiled Muusamali clan, from which they profess to belong, was prohibited from returning. So, of course, that made it clear they were impostors. When I received the report of these two, the mention of Muusamali and the exodus aroused my curiosity to delve deeper. True to my character, I'm always digging for more."

His answer didn't satisfy Nuumyu, and he asked, "What names did these two gives?"

"I doubt that the border guards even got names," Duugawdu lied becoming uneasy. "As I've said, they were clearly impostors and were immediately sent back to the swamps from which they came."

With that, Duugawdu started to leave, but again the old emperor stopped him with another question. "It troubles you that another clan of Cuuzan exists, doesn't it?" Nuumyu said this with a smirk playing across his lips while watching for the reaction of his brother. Duugawdu was taken back by the bizarre expression on the old man's face. What Nuumyu said next confirmed his fears about the two swampers.

"It better trouble you, you and the rest of your bewitched devil disciples on the Imperial Council. You're trying to whitewash our great black constitution with your so-called reform amendments. Your disgraceful allegiance with the white European devils goes against the most fundamental principles on which our constitution was founded. Even though I don't have the strength and health to fight you and your treacherous reforms, the seeds I sent into exile for safekeeping carry my most orthodox philosophical genes. And if I know my brother Muusamali, he has undoubtedly cultivated those exiled seeds and mustered a powerful, disciplined Cuuzan clan.

"That is your worst nightmare, Duugawdu. A pureblood clan of Cuuzan exists untainted by the white poison running through your bewitched veins. You fear that these purebloods may come home to claim the land of their birthright—don't you? That an army of Muusamali's fighters, devil killers, led by my great general Zuuox will return to Cuuzanland. They will spare no white devil in our land masquerading as a priest. Neither will they tolerate black devil disciples like you and your puppet council members!"

Duugawdu turned and headed for the door. This time nothing would stop him. Nuumyu's rage was unrelenting. "You think the Puma War soiled the valley floor with blood? Wait until my brother's army of purebloods return to claim their heritage!"

That was all Duugawdu heard as he ducked out the door, slamming it shut behind him. He paused and took a deep breath and then exhaled as if he were relieving himself of Nuumyu's wrath. He didn't waste a moment as he stepped past the two royal guardsmen standing like armed statues on either side of the threshold. He moved quickly down the long corridor which led to the crowded streets of the capital city.

What used to be wide open, dusty grassland dotted with straw and mud huts called Cuuzanland was now the main metropolis of the Kongolian Empire. The streets were paved. The houses and buildings were made from brick, and plum trees now lined the sidewalks. Gas lanterns ran along the borders of the roadways in neat precision.

The two-story royal palace from which Duugawdu had just emerged had once been King Nuumyu's old mud hut. After descending the wide flight of brick stairs, he found his enclosed, wheel-less litter-coach waiting for him. It was manned by four large muscular Africans and was surrounded by a number of armed bodyguards with shields and spears in hand; some were toting rifles.

Duugawdu boarded the coach and settled into the plush, silk pillows of his lavish reclining seat. A large crowd of onlookers had gathered hoping to catch a glimpse of the Cuuzan prince and overlord of the Imperial Council. Several men and women wearing common garments and with pleading expressions stamped upon their faces, stepped from the crowd and toward his litter-coach. However, the guards quickly but gently subdued them and pushed them back behind the lines with their shields.

The four shirtless coach bearers, their black skin shining against the noonday sun, each grabbed hold of one of the coach's poles. In perfect unison, upon command of one of the armed guards, they gently lifted Duugawdu and his bed of luxury up on to their shoulders.

At that point, two of Duugawdu's personal bodyguards quickly approached the coach. They carried rifles and were dressed in matching khaki pants and shirts. The belts which were strapped across their shoulders were filled with ammunition: bullets to guard their leader and their land. Duugawdu demanded of them, "Those two swampdwellers who attempted to cross the western border yesterday? Where are they?"

"Intelligence tells us they are with the Oupa Ra bitch," one of the guards answered. Duugawdu said, "Go—go and get them. They are not to speak with anyone else. Take them to the prison. I will meet you there." He paused and, leaning forward, spoke directly into the guard's face, "I want them alive and well!"

"Yes, your highness," the guard replied, bowing his head. "As you demand, it shall be done."

Duugawdu continued, "Also, get a message to the European ambassador. Tell him that I wish to see him at the prison immediately."

"Yes, your highness, as you demand, it shall be done," the guard said once more then turned and hurried off into the crowd.

The crowd of bystanders grew larger and louder as hands waived in the air and voices pled for Prince Duugawdu's attention. On occasion, he would single out a dozen or so from the crowd and order them brought to the royal palace. There he would sit on his brother's royal throne in the great hall and listen to their grievances. It was considered a great honor to be chosen for a private audience with the Cuuzan prince in such a way. At least once every three months Duugawdu would play God to a chosen lucky few. Regardless of their grievances, he always made it a point to rule in their favor on these quarterly occasions.

On this day, however, Duugawdu was not singling out the lucky dozen to dispense a blessing. With a stern expression on his face, he nodded in the direction of his guard commander. In turn, the commander raised his rifle overhead. When he lowered it to his side, the entire entourage moved forward. The squad of bodyguards circling the moving coach used their shields to keep the anxious onlookers at a distance.

Duugawdu calmly reached up and pulled shut the curtains of his coach. Once done, he had completely shut himself off from the rays of the hot sun and from the pleading black faces seeking their chance for an audience with him.

On the western fringes of Kongolia, midway between the Puma Valley and the capital city at Shacuwa, is a huge shanty town called Bawku. It's the largest province governed by the Kongolian Empire. Bawku was once a small village and home to a tribe of farmers called the Timba people.

With the merger of the seven warrior kingdoms, and the birth of the mighty Kongolian defensive force, a mass migration of Africans fleeing their homelands to avoid being enslaved by European invaders, sought refuge under the powerful umbrella of the newly formed Kongolian government. These refugees weren't allowed to cross the border into the capital city itself. Nevertheless, all who reached Bawku were safe from the invaders since Bawku was located well inside the Puma Valley and beyond the front lines where the Kongolian defense force kept the invaders in bloody check throughout the war.

Bawku's population grew enormously after the war. Kongolia's victory over the Europeans in the Puma Valley made the Kongolian territory and all its neighboring provinces a safe haven for the homeless and defenseless African peoples. However, those Bawkuians and other refugees taking up residency in one of the shanty towns or other villages surrounding Shacuwa, could only dream of becoming a Kongolian citizen and living on the inside of the fortified city walls.

Shacuwa was luxurious compared to the slum-ridden Bawku. But not everyone was willing to live inside its confines. Many of those refugees who could easily afford to buy their way into citizenship, the wealthy yet homeless, resisted the idea.

The curse of the Oupa Ra hung over Shacuwa like a dark and menacing cloud. The curse evolved from ancient African warnings that survived among the Timba people. "Once the white man enters the land of the blacks, the land will die."

Oupa Ra is the name given to the "keeper of the shrine," the sacred shrine of Igun, meaning "God of Africa." The Timba people were the initial founders and guardians of Igun's shrine. The Oupa Ra is one who is ceremonially chosen at a young age to be the earth's representative unto the god, Igun.

The chosen one is always a female and routinely a native of the Timba tribe. Several other farming tribes in the region adhered to the Igun cult in spite of having their own god whom they worshipped separately. The Timba were a good-natured people and were devoted to the earth and to all black-skinned peoples who inhabited it. Other tribes had such respect and compassion for them because they naturally had a deep reverence for Igun. Igun was thought to be good for all black-skinned people living in the land.

The Oupa Ra was treated like a queen bee by her own tribe as well as many other tribes who respected Igun. From the moment she was chosen until her death, she would be pampered and worshipped and relied upon for rain and a good harvest, blessings of good will, and good health for all.

There was also a malevolent side to the Oupa Ra. She could create fear and dread simultaneously in a multitude of minds. Many Oupa Ras had come and gone, but none had been as powerful and as feared as the present one.

Her birth name was Nomaa. She happened to be the first Oupa Ra chosen who was not a purebred Timba. Nomaa's father was the voodoo chief of the Bandunda tribe. Her Timba mother was just one of the voodoo chief's many wives.

At the time of Nomaa's birth, two decades before the Puma War, fortune tellers predicted that the rich farmlands belonging to the Timba and Bandunda people were going to attract a host of desert tribes into the region. As none were warriors, the Timba and Bandunda people united their homelands through a marriage of convenience between Nomaa's mother and the chief of the Bandunda. It was a powerful merger in its own right: the guardians of Igun's shrine and a voodoo tribe whose chief was renowned for his strong magic. To strengthen the alliance, the chief's daughter by his Timba bride of convenience was chosen a Oupa Ra . . . the keeper of the shrine.

Nomaa was deeply rooted in the practice of voodoo, and she alone had the power to pray to the sacred shrine and receive blessings of fortune or curses of dread. She was as feared and revered as any single individual within the land, second only to the Kongolian emperor himself.

The Oupa Ra was an old woman now with two grown daughters of her own. The three of them lived in a modest house on the west side of Bawku. She had mothered two sons also, but they had both died in battle early on in the Puma War. It wasn't the death of her sons that made this Oupa Ra pass judgment on Shacuwa because, in her view, they were martyred for a just cause. However, the cause was betrayed by the unofficial yet very active peace treaty between the white enemies and the Kongolian government.

The Oupa Ra declared that the Kongolian government had not respected Igun. She said they had spit on the land by allowing the white enemies to tread on its soil which held the divine blood and bones of ancient and great ancestors. She declared they had spilt the blood of fallen Kongolian fighters, her beloved sons among them—those who had died in the struggle to keep the ancestral dream alive. This was the great African dream: keeping the land in the hands of the black man. It was their birthright.

Ali Hakim Nadir, being the shrewd opportunist he was, didn't intend to part with his unusual catch without making a profit. He could have easily sold Tuuwee and Kuula to Arab slavers for a sizable fast buck had he not been taken in by Tuuwee's story that he and Kuula were long lost relatives of the emperor. Favors in high places could often be more valuable than cash, and Ali opted to present his catch to the highest authority in the territory.

The Oupa Ra was not exactly Ali's first choice. Initially he tried to cross the border into Shacuwa with Tuuwee and Kuula to turn them over to the imperial palace. But the border guards didn't buy his story that he had found two lost gems from the royal family. They turned him away but not without reporting the incident to the palace authorities.

The Oupa Ra was surprised and thrilled when Ali dropped Tuuwee and Kuula off at her doorstep. Along with them, and at the Oupa Ra's request, Ali also left a lock of his woolly hair. She promised to appeal to Igun on his behalf not just for a blessing of good fortune but also for a long and healthy life.

A small crowd of townspeople dressed in the more traditional garments of the day, trousers and skirts, had gathered on the street in front of the Oupa Ra's house. The onlookers were curious about the two new strangers, who were naked except for loincloths tied around their middle with string, spears and shield in hand.

Tuuwee still had the white powder smeared over his body. However, it wasn't so much their primitive appearance which evoked such curiosity as it was their untamed behavior. Tuuwee and Kuula were unlike most backwoods relatives who, from time to time, ventured into town from the desert plains and rainforest regions of central Africa. Tuuwee and Kuula behaved like two wild cubs, eyes wide with fear, yet unmistakably ready to strike out at anyone who got close. They were either walking backward or snapping their heads from side to side allowing nothing to move without first catching it in their range of vision.

For a long moment, Tuuwee and Kuula were hesitant about entering the Oupa Ra's house. Tuuwee didn't understand why they weren't standing on his uncle's doorstep. Why weren't they taken to King Nuumyu? Instead, here they were standing in front of a grinning old woman who feasted her eyes on them as if they were a much-needed meal.

"Come. Come in," the Oupa Ra said to them. With a motion of her hand, she beckoned them to enter as she politely stepped to one side allowing them passage.

Kuula peered inside the dimly lit front room and spotted the Oupa Ra's two daughters standing in the foreground. Tuuwee, however, was focused on the street behind them. He watched as Ali and his driver/bodyguard left on foot up the dirt road. They were heading toward the border crossing from which they had just come. Tuuwee desperately wanted to turn from the Oupa Ra and follow Ali up the road, but, just then, a hand touched him gently on his arm.

"Your place is with me, I assure you" the Oupa Ra said. Tuuwee turned to find Kuula already in motion and inside the front room. Reluctantly, Tuuwee allowed himself to be led inside as well, and fell in step behind Kuula. Tuuwee leaned forward and spoke softly into Kuula's ear. "Our place is with our people" he said. Then he turned to the Oupa Ra and, standing squarely in the middle of the front room, he said "We've traveled far and risked much to get here. Why must we delay any longer from joining our uncle, King Nuumyu?"

"It's a long story, my son" the Oupa Ra said as she closed the door. "I promise to satisfy all your curiosities in due time. I hope, too, that you will also provide me with some answers to some very important questions. But first we must make you comfortable with, perhaps, some food." The Oupa Ra paused as she quickly scanned their dirt-smeared bodies. With a noticeable frown, she then added, "And water, that's for certain. And maybe something refreshing to drink."

For the first time, Tuuwee noticed the Oupa Ra's daughters while Kuula had noticed nothing else! The Oupa Ra turned toward the girls and snapped, "What are you standing there for. Go and fix two hot baths for our guests!" The two young women giggled and dashed off into the adjoining room to do as their mother had asked.

"We've eaten our fill already," Tuuwee said in a sharp tone. "Now lead us to our uncle!" The butt end of Tuuwee's spear came down hard on the wooden floor as he used it to emphasize his urgency.

"Now just a minute, young man. Don't you raise your voice and rattle those toy weapons of yours in my house," the Oupa Ra shot back with an equally harsh voice. "I have a mind to help you in your quest to meet your uncle, the emperor. In fact, I am the only one outside the walls surrounding Shacuwa who can help you! That's why Ali turned you over to me. But unless you cooperate with me fully, you will likely never see King Nuumyu. He is very sickly—close to death, in fact—and has taken to his bed. The first thing we must do is wash your filthy bodies. If the emperor were to permit you into his chambers the way you are now, the smell of you would kill him. Now, put those crude weapons down and work on getting cleaned up."

The Oupa Ra stepped forward with her hands out in front. She wisely stopped short of grabbing Tuuwee's and Kuula's weapons. Instead, she stood with her hands on her hips . . . waiting. Tuuwee's gaze was fixed on her. He was trying to read what her next move would be. At that moment, he had no intention of handing over his spear or shield.

Kuula, on the other hand, watched the Oupa Ra's hands. They seemed harmless enough to him. He raised his eyes and looked into her face. What he saw was a caring old woman who meant them no harm—only good. Kuula handed her his spear and shield. Ever so gently, she took them and set them against the nearby wall. She then turned and approached Tuuwee, hands outstretched. "You have nothing to fear and nothing to lose by cooperating with me. But you have everything to gain by doing so. I am here to help you. Trust me."

Tuuwee hesitated a moment longer, finally giving in and handing her his weapons. This was a giant leap on the part of the Oupa Ra in getting her two visitors to lower their guard. Her next step was to put them at perfect ease as she and her daughters gave them a hot bath and fed them with fresh fruit and cheese.

A short while later, Tuuwee and Kuula found themselves in a room draped floor to ceiling in animal skins. They were now dressed in colorful African garments which covered their tawny black skin from their chins down. They sat on giant pillows, with the Oupa Ra sitting opposite them on a fur-lined chair elevated a couple of feet higher than their own particular perches on the floor.

In one corner of the room sat a life-sized bronze statue looking much like a lion sitting upright on its hind legs. However, its head was that of a man resembling the famous Egyptian sphinx with a large, broad nose. But this Sphinx lookalike was the sacred shrine of Igun. It was said to be older than all the monuments of Egypt. And it was the source of the Oupa's power and influence over all the Africans throughout the West Central region.

Over the course of several hours, the Oupa Ra sat and talked with Tuuwee and Kuula. Kuula mostly listened, allowing Tuuwee to speak for them both. The Oupa Ra seemed to have a deep interest in Tuuwee's father, Muusamali. She quizzed him more and more about his father as their discussion continued. She also probed for information regarding the strength and size of the Cuuzan warriors living in exile with Muusamali.

Tuuwee was finding the old woman pleasant to be with. Her face had aged sweetly with time and was not at all hard to look at. What wrinkles lined her brow were set well and positioned evenly on her brown, glowing complexion. Her teeth were white and straight, giving her a warm smile. And Tuuwee found he could make her smile quite easily when telling her stories about his father. But her probing eyes, which seemed to know each of his answers before he'd given them, made Tuuwee uncomfortable. There was a certain wisdom about this woman, which made her both disquieting as well as fascinating.

"You must have known my father well to have such a fondness to hear about him," Tuuwee said. "Yes, I did know him well. It was back when we were both quite young," the Oupa Ra answered. She paused and looked off into the distance as if pondering a pleasant and warming thought. Finally she went on. "Muusamali and I often attended religious conferences together with our fathers. Although your grandfather, King Fuuru, died a premature death before Muusamali turned twelve years old, he lived long enough to instill in him a hunger for spiritual knowledge and a desire to be a great Huzza priest."

"I, on the other hand, was born for one purpose, and forced into the mystic arts by virtue of who my father was. He was a priest who attracted the likes of young men like Muusamali from all over the territory. He thirsted for ancient knowledge as well as the secret arts.

"Your father was always the cheerful one. During my many moments of boredom, he would always make me laugh by whispering something funny in my ear. Usually, the funny remarks were directed at my father as he would be standing before a crowd teaching. Muusamali could find amusing flaws in anyone. Once he said that I reminded him of the world turned upside down. He said this because each time I smiled, I made his world spin." The Oupa Ra paused again and stared off in dreamy wonder, smiling. "So," she began again with the stern look returning to her face, "whenever Muusamali came to our village to listen to my father's lectures, I would always put on this ugly mask and pretend to be bored senseless— yet all the while smiling. What laughs he must have gotten while making fun of me."

"One cannot look at a beautiful flower and make fun of it," Tuuwee said as he stared at her. The Oupa Ra was caught off guard with the remark. She was surprised that such sensitivity was coming from the young swampdweller. All she could so was blush and allow yet another grin to cross her lips. This, of course, prompted Tuuwee to be more generous with his praise. "If the smile I'm looking at right now is the same blossoming flower my father witnessed, then I'm sure he has never made fun of you!" Tuuwee added with a grin of his own, bringing yet another blush to the old woman's cheeks.

Kuula was in agreement with Tuuwee's remarks and vigorously nodded to show it.

Tuuwee hadn't heard his grandfather's name mentioned since he was a young boy. Even then it was Zuuox who took time to satisfy his curiosity.

Muusamali seldom spoke about his father, so Tuuwee asked the Oupa Ra questions about him. She was glad to oblige and revealed all she knew about King Fuuru. Even Kuula had a question or two about his mother's father.

Tuuwee and Kuula hung on every word as the Oupa Ra spoke. After a while, she called out to her daughters, who emerged from the adjoining room. As the two young women stood beside their mother, the Oupa Ra stared at her guests, most especially Kuula.

"This is Nala and this is Ty," she said pointing to each girl in turn. She seemed to be speaking exclusively to Kuula. As she looked away from him, she held her gaze on Tuuwee and continued, "I wish to hear more about your people in exile and about your swamp home away from home. Also, I'd like for you to share with me what your father taught you about the art of Huzza. But of course, if Kuula is not versed in the secret arts, he will only be bored by our conversations."

The Oupa Ra motioned for her daughters to lean down. Together, Nala and Ty bent toward their mother as she whispered instructions into their ears. Tuuwee and Kuula watched the exchange silently. When the girls straightened again, they looked directly at Kuula, who met their stare with some apprehension.

"Kuula and I have traveled far," Tuuwee spoke up. "And to be so close to our uncle and our people and yet not be in their company is something we cannot abide with much longer." Tuuwee had barely finished speaking when Nala and Ty stepped up to Kuula and, without a word, reached down each grabbing an arm and gentling pulling him to his feet.

"I understand your eagerness to meet your uncle, the emperor, and join your people," The Oupa Ra said as Tuuwee sat dumbfounded watching Kuula being led away to the adjoining room. "But such a meeting will not come easily. The man responsible for making it so hard, maybe even impossible, for you to ever meet your Uncle Nuumyu is another of your uncles. Duugawdu. He is the one who is standing in your place as the next king of the Cuuzan and next emperor of Kongolia."

Those last remarks captured Tuuwee's undivided attention. He didn't even notice Kuula turn back and look at him, his lips seeming to move. Tuuwee took no regard to Kuula's words, as the door shut silently behind him.

For the rest of the night and into early the next morning just before dawn, Tuuwee and the Oupa Ra sat together and talked in front of the gas lantern. They remained under the watchful eye of Igun, the half-man, half-beast god of Africa.

Kuula hadn't been seen since the night before when he entered the room with Nala and Ty. The girls, however, came out from time to time, half-naked, when their mother clapped her hands, signifying she had a need for them to attend to. Those needs consisted mainly of keeping Tuuwee's and her drinking cup filled with hot tea laced with an herbal stimulant. It was a strong concoction which caused Tuuwee to lose all track of time. He and the Oupa Ra engrossed themselves in a verbal marathon: nonstop talking and tea drinking.

The Oupa Ra learned as much as she could hope to learn from Tuuwee. She heard about the exiled Muusamali clan of Cuuzan living abroad. She heard about the secrets of Huzza from Muusamali's point of view. At one point, she had to rebuke Tuuwee for his reckless eyeballing. Each time one of her daughters would appear wearing little more than a smile, Tuuwee would ignore the Oupa Ra with lust-filled eyes following her every move. "Young Tuuwee Cuuzan," The Oupa Ra said in a sharp yet calm tone. "I'll have you know that being a stud is beneath the dignity of any true Huzza priest or voodoo master. Your cousin's male attributes hang between his legs like a third arm. That's why I chose him to mate with my daughters. At best, your breeding equipment will produce girls. But your god has blessed you in another area. He has given you a giant mind and the birthright to an emperor's crown! The power to rule men, their women, and children is within your grasp. You, unlike your cousin, are destined for greatness! Let wisdom, knowledge, and understanding be your only desire right now. There will be plenty of time to satisfy the trifling urges of the flesh later on."

The Oupa Ra went on to bring Tuuwee up to date on the latest political turbulence rocking the empire. His uncle Nuumyu's failing health and his other uncle Duugawdu's clever plot to take overpower. She told him that Nuumyu never fathered any male offspring. This meant that Tuuwee had a legitimate claim and could easily challenge Duugawdu to succeed Emperor Nuumyu to the throne.

She told him about the Puma War and about the ongoing struggle to keep the land black and the people free. She fed Tuuwee a host of revelations and information about the future of Kongolia and the efforts on the part of the Puma Dorrs to remove Duugawdu and his puppet cabinet members from power.

At daybreak, with Tuuwee looking exhausted and the Oupa Raw herself in need of sleep, she sent one of her daughters out into the early morning dawn to deliver a secret message to someone at a clandestine location. When Nala returned, Tuuwee was fast asleep, and so were Kuula and Ty.

The Oupa Ra was in her room lying awake in her bed. She fought off sleep until she was certain that every piece of her plan was set in motion. "Comrade Luba Zandi sends his respects and says he will arrive at the house as you requested at noon today," Nala said as she stood next to her mother's bedside. "Good," the Oupa Ra answered as she lay propped up on her pillows and gently stroking the spotted head of her pet ocelot as the cat lay prone beside her. "That will give our new friends some time to rest before they meet their future comrades in arms. Now remember, I don't want you or your sister to lay with anyone except Kuula or Tuuwee for as long it takes one of them to impregnate one or both of you! When I'm done with Tuuwee, I will turn him over to you. The political advantages will be enormous if we can convince them to join the Puma Dorrs. And if Igun is willing, you or your sister will give birth to a situation which will give us insurance as well as additional bargaining power."

"We will do our best Mother . . . our best for the cause," Nala said in an unusually calm manner. "Yes, daughter, for the cause," the Oupa Ra said as she finally closed her eyes in sleep. Nala turned and headed for the door without another word. For her and her sister, as well as the entire population of Bawku, the queen bee's wishes were all that mattered.

The horse-drawn wagon crept slowly up the street. A lone black driver sat behind the reins. He looked inconspicuous enough although he wore a hood over his head and gray-colored Arab robes. Arab garments were common dress in and around Bawku. The large crate which sat in the back of the wagon didn't exactly draw attention until the wagon pulled up to a stop in front of the Oupa Ra's house.

The driver slowly climbed down from his seat. Something heavy was concealed beneath the robes of his right arm. When he reached in the back of the wagon, he tapped three times on the giant crate before reaching up and unfastening the latch. As the door flew open, three men exited in single file and hurried toward the Oupa Ra's front door. Their long robes were flowing behind them in the breeze and their faces were partially hidden, wrapped in scarves. Just like the driver, these three men kept one arm locked in place as if carrying a heavy bundle beneath their robes. Nala was already at the front door holding it open as, one by one, the four filed inside her mother's house.

Tuuwee and Kuula had just awakened. The Oupa Ra gathered them all together in the front room to await the arrival of Luba Zandi and his Puma Dorr comrades. As the four men entered the room, they immediately took up their positions. One man posted himself at the front window overlooking the street outside, while another went to the rear of the house to stand guard at the back door. A third, the tallest of the four, stood in the center of the room and kept an eye on Tuuwee and Kuula, who were standing awkwardly next to their spears and shields.

The fourth man was the first to pull the veil from his face and remove his hood as he stepped in front of the Oupa Ra. Thick red dreadlocks hung to his shoulders. The man was in his thirties, dark-complected, with a wide smile that revealed a set of large, even white teeth. "My, my, Oupa Ra. Your beauty intensifies each time I feast my eyes on you."

"And your lies get sweeter and sweeter, Luba Zandi," the Oupa Ra said as she stood fast, allowing the man to embrace her in a one-arm bear-hug. Luba Zandi kept one arm around her shoulder as he turned and faced Tuuwee and Kuula. "And I presume these are the two swampers who claim to be the emperor's nephews?"

Tuuwee didn't appear to hear a word as he stared at the other man before him. Kuula, however, stepped up immediately and faced Luba Zandi. "Do not make the mistake of calling us swampers again. We are Cuuzan warriors!" Kuula said as he looked Luba Zandi squarely in the eye.

Luba Zandi seemed shocked for a moment as the ever-present smile was momentarily wiped from his face. Slowly he removed his arm from the Oupa Ra's shoulder. As the man at the window turned and removed a rifle from beneath his robe, Luba Zandi held up a hand signaling the man to freeze.

"Our young friend here is very convincing," Luba Zandi said. In spite of the forced smile playing on his thick lips, his eyes revealed his anger, and his words held a warning. But there's only one man in this room whose word will convince me of your true identity. And you'd better pray that you are who you say you are!"

With that, all eyes turned to the tallest man in the room. As he slowly unveiled his face, Tuuwee's face went flush. Kuula's mouth dropped open in surprise as he uttered in a disbelieving tone, "Zuuox!"

"It is you!" Tuuwee managed to say. "Yes, my Prince," Zuuox answered in his deep and roaring voice. "You were not completely fooled, were you?" "From the moment you walked through the door, I sensed it was you," Tuuwee said.

"So did I," Kuula lied as he stepped over and embraced Zuuox. "We missed you," Kuula added as he looked over at Tuuwee. Surprisingly, Tuuwee's expression remained unchanged and cold. "Not everyone missed me, it seems," Zuuox added as all eyes were on Tuuwee.

"Why did you leave without me? After everything you revealed to me in secret about the homeland, how to reach it, and about my place being here and not the swamps. Yet you packed up and left me behind. I don't understand," Tuuwee said.

"I gave your father my word that I wouldn't bring you with me!" Zuuox said with a solemn expression. Kuula was still glued to his side, and he nodded his head up and down to show his support of Zuuox's explanation.

Tuuwee, however, was not so quick to consent. "But you alone planted the seed and cultivated the desire that drove me to leave," Tuuwee said. Zuuox quickly jumped in saying, "Something I didn't promise your father I wouldn't do. So I did it. And here you are! Here we are—together—as the gods obviously intended." Tuuwee added, "I did miss you very much."

Zuuox continued, holding out a long arm, "How can I believe such when you won't even embrace me?" With that, Tuuwee smiled and walked into his outstretched arms.

With Tuuwee under one arm and Kuula under the other, Zuuox proudly introduced them as the two bravest Cuuzan warriors of all time! Luba Zandi stepped up first and then the other, named Sipiho, walked away from his window perch long enough to shake Tuuwee's and Kuula's hand. The man named Sipiho removed his hood, revealing a head of reddish dreadlocks not quite as long as Luba Zandi's rope, but they clearly distinguished the two as Ikeele tribesmen.

"It's obvious our guests are true to their claim," Luba Zandi announced, looking away from Kuula and toward Zuuox and Tuuwee. "Why don't we allow comrade Zuuox a private moment to reunite with his young tribespeople? I'm sure Tuuwee and Kuula Cuuzan have a lot to tell. And most certainly, comrade Zuuox will thoroughly acquaint the emperor's nephews with the Puma Dorrs and the 'people's cause,'" Luba Zandi said, looking Zuuox squarely in the eye.

Zuuox kept his poise and said only "they will be enlightened." Luba Zandi then led the way out of the room as the Oupa Ra paused in front of

Zuuox and said with a hint of insincerity, "It's always a pleasure to see you, Zuuox." "The feeling is mutual, of course," he answered dryly.

The Oupa Ra was already headed out the door when she suddenly stopped and turned. "Oh, I almost forgot. I kept your presence in Bawku a secret so that I could enjoy watching the joyous surprise on the faces of Tuuwee and Kuula Cuuzan. And what a happy moment it was indeed!" After saying this, she abruptly turned and walked away.

As Sipiho exited behind the Oupa Ra, he pointed to the window. Zuuox responded by signaling Kuula to take his place at the front window. "Keep your eyes peeled for anyone approaching the house!" he ordered.

As Kuula took his position, Zuuox and Tuuwee slowly followed him arm-in-arm as they stopped just short of the window and sat in two chairs along the wall. Zuuox raised his robe, revealing a bolt-action .22 rifle hanging beneath his arm from a leather strap tied around his shoulder. Tuuwee watched with a curious expression as Zuuox unhooked the rifle from the strap and gently set it upright against the wall.

"No better weapon exists for killing than this," Zuuox said. "Yes, so I'm told" Tuuwee replied and then went on to tell Zuuox about how Ali, the merchant, found them in the canyon and brought them to Bawku. Along the way, Ali took time out and gave Tuuwee and Kuula a little demonstration of what a rifle could do by shooting a wild dog which was running on the open plain.

Tuuwee and Kuula took turns telling Zuuox about their fight with the Foliose and about the Gatooma pygmies rescuing them from the jaws of death. They went on, explaining in great detail, the other hair-raising tales from their journey.

"From what you tell me, you and Kuula owe Cuuz the almighty a great debt of gratitude," Zuuox commented. "Well, I haven't had much luck in completing a sacrifice as yet," Tuuwee said.

Kuula fought off the urge to laugh. Nevertheless, the muffled sounds of a snicker crossed his lips.

Zuuox smiled slightly, and Tuuwee pretended not to have heard Kuula's attempt to contain his mirth. Instead, Tuuwee launched right into a flurry of questions. First, he inquired about Zuuox's supposed accidental death. "I informed King Muusamali years ago that I did not intend to live out my life in the swamps."

As Zuuox reared back in his chair, Tuuwee noticed for the first time that he had grown a beard, as he continued, "He knew that any day I would go on a hunt and not return. When that day finally arrived when I really did not come back, your father must have told Suubala and the others to fake my death rather than tell the truth and risk having others try to follow me to freedom."

"In spite of what you might believe about your father, he does care about you, Little Eagle." Zuuox paused and gave Tuuwee one of his intense looks, as if he were trying to measure the impact of his words. But Tuuwee was unmoved, or so it seemed, by any mention of his father. What did raise his brow was hearing his pet name, Little Eagle, the one Zuuox had given him as a tiny tot. Zuuox continued, "It's mostly because of me that Muusamali's feelings grew cold toward you. He wished for nothing more in life than to see me leave and to see you stay. If he really didn't care for his firstborn son, he could have easily told me to take you, and I would have done so before you were big enough to walk.

"There is something else you should know about your father which I was forced not to reveal to you all these many years." Zuuox paused and looked Tuuwee squarely in the eye. "Your father didn't desert the homeland by choice. King Nuumyu ordered him to go into exile with a share of the tribe in order to ensure that the white invaders would not wipe our entire Cuuzan race. Your father is living in exile by King Nuumyu's decree!"

Tuuwee looked bewildered. "By decree?" he questioned with a startled voice. Then he stared at the floor and added, "But I thought he abandoned the homeland to keep from fighting?"

Zuuox shook his head from side to side.

"Then he is not a coward after all," Tuuwee said with some relief in his voice. Tuuwee didn't know what to think or say. All his life he held his father solely responsible for the exiled clan being forced to live in the wretched swamp land. And all his life, he despised him for it!

Zuuox realized Tuuwee's dilemma and quickly decided to change the subject. "Was there no way that you could shake Kuula off your tail long enough to leave without him?" Zuuox asked as he reached over with his long arms and gave Kuula a judo chop behind the knee. Kuula's legs suddenly buckled, and he was forced to grab the window ledge for support.

In response, Kuula hit at Zuuox playfully and, as the two of them exchanged open-handed blows, Kuula happened to look up and see Luba Zandi standing in the next room with Nala and Ty by his side.

"Kuula and I are inseparable," Tuuwee said. "I would have never left without him. But don't tell him that!" Tuuwee was trying his best to engage Zuuox and Kuula in pleasantries in spite of his confused heart over what he'd just learned about his father.

Of course, Kuula was well within earshot and as Tuuwee and Zuuox looked at him for his reaction, they found Kuula in a trance, staring across the room at Luba Zandi, Nala, and Ty.

Zuuox followed Kuula's gaze, but the sight of the two daughters with Luba Zandi meant nothing to him. It only made him think of the Oupa Ra.

"So, you've been with the Oupa Ra all night and she just decided to send for us this morning?" Zuuox questioned.

"Yes," answered Tuuwee, whose attention was divided as he looked from Kuula to the other room and back again at Zuuox. "Yes, we talked for quite a long time."

"I'm sure that she asked, and you answered, a lot of questions about your Huzza training and other matters about the exiled clan of our people," Zuuox said.

Tuuwee nodded his head as Zuuox continued, "She is dangerous. Tuuwee. Treat her as you would a creature with sharp teeth . . . very sharp teeth!"

"But she is such a nice, gentle old lady," Tuuwee said. "Yes, just as meat-eating plants are beautiful and gentle looking flowers, But . . ." Zuuox paused and gave Tuuwee that look of his which demanded an answer without asking.

"They eat insects," Tuuwee said. "Correct," Zuuox replied. "And the Oupa Ra has fed on you. Her head is fat with knowledge and information which you provided. Did you reveal any Huzza secrets?" "Yes," Tuuwee answered sadly. Then he raised his head and added, "But she revealed voodoo secrets to me in exchange."

"Probably elementary stuff. And she likely already knows twice as much as you do about Huzza medicine. But like a blood-sucking creature, she lives to suck information from the people. She uses information any way she can to maintain her power over people. Do you understand what I'm saying?"

"Yes, I believe so, "Tuuwee answered feeling very much at ease to once again be in Zuuox's company.

"And do you also understand that the Oupa Ra is not the kind, sweet old lady she pretends to be, Kuula?" Zuuox looked up at him as he spoke. However, Kuula's mind was still on the next room as he continued to stare at Luba Zandi entertaining the sisters.

"I will return shortly," Kuula announced and then hurried off. Zuuox looked at Tuuwee with questioning eyes. "Kuula laid with the sisters all night," Tuuwee said with a shy smirk. "I think he feels as though these women are his property now."

Zuuox didn't look too surprised as he shook his head and said, "That old woman is some shrewd operator."

"Some what?" Tuuwee asked frowning.

"Never mind," Zuuox replied. "I must get you and your cousin out of here."

At that moment, Zuuox heard the thundering sound of footsteps as they stormed on to the front porch. He immediately reached for his rifle. Just as he grabbed it, the front door swung open, and soldiers with rifles of their own rushed in. Before Zuuox could level his weapon, he and Tuuwee were overrun as they got to their feet. Several rifles were pointed at their heads and Zuuox's own rifle was snatched from his hand.

"Don't move or we will kill you on the spot!" one of the soldiers warned.

"Do exactly as they say, Tuuwee!" Zuuox said as they both stared down the barrels smelling of gunpowder.

Tuuwee, however, seemed oblivious to the gun in his face. He was more concerned with what was happening in the next room. He couldn't see what was taking place, but he watched with dread as a half-dozen soldiers stormed across the floor and rushed to where Kuula was in the adjoining room. He feared the worst might happen to his cousin and friend.

Suddenly, a gunshot rang out! The sound was loud and chilling. It caused a paralyzing effect to his nerves. Tuuwee was suddenly driven to action as he brought both hands up simultaneously slapping two gun barrels away from his face. In the same motion, he lunged forward slipping past the first two soldiers, only to meet with a third who rammed his rifle barrel into Tuuwee's unprotected midsection. The blow caught Tuuwee off guard and knocked the wind out of him as he dropped to his knees and hugged his stomach gasping for air.

Zuuox flinched as if to aid Tuuwee, but a gun barrel was suddenly jammed beneath his chin. His head was forced so far back on his neck that he was forced to stand on his toes to keep from choking.

"Put them in chains. Quickly," A voice called out. "Or we will be forced to kill them."

"This is an outrage. You dare invade my home like this!" The Oupa Ra's voice was heard saying over the noise of the soldiers' stomping feet and commanding voices, ordering everyone to get down and not move. So quick and forceful was the surprise raid that the whole house was taken over in a matter of minutes.

A large crowd of men, women, and children began to form across the street from the Oupa Ra's house. Each and every shiny black face was marked with fearful anticipation of what was to come. The crowd peered over the shoulders of armed soldiers who stood facing them as they lined the streets in double formation. There were about thirty-five soldiers in all, the front row of which were armed with large metal shields and broad double-edged swords. The soldiers came well prepared, knowing that crowd control would be a prerequisite to arresting and removing anyone from Bawku.

The raiding party did not anticipate capturing any Puma Dorrs in their surprise attack on the Oupa Ra's house. Least of all, they never expected to find one of the main Puma Dorr generals, Luba Zandi!

As the first prisoner was marched out onto the front porch, a loud murmur rose from the crowd of spectators. The front line of soldiers responded by bringing their shields to the ready. The snapping noise their shields made got everyone's attention. And for a moment, the crowd quieted down.

The prisoner on the porch was Sipiho. He was surrounded by three soldiers who carried their rifles in leather slings around their shoulders. Holding him by the arms, they pulled him down the steps. His legs were in shackles and his wrists bound by a chain around his waist and midsection. Sipiho was marched out and down the front street.

"Power to the people!" Sipiho yelled as he passed in front of the onlookers. The crowd immediately responded, loudly and in near-perfect unison, "Long live the Puma Dorrs! Long live the Puma Dorrs!" Over and over they chanted. As the crowd stirred closer, the front-line soldiers tightened their ranks and began forcing them back.

Next, Kuula was dragged from the house on to the porch. A soldier on each side gripped his arms and forced him down the steps and on to the street. The crowd became more enraged as they shouted obscenities at the soldiers and spit on the ground to emphasize their disgust at the way in which Kuula was being treated.

As Kuula fought against the soldiers' efforts to drag him down the street, he kept looking back over his shoulder for Tuuwee. Nothing else mattered to Kuula—not the crowd, not even the continuous pain he felt as the soldier at his side, the one wearing the uniform of a sergeant, kept poking his ribs with the butt end of his rifle.

Tuuwee was the next to appear. Slumped over in pain, he was half-dragged and half-carried down the porch steps and onto the street. The rattling sound of the chains binding his ankles rang out and strangely mixed with the shouts from the crowd to "free the Puma Dorrs"!

Tuuwee looked up and caught sight of Kuula trying to break free from his captors. Tuuwee could barely stand on his own because of the pain being administered to his stomach so effectively. But he forced himself to straighten up, not wanting Kuula to become any more enraged by seeing him in distress. Tuuwee sensed that cooperating was the only way to avoid further pain to himself or to his cousin.

"Stay calm, Cuuzan!" Tuuwee yelled over the noise of the crowd. His voice was weakened and strained. But from the forty-yard distance between him and Kuula, his words were still heard.

"Listen to your friend," said the sergeant who had been jabbing Kuula in the side. "You listen to me," Kuula replied with tight jaws as he glared at the soldier with hate-filled eyes. "If ever these chains come off, I'm going to wrap them around your fat neck!"

"But they won't ever come off, swamper! Not until you are tried, convicted, and hung for your crimes against the empire. You Puma Dorr pig!" the soldier snarled.

"I am a Cuuzan warrior!" Kuula loudly hissed through clenched teeth, spitting on the soldier's face. The sergeant turned ugly with rage. He brought the others to a halt as he stepped around and stood directly in front of Kuula. With two other soldiers holding Kuula by the arms, the sergeant drew back his rifle like an overhead battering ram. Without a second thought, he drove the butt end toward Kuula's face with all the power he could muster. Kuula managed to turn his face just in the nick of time, missing the full force of the blow. Nevertheless, the gun butt caught him on the temple, viciously jerking his head to the side. He then fell limp as his chin came to rest on his chest. The two soldiers held his motionless body as they stared in disbelief at the sergeant.

"You saw what that pig did," the sergeant snapped as he wiped the spittle from his face. He then reached and checked Kuula's neck for a pulse. After a moment, he looked at the others with a twisted grin and said, "He's fine. Now get him out of here!"

The voices from the crowd screamed, "Murderers, murderers! Cowards! Down with Shacuwa. Long live the Puma Dorrs!"

Then Tuuwee's voice was heard calling out Kuula's name. As his two captors marched him arm-and-arm down the street, they approached the sergeant who stood in the center plaza. Tuuwee looked past him and watched as Kuula's limp body was being dragged further down the road toward the waiting wagon. "What have you done?" Tuuwee screamed at the sergeant. The sergeant stood blocking their passage, forcing the other guards to bring Tuuwee to a halt.

Tuuwee found himself staring into the face of a madman. The same twisted grin which Kuula had just been forced to witness displayed itself once again across the sergeant's face. The sergeant had a clean-shaven head and very prominent, high cheekbones, all the characteristics of the Kodok. The Cuuzan and Kodok tribes were once long-standing and bitter enemies who used to kill each other on sight. It was the urgent need to unify the homelands to survive the European onslaught that forced them to swear a peace treaty with each other, thus merging with the other five tribes into the Kongolian Empire. But deep-seated hatreds remained between the Cuuzan and the Kodok. And unfortunately, Kuula was painfully experiencing some of the violent backlash in spite of the fact that neither he nor Tuuwee had ever met a Kodok before this day.

None of the other soldiers attempted to intervene on Kuula's behalf even though the ranks of soldiers present were noticeably diversified. The number of Manono, Warri, Bakuwa, and Owada were greatest among the nonranking troops. Practically all the ranking officers who made up the Kongolian army and police were Kodok, Ikeele, and Cuuzan nationalists. Those three tribes were always the most dominant ones in the territory and were the fiercest fighters during the Puma Wars.

Tuuwee suddenly lost control of his own better judgment. "I'll kill you!" He screamed and lunged at the sergeant in an effort to use his forehead to strike the man. But the two other soldiers, gripping Tuuwee's arm, held him back. It was a close call as his forehead came within inches of ramming the sergeant in the nose.

The sergeant became enraged once again. Just as before, he drew his rifle back, aiming the butt end at Tuuwee's face. He was just about to deliver a crushing blow when the sound of a fast-approaching horse filled his ears and a voice yelled at him to halt.

The man on horseback rode up and leaped from the saddle. He wore the traditional officer's uniform, cut-off khaki pants with matching short-sleeved shirt. A holstered pistol was strapped to his side. As he reached for the sergeant's rifle, he kept his other hand on his pistol.

"You damn fool!" he yelled as he wrested the rifle from the sergeant's hand. "You were given orders not to harm these men in any way."

"But Captain," the sergeant said with a look of surprise, "these pigs are Puma Dorrs!"

"The captain shook his head, stared into the sergeant's eyes, and said, "If only you knew who these men truly are, you'd put this rifle in your mouth and pull the trigger!" The captain held the sergeant's rifle up to his face, within inches of his wide nose which flared ever wider in anger. The sergeant retrieved his rifle. A twinkle of curiosity flashed in his eyes, but, overall, he was able to maintain a defiant expression as he asked, "Is that all, sir?"

"Yes. You are relieved of duty. Now get the hell out of here."

The captain turned and faced Tuuwee. They looked at each other in a most peculiar manner. The captain's eyes settled on the distinguishing Cuuzan tribal scars lining Tuuwee's forehead from hairline to hairline. The captain wore a cap tilted low over his forehead but possessed all the physical features of the Cuuzan.

"What happened to Kuula?" Tuuwee asked, his voice filled with anxiety. The captain took a step closer as he gave Tuuwee a look of grave concern. "You should not have come here!" the captain said.

Tuuwee looked at him with a frown. He wanted to speak, wanted badly to tell this man that Cuuzanland was his home. Tuuwee's voice betrayed him. His heart cried out in anguish as he suddenly realized the mess he and Kuula had gotten into.

The captain must have sensed Tuuwee's frustration and hurt. And so, he laid a hand on his shoulder. But Tuuwee jerked away violently, causing the captain to withdraw. Tuuwee sought relief from his misery and found it momentarily in that instant when he snubbed the captain's attempt at consolation.

The captain's expression was one of understanding as he stared back at Tuuwee and said, "As long as this young man does as he is told, he is not to be harmed." The captain stepped to one side and noticed Tuuwee's face was set in stone as the two soldiers, one Warri and the other Manono, began marching him off down the street.

The captain turned and walked toward the house where several other soldiers were being led from the front door, with Luba Zandi in chains.

"Beware of the curse!" came a cry from the crowd as the captain walked past.

"Cowards! Shacuwa is doomed!" The verbal assaults seemed not to affect the captain. His expression was one of urgency, and his anxiety had nothing to do with the harmless bystanders.

As the captain climbed on to the front porch and stood before Luba Zandi, he was met with another pair of different eyes, eyes that burned with contempt. The captain's expression turned to surprise.

"Is this who I think it is?" the captain asked as he stared at Luba Zandi's red dreadlocks. The soldiers standing at Luba's side nodded their heads in the affirmative. Luba Zandi stood silent, staring back at the captain.

"Your luck has finally played out, Luba Zandi!" the captain said, his tone more sympathetic than hostile.

"That is your misconception," the Puma Dorr general answered. Luba Zandi was a couple of inches shorter than the captain, but with his chin so high in the air as he stared down his nose at the man, you would think they were the same height. "My fate will not be determined by luck. And surely a lowlife captain like you will have no say about my future. I am an Ikeele citizen—first and foremost!"

The captain smiled in a sad kind of way. Then he stepped to one side as he said, "Lucky you!" With that, he motioned to the soldiers to move out.

As the soldiers escorted Luba Zandi down the short flight of steps and out into the street, the crowds' anger grew louder and more hostile. Someone screamed, "Free the red comrade," which was Luba Zandi's name in translation. The wave of bystanders suddenly rolled forward as Luba Zandi was marched past. The front line of soldiers was, for the first time, forced back on its heels. The support troops quickly stepped up into position as shouts of "free Luba Zandi" rang out followed with stones and such being thrown at the soldiers.

The soldiers' sudden response was brutal and without mercy. Using their shields to hold the crowd at bay, they began jabbing people with their bayonets and hacking others on the arms and hands with their razor-sharp swords. Blood spilled and screamed of pain filled the air. The unarmed crowd was no match for the soldiers. The wave of spectators was rolled back as their faces filled with terror. They quickly broke off and ran their separate ways.

The captain turned his back on the ruckus as he walked through the front door of the Oupa Ra's house. One look at Zuuox standing in the middle of the room between two soldiers caused the captain's face to drop. Zuuox returned the stare. Instead of surprise, his expression revealed a warm smile. The captain's eyes fell on Zuuox's hands and feet, which were bound by rope. Another long strip of rope was attached to his ankles on one end, while a soldier held the opposite end in his hand.

Without warning, the captain reached and snatched the end of the rope from the soldier throwing it to the floor in one motion. "This man is not a dog!" the captain roared. "But Captain, we ran out of chains" the soldier pleaded.

Just then, another soldier wearing an officer's uniform entered from an adjoining room. All eyes looked his way. The captain spoke immediately. "Was it not clear to you, Lieutenant, that this operation was to be low-key and the men treated decently?"

"In case you haven't noticed, Captain, these so-called men are Puma Dorrs!" the lieutenant answered as he stopped and stood next to his leader. The lieutenant was an Ikeele. His long hair was in dreadlocks, tiny ropes which hung no further than his ears. However, the reddish tint was absent. In keeping with tradition, all Ikeele wore dreadlocks. But it was the reddish tint which distinguished the "traditional thinkers" from the "liberal reform–minded" Ikeele. The redder the tint, the more orthodox the person's views were.

"I don't care who they are, Lieutenant. Orders are to be obeyed, not at your discretion, but at the wish of your superiors," the captain said in a stern voice.

The lieutenant couldn't hide the resentment he felt and which was evident in his voice. He nodded and replied with a grumble, "Yes, sir."

The Oupa Ra appeared in the doorway at that moment, followed by two soldiers carrying the dead body of a Puma Dorr who'd been shot. "I want this man's body to remain with me," the Oupa Ra was saying. "He deserves a proper burial, something I wouldn't trust the Shacuwa government to do. These other men are to be released at once!"

The captain's mouth dropped open at the sight of the dead man. He hurried over and stared down into the dead man's face. After seeing something he either did or did not want to see, his face relaxed somewhat. He then turned and walked back over to the lieutenant and gave him a hard, questioning stare.

"He resisted," the lieutenant said quickly. Then, in a softer tone, he added, "It was either him or one of my men."

"It was murder!" the Oupa Ra shouted from her place. "The blood of this man is on each of your heads. Igun's bitter judgment will befall every one of you! Such pain and suffering like you've never seen will someday rain down on all of you like a hellstorm."

"Look, just leave the corps where it is," the captain said to the soldiers as they stared wide-eyed at the Oupa Ra. Without hesitation, the men set the body down on the floor and slowly backed away.

The captain then turned back to Zuuox and the two soldiers guarding him. Zuuox was standing tall with an almost nonchalant expression on his dark, imposing face. "Leave this man with me and go," the captain ordered.

The young lieutenant who couldn't have been more than twenty-five years old, stared at Zuuox's tribal markings. The five tiny and knotted scar tissue lines across Zuuox's forehead were old but still plainly visible.

Although the captain wore his cap tilted low over his forehead, the young lieutenant was nevertheless well aware that the cap concealed more than just hair. "What should we do with the Oupa Ra?" the lieutenant asked as his eyes switched from Zuuox and fixed on his captain.

"You will do nothing with me," the Oupa Ra shouted. Neither me nor my daughters. And if you value your health, you'll release these other men immediately!"

"Take her out of here," the captain said, frustration mounting in his voice. "Take her out on the streets . . . somewhere . . . anywhere . . . everyone just leave!"

The lieutenant hesitated just a moment, finally saying, "As you wish, Captain." He took one last look at Zuuox then turned to the Oupa Ra.

"Don't put your hands on me!" she warned. The lieutenant complied, and the Oupa Ra turned and slowly followed Nala, Ty, and the soldiers toward the front door. She hesitated in the doorway, with the lieutenant on her heels, just long enough to look back at Zuuox. They exchanged nods, an acknowledgment of sorts.

"Whatever you do, young fool, don't put your hands on me or my daughters," the Oupa Ra said as she turned and headed out the door.

"Hello, little brother," Zuuox said with a grin. "You broke the king's decree by coming back here," the captain responded.

"Yes, I know," Zuuox answered, looking his brother squarely in the eye. "I got tired of living like a swamp gator." The captain's head dropped as he shook it sadly from side to side. Then he looked up and said, "Do you know what we are doing to captured Puma Dorrs? We put them on trial and then hang them the very next day!"

Zuuox looked behind his brother at the dead Puma Dorr laying on the floor. "Some trial he got," he said, looking back at the captain. Zuuox's expression was serious, but his little brother had a look of urgency in his eyes as he shot back, "Don't make light of it. It could have easily been you!"

"Yes. Me and about three of your soldiers," Zuuox said a slight touch of vanity in his thundering voice. Then he added, "Had King Nuumyu's nephews not been present, of course."

The captain looked off, as if calling to mind some reality long forgotten over time. "I believe you," came his nervous response. "Now, what will I do with you?"

"First of all, tell me what will become of Tuuwee and Kuula?"

"They will not be harmed. They are royal Cuuzan blood. You know the law."

"A lot has changed, Wuuta, that's all I know for certain," Zuuox answered with a sign of sadness on the one hand yet relief on the other.

"Change is inevitable," Captain Wuuta said. "So I see," Zuuox replied with that subtle grin now creasing one side of his mouth. "One brother will enslave another like an animal," he added as he pulled on the ropes binding him wrist to waist.

With little hesitation, Wuuta abruptly whipped out his knife and cut his hands and feet free.

"It's not a younger brother's place to question the actions of an older brother," Wuuta said as he released him from his bindings. "But why do you keep company with the hated Puma Dorrs?"

"Why were two members of the royal family carted off in chains and not picked up in a royal coach?"

"That is a situation involving royal family business," Wuuta said as he watched his brother cross the room and post himself by the window. "And it is not your place to question the royal family."

Zuuox spoke up as he peered out the window into the streets. A crowd of supporters was seen milling around the Oupa Ra. Like a beehive's ritual, the horde of black bodies constantly buzzed and shifted, as individuals in the back of the crowd worked their way toward the center to touch her. They did this either as a means of assuring themselves of her well-being or just to convey their devotion through the simple act of physical contact.

The lieutenant and several of his soldiers stood quietly to the side. The lieutenant's attention was focused not on the Oupa Ra but rather on her house. "Prince Duugawdu especially does not like his orders questioned," Wuuta said to Zuuox as he stepped closer to his brother.

"You've answered your own question as to why I joined the Puma Dorrs," Zuuox said as he turned to Wuuta. "Duugawdu is misusing his power. Somebody has to question his actions and the Puma Dorrs are the only ones brave enough to do so."

"You've changed, Zuuox," Wuuta said. "The brother I remember respected tribal law and was unconditionally loyal to the royal family. I am a royal guardsman because, as a child, I wanted to follow in your footsteps. And here I am. A product of your teaching and influence, a carbon copy of what you were. What happened to you? You don't respect the law and you bad-mouth the prince."

Zuuox stepped away from the window and approached his brother with an apologetic expression. "I would like nothing more than to stand here and discuss these differences with you, little brother, but there are restless soldiers out there waiting for you to march me out of here so they can throw me in prison."

"Prison would be a safer place for you, Zuuox, than with the outlaw Puma Dorrs. They are enemies of the empire and usually shot on sight!"

Zuuox gently laid his hand on Wuuta's shoulder. "Quickly, tell me how much larger has our family grown by your male prowess."

"You have eight nephews and three nieces."

Zuuox's eyes lit up. "You've been busy," he said as he gazed proudly into Wuuta's eyes.

"And you, Zuuox?"

Zuuox hung his head. "Our parents would not be so proud of my male prowess, I'm afraid." He spoke softly and sadly. Then he asked with renewed vigor, "How are they—our parents?"

"Growing old," Wuuta said. Then he smiled and said, "Gracefully, I must add, and wiser by the day."

"Well, give them my regards, will you?" Zuuox asked. Wuuta's replied, "Of course I will."

"And don't forget to name one of your man-children after me before you grow old and your male prowess dries up."

"My firstborn son is named Zuuox Cutun," Wuuta said. Then he reached over and tapped Zuuox on the arm and added, "After my one and only brother whose loyalty to the king and tribal law compelled him to sacrifice everything, even his homeland."

"I'm greatly honored," Zuuox said.

"Perhaps you will settle down and raise a family, my brother?" Wuuta said in a leading manner.

"There's no need. Not this late in my life. I've had the great privilege of helping with the raising of the king's first nephew, Tuuwee. A mission from the gods. And a mission with which, I would venture to say, the gods are well pleased. But seeing the firstborn son of Muusamali carried off in chains must have the gods frowning. What do you think, little brother?"

Wuuta carefully pondered the question before saying, "I don't try to second-guess the gods these days. Things happen too suddenly, like the untimely arrival of the emperor's nephews. They should not have come here. They came at the worst possible time. The land is already filled with turmoil. The survival of the empire depends upon a peaceful, diplomatic compromise between opposing forces. Forces which are weakening the empire's very foundation by fighting with each other for power and control.

I am worried that the emperor's nephew will be thrown into the fray and will create a feeding frenzy. Our Kongolian Empire could be devoured and left bare like a bone on the desert floor."

"Well stated," Zuuox said as he placed a heavy hand on Wuuta's shoulder, almost knocking him off balance. "But the only forces worth fearing are the gods, little brother. Remain true to the gods and the real forces of life will be with you and not your enemies."

Wuuta looked at his brother tenderly but said nothing more. To speak further on the matter where the gods were cited as the authority endorsing the message would be to disrespect both the gods and the messenger.

"What will you do now, Zuuox?" Wuuta finally said.

"I will do whatever the gods inspire me to do." Zuuox then rubbed his temple with his long, slender index finger and added, "As long as I am being guided in the direction which will serve the best interests of the true crown prince, Tuuwee Cuuzan."

With that, Zuuox slowly turned and started off. Wuuta was left with his mouth open and eyes staring at the empty space where Zuuox once stood.

"Wait," Wuuta shouted and spun on his heels. Zuuox stopped and turned. "Hit me," Wuuta commanded as he walked up to Zuuox with his chin out. Zuuox hesitated. "Hit me and leave a mark proving that you attacked me and escaped!"

"I cannot," Zuuox said. But before he could finish his sentence, Wuuta delivered a gut shot to Zuuox's midsection and he buckled over in pain. When he started to straighten again, he glared into Wuuta's eyes and said, "So that's how it's done." He drew his right hand back over his left shoulder and, with enough force to knock Wuuta back on his heels, delivered a smashing backhand across his face.

Wuuta's nose instantly sprang a bloody leak. "Now, get out of here," Wuuta said as he brought his hand up to stop the crimson flow. Still, Zuuox hesitated. "Go, damn you, before all of this turns out to be for nothing! Mind you now, travel north in your flight and I will lead my men south."

"Peace be with you, my brother," Zuuox said and ran toward the back of the house.

The Gorma prison compound was a cluster of wooden barracks surrounded by barbed wire fences and guard towers and patrolled around the clock by armed sentries with their guard dogs.

Gorma was once just a holding facility for draft dodgers during the Puma War and a holding facility for captured European soldiers. At the end of the war, and with a measure of peace and prosperity covering the land, Gorma had to be enlarged to accommodate the influx of a new breed of outlaw. They ranged from common thieves to radical revolutionaries.

Gorma was now a dual facility. The newly built main jail was used to house preconvicted prisoners awaiting trial. It was decent in appearance and because the jailed residents were merely alleged lawbreakers, they were treated decently as well.

The old prison barracks, on the other hand, housed convicted prisoners serving long sentences for serious acts of disobedience toward the authoritarian system of government being enforced by Duugawdu and his imperial counsel. It featured a hot, mosquito-infected dungeon atmosphere and an appalling treatment of inmates.

Seventy percent of the inmates being warehoused at the old facility were political prisoners, deemed "enemies of the empire" for little more than speaking and protesting publicly against dictatorial governmental policies.

One of Duugawdu's many governmental titles was minister of defense. His overzealous police force was unscrupulous in identifying lawbreakers. They were very active in rounding them up and throwing them in jail.

The court system was yet another machine of injustice functioning in the shadows of Duugawdu's tough stance against disobedient behavior. His kangaroo court was swift in the process of convicting "enemies of the empire" and either putting them on the shelf to rot in Gorma prison or arranging for their hanging. But years of stacking prisoners like sardines inside Gorma was beginning to take a dangerous toll. Riots were commonplace, but, so far, the force of arms from the prison guards had kept the uprisings in check. However, the prison population was growing more desperate and was smoldering on the brink of an organized takeover.

Politically, Duugawdu faced mounting criticism from certain liberal members on the Imperial Counsel. Screams of injustice from the inmates' relatives highlighted the appalling human conditions inside the crowded Gorma walls. Their cries were beginning to reach the ears of the liberal council members. All the members were kings of their particular tribal clans and, as such, had a moral obligation to protect the health and welfare of their people, in or out of prison.

Since decisions of governing the empire were made by a body of legislators, and policy dictated through voting among the members, most of the kings had grown out of touch, lazy, and insensitive toward the individual pulse of the people. But violent and radical extremists such as the Puma Dorrs were making a lot of noise and their numbers were growing like wildflowers. Mass arrests were being made against the Puma Dorr members, and this was overwhelming Duugawdu's prison system. It was also waking up the sleeping kings to the inhumane treatment of their people.

The light of day had crept away, and darkness settled over Gorma's gray dungeon barracks with a ghostly hue. The warden's office, however, was especially bright. It was a little bungalow that was set off from the main housing facility. A combination of men with arms stood outside in the courtyard underneath the lights of several gas lanterns mounted on tall poles. Royal guardsmen with their steel swords strapped to their hips, soldiers with rifles, prison guards with wooden batons, and several of Duugawdu's own personal body guards stood vigilantly.

Duugawdu's presence on the prison grounds was a first. It was an extraordinary phenomenon like witnessing a surprise eclipse of the sun. Everybody's attention and nervous energy was focused on the warden's office. As they watched and waited, the suspense of the moment had everyone holding their breath.

Inside the luxurious offices, Duugawdu sat in a high-backed leather chair behind the warden's massive walnut desk. The other two chairs in the room were situated in front of the desk and were occupied by the white ambassador and his black European interpreter. The ambassador was clean-shaven, with blue eyes set in a darkly tanned face and black hair trimmed short. His starched high-collared shirt with the ruffled sleeves made him look stuffy and uncomfortable in the midst of the nighttime heatwave.

The black interpreter looked equally uncomfortable in his three-quarter jacket and ruffled shirt although his demeanor, especially for an interpreter, was subtly yet visibly ostentatious. He had the slight, sharp features of a European but had tight woolly hair and darkened skin, not darkened by the sun but is rather clearly due to his African ancestry.

The stockily built warden, who was ordinarily an imposing man with a full bushy head of hair and a large, broad nose set in a dark, blue/black face, stood timidly against the far wall behind the ambassador. He appeared to be an inconsequential guest in his own office.

Two of Duugawdu's shirtless bodyguards stood flanking him behind the desk, with their muscular arms crisscrossing their massive chests. Each clutched a naked broadsword in his fist: a short, double-wide version of the deadly weapon. And as the polished razor-sharp blades hovered in the air, they cast reflections on the wall-like steel mirrors.

"It's all very practical, prince," the ambassador was saying in his native, European, tongue. His voice was low, and he was choosing his words carefully so that his interpreter could translate with ease into Bantu. The ambassador had spoken with Duugawdu several times on this matter, and in spite of feeling frustration toward his stubbornness over the past few years, the ambassador presented his case as if he were doing so for the very first time.

Duugawdu sat steely-eyed in his chair, elbows up and hands locked together to support his bearded chin. He watched and listened to the overdressed white man as if he were hearing the same old sales pitch for the first time. The ambassador continued, "You're sitting on a pressure cooker that's about to explode. You need to create a relief valve. A tiny crack at the backdoor will release enough pressure to prevent a catastrophe. Such a crack will allow your justice system to resume normal operations, arresting these anarchist radicals and putting them away where they will no longer be a threat to the empire. This problem you're having with the terrorists trying to upset and overthrow your government will forever be a thorn in your paw.

"Homegrown terrorism is like wild weed. You pluck one and two more spring up in its place. Like tending a garden, you must constantly pluck your empire of these deadly pests, one by one, through a system of 'removal and disposal.' In the front door, and out the back through a tiny secret crack in the structure that no one knows about except you and your closest confidantes.

"Who cares what you do with troublesome pests once you've removed them from society? No one except, perhaps, their family members. But their cries would only last so long. They would be like a small tear shed in the ocean compared with other more important concerns of government. And of course, there are the liberal elements within your governmental body. They, perhaps, may cower at the sight of a chicken's neck being wrung. But keep in mind that it's these very same spineless liberals who would be responsible for the downfall of your government. If not for the wise, courageous, and practical use of secret systems to remove and dispose of such deadly pests, your empire is doomed.

"Now on the surface, the system looks like nothing more than a wise idea to reap profit from a problem. A method utilizing a massive, ready labor force that is otherwise wasting away here at Gorma like ripe, unpicked fruit. Keeping a prison packed with dangerous criminals beyond the maximum capacity is very risky business and costly to your economy. Your wise and practical ideas before the public and your liberal counterparts is to export strong and able-bodied inmates as commodities overseas to work off their sentences in labor camps. This practical system will not only bring your prison population down to a normal and safe level. It will also keep it at a minimum and pay you a hefty profit in foreign currency which would fatten the state treasury and shower you with other luxuries."

The ambassador paused and calmly reached for a glass of water from the desktop. Slowly and with confidence, he took a sip. Duugawdu watched him with unwavering eyes. The room was still except for the interpreter as he uttered on in Bantu the final words from the ambassador's speech. By the time the ambassador sat his glass back down, the interpreter had concluded. Everyone waited and watched the two main attractions. Finally, after tapping his top lip ever so gently with a white handkerchief, the ambassador went on in his native tongue. "Not only will this system of 'removal and disposal' solve your immediate problems, but—"

Suddenly, Duugawdu raised his hand in the air signaling the ambassador and interpreter to stop. "Tell your master," Duugawdu began in a sharp, composed voice, "I am offended by his suggestion that profit and foreign luxuries would sway my thinking on matters of morality. Urgent necessity, not greed, is the motivating factor prompting me to consider these extreme measures. I caution your master to keep that firmly in mind." Duugawdu dropped his hands in his lap and leaned back in his chair.

Slowly the black interpreter pried his eyes away from him and leveled them on the ambassador. He leaned toward him and said, "It's taking every ounce of strength in my person to avoid telling this heathen that he's speaking to a gentleman and not some damn servant!"

The ambassador swallowed hard but somehow managed to keep a straight face. "You had better have plenty of reserve strength, Mr. Dunbar," he whispered between clenched teeth. "This fool trusts you as a servant. So that's what you will be until your mission here is complete. Now get on with the business at hand!"

"My master," Dunbar said, turning back to Duugawdu, "apologizes for his shortsightedness. Of course he respects and realizes the moral dilemma you are facing in choosing an effective remedy to your situation."

"Good, then we understand each other," Duugawdu answered.

"He wants us to believe that he's not interested in monetary gain. In fact, he pretends to be offended by the idea." Dunbar related to the ambassador. The ambassador put on his most somber expression as he nodded his head signifying his reverence for Duugawdu's wishes.

"I may be tempted to test this weeding procedure. How soon can this operation begin?" Duugawdu asked.

Dunbar addressed the question to the ambassador. After what seemed like several minutes of consultation, Dunbar relayed the ambassador's response to Duugawdu. "Well, there are procedures to be ironed out, people I must contact. But it shouldn't take more than two weeks before we can begin shipping."

"Not suitable!" came Duugawdu's reply as he raised a little in his chair. "If we are to ever deal in this area of business, I need to see a demonstration tonight."

Dunbar was hesitant as he turned to the ambassador and relayed the message. An eager glint sparkled in the ambassador's eyes as he sat straight and tall in his chair and listened. "Tell him okay. If it is a demonstration he wants, he shall have it."

"Be serious," Dunbar whispered back as he fought to keep the tension from his voice. "We're not prepared to move slaves tonight."

"Keep your head, Mr. Dunbar," the ambassador said. Somehow he managed to maintain a half smile as he looked on Duugawdu with a respectful stare. "We've waited years for this moment. Now, do your damn job! Tell him we'll need some assistance in transporting the cargo from here to the coast. Tell him the number of cargo shall be considerably small during this demonstration. However, he can rest assured that in the very near future the shipments shall be such that the prison population will see an immediate decline and all parties involved will recognize a substantial monetary gain—no, scratch the mention of money!" the ambassador concluded with a twisted grin as he leaned back in his chair with an air of self-satisfaction.

The east cell block was the largest and noisiest housing unit on the compound. It was long and narrow like a giant chicken coop, but with steel-doored cells on either side of the two long corridors, running parallel.

The foul odor of rotting flesh and death was thick in the air. Mixing with the humid heat, the smell hung in the nostrils.

Tuuwee and Kuula were confined to a small 10' x 5' cell, along with Luba Zandi and Sipiho. There were only two bunks attached to the wall, one atop the other. There were no windows and only a narrow tray slot cut into the center of the thick cell door.

The tiny cell was in near darkness with just a faint stream of light flowing through the tray slot. Tuuwee and Luba Zandi had Kuula positioned on the bottom bunk whereby the stream of light could shine on his head as he lay on his back. The left side of his face had swollen beyond recognition. He hadn't opened his eyes for the past several hours, or perhaps it was because the swelling had not allowed him to do so. In either case, Tuuwee kept constant vigil as he sat on the edge of the bunk at Kuula's side, watching and waiting. Every now and then, Kuula's lips would move, and Tuuwee would hurry to put an ear to his mouth, yet only a strained, dry moan would escape him.

"I am here, Kuula," Tuuwee said with tears in his eyes. "Water, he needs water," Tuuwee uttered in despair.

Luba Zandi stood with his back to the cell door looking on with sorrow. The guards had promised to bring them water an hour ago but, so far, none had arrived. In remembering tales, he had heard about Gorma's harsh and merciless environment, one description stood out in his mind. "The only chance a man had of surviving here was if he had entered in perfectly good health."

"Comrade, perhaps you would like to lay down for a while and I will take your place standing?" Sipiho asked from his place on the top bunk. He was laying, stomach down, resting on his elbows. Just as Tuuwee's attention was focused on one person in the cell, Sipiho was tuned into Luba Zandi's every move. He was ready to serve and protect his commander under any circumstances. But Luba Zandi was silent in his grief.

Outside the cell, a loud, disorderly symphony of voices rocked the block. Some voices shouted back and forth at each other from cell to cell. Others sang and chanted. Occasionally screams of agony cut through the noisy ruckus in chilling tones, bringing the entire cell block to a standstill.

Luba Zandi never did answer Sipiho. Instead, he kept staring silently at Tuuwee's woeful effort to comfort a dying companion. Finally, Luba Zandi could take it no longer. Placing his mouth to the open tray slot, he yelled out into the corridor, "Comrades of the struggle, Puma Dorrs, listen up." A few noisy cells in the immediate area quieted down. "There's a sick comrade in here. We need water."

"Who goes there?" a voice yelled out over the distant ruckus.

"Luba Zandi."

Suddenly, Luba Zandi's name went flying up and down the corridor as more and more cells fell silent. Then a deep commanding voice from somewhere, not far away, thundered, "This is Kafka of the Monduli, commander of Gorma. Welcome, comrade, to your new home. I regret to say that water is a very scarce commodity here. It's only issued twice a day. The next water run is . . ."

Just then, the sound of rattling chains and many footsteps was heard marching down the corridor.

"Jackals walking!" a loud voice from one of the first cells screamed out into the corridor as the guards passed by. That initial warning started a chain reaction of shouts and yells, "Jackals walking!" This was repeated several times from cell to cell, all the way down to the farthest end of the corridor.

The army of footsteps stopped in front of Luba Zandi's cell. Keys were inserted into the locks, and the door swung open. Seven guards were posted outside the door. "All right, one of you at a time. Step out of the cell."

Sipiho was the first to respond as he jumped down from the top bunk to shield Luba Zandi. "For what purpose should we submit to being chained up?" Luba Zandi asked as he gently pushed Sipiho to one side.

Another prison guard stepped up from the rear of the pack. He was the only one with a pistol wedged in his waistband and the only one not carrying either a twenty-four-inch baton or chains.

"I am Bacchus (man eater), captain of the guards. I know who you are, Luba Zandi, and everything about you. But what's important is for you and these other newcomers to know and fear me. I squash all troublemakers who do not obey the rules and follow orders. Take heed to that and your stay here at Gorma will be a relatively healthy one." Bacchus took several steps backward and concluded by saying, "Now the warden has summoned all of you to his office. We can accomplish this the easy way, or the hard way. The choice is yours."

Luba Zandi, Sipiho, and Bacchus had matching dreadlocks. Bacchus's hair, however, was cut much shorter than their long ropes and Bacchus's dreadlocks did not have the red tint. Bacchus's high cheekbones and those of Luba Zandi and Sipiho, along with their dreadlocks, set these three apart from all the rest. All three were Ikeele tribesmen. Putting natural physical similarities to one side, a deep-seated hatred radiated from each of them, casting a thick cloud of tension throughout the cell which you could cut with a knife. As Luba Zandi and Sipiho stared at Bacchus, he glared back at them with a twisted smirk on his lips that said, "Yes, I am everything you heard, and more."

What was known about Bacchus and his cruel treatment of inmates—and his own tribespeople in particular—was enough to turn Luba Zandi's and Sipiho's stomachs in disgust.

"He's dead!" came Tuuwee's tormented voice, breaking the awkward silence. "You've killed my cousin!" Slowly Tuuwee rose to his feet and backed away from the bunk which held Kuula's lifeless body. An intense look of pain, anguish, and horror lingered in his eyes as he stared at Kuula's limp form. One small backward step at a time, Tuuwee squeezed past Luba Zandi and Sipiho, never taking his eyes from his Kuula.

Tuuwee was clearly in shock and torment as he backed right into the arms of the waiting guards. Two of them grabbed him by the arms and suddenly Tuuwee's instincts took hold. He became enraged like a man possessed.

In one ferocious motion, he yanked his right arm free from one guard and, in an instant, swung his fist toward the other, catching him right on the Adam's apple. Immediately upon impact, Tuuwee's arm was released and the guard fell to his knees gasping.

The other guards rushed in to help, but before anyone could lay a hand on Tuuwee, he locked his fists together and used them like a single deadly club. He swung on the approaching guards with a vicious roundhouse motion, striking the first one in the jaw. The force of the blow knocked his jawbone out of line, and he went flying off to one side.

One of the guards wielding a massive club struck Tuuwee hard on the back of the neck. As he went down, the guards rushed him from all sides. Just as another with a billy club was about to strike Tuuwee a second time, Luba Zandi stepped in. Balancing himself on his left foot, he drew his right foot back and aimed for the guard's kneecap. He drove the heel of his foot home and the sound of bone breaking was chilling, matched only by the man's tormented screams.

Sipiho sprang from the cell. Rushing out in front of Luba Zandi, he dove at Bacchus just as he was drawing his pistol from his waste. The sound of the firing gun was ear-shattering and drew everyone's attention.

Tuuwee was pinned on the floor as several guards wrestled with him and placed irons on his wrists and ankles. Luba Zandi was still on his feet but well restrained by two burly guards on either arm, a third guard standing behind him. Using a billy club, he had Luba Zandi in a deadly choke hold as he knee-wedged him in the back.

Sipiho and Bacchus were locked in a still embrace. A cloud of smoke from the pistol hovered above their heads. Slowly, Sipiho's limp body began to fall as the guards stepped over and grabbed his arms. Sipiho was dead.

Bacchus stepped around his men and walked up to Luba Zandi. He pointed the smoking pistol to Luba Zandi's head and said with teeth clenched, "That was meant for you."

Blood from Sipiho's wound smeared the gun barrel and Bacchus wiped a portion of it off on Luba Zandi's cheek. Luba Zandi tried to move, but the guard with the club wedged it against his throat and applied still more pressure, cutting off his wind. "Welcome to Gorma," was all he heard before passing out, as Bacchus's fist drove squarely into his stomach.

Half-naked, bruised, and battered, Tuuwee and Luba Zandi were hustled across the prison yard in chains and through a giant steel gate into the courtyard where the warden's office was located.

In addition to the host of soldiers and guards standing about, the ambassador and Dunbar were also there having been excused from the office at Duugawdu's request. As Tuuwee and Luba Zandi were marched past the bench where they were seated, the ambassador stood up and tipped his top hat in Bacchus's direction. He acknowledged this pleasantry with a simple nod of his head but kept walking, leading the march of prison guards.

The courtyard was hushed, and all eyes were on Tuuwee. Tuuwee struggled and fought against his captors. A dazed and limp Luba Zandi was being supported by the arms and being dragged across the yard.

At one point, Tuuwee ceased struggling when he caught sight of the white ambassador standing among the sea of shining black faces. As he shuffled past the place where the ambassador stood, he strained his neck to gawk at this white man. His first thought was a flashback account of a healing ceremony which was conducted on his mother, Puulu, when he was a tiny child. Puulu was laying on her bed sick with swamp fever, and Tuuwee was kneeling at her side. The room was dimly lit with only one small candle. A host of concerned tribespeople stood around the bed peering down at her. Everyone was waiting for the old Huzza doctor to make his grand entrance. Tuuwee insisted on staying with his mother and wouldn't allow anyone to pry him from her bedside.

Suddenly and without warning, the old Huzza doctor appeared wearing a long, shoulder-length wig made of animal tails. His entire face and body were smeared with a white ash. A set of lion fangs were fitted in his mouth and painted red. Fake claws, made from wood, covered each of his fingers.

The Huzza doctor lunged toward Puulu and Tuuwee, growling and screaming like an enraged beast. The tactic was meant to frighten the evil spirits from her body. That night, it took several long minutes to persuade Tuuwee to come out from beneath her bed. In a few days, however, Puulu recovered from her illness.

Tuuwee had long since gotten over his fear of a painted white face. But somehow, he sensed what he was seeing in the ambassador—for the first time in his life—was a real, live boogeyman.

In spite of the deadly fast pace and mind-blowing turn of events, Tuuwee found in that brief moment of watching the ambassador a notion to rationalize why Kuula had to die and why all this was happening to him. "Once the white man enters the land of the blacks, the land and its people will surely die." That old ancestral warning haunted him as he stared at the one white face among so many black, so composed, yet so disturbing in Tuuwee's mind.

The warden, along with four of Duugawdu's sword-carrying bodyguards, remained in the room. He had ordered that the highest-ranking officer who participated in the raid on the Oupa Ra's house be brought to him. The sergeant was the only officer on the prison grounds.

"So you say that the Puma Dorr who escaped was a Cuuzan nationalists?" Duugawdu asked from his place seated behind the warden's desk. The warden was still on his feet leaning against the far wall, while the sergeant stood at attention in front of the desk.

"Yes, my prince. I overheard the lieutenant mention that the Puma Dorr who remained alone in the house with Captain Wuuta wore the tribal markings of the Cuuzan just like the captain and, of course, you—your greatness."

"Where are the captain and the lieutenant? Why aren't they reporting these matters instead of you?"

"Captain Wuuta took it as a personal crusade to recapture the escapee, since it was he who lost the prisoner. And Lieutenant Buta, I suppose, went to—"

"I've heard enough!" Duugawdu interrupted, warning the sergeant off. The sergeant backed up toward the far wall to join the warden. As he did so, Duugawdu nodded his head toward the guards flanking the door. One of them opened it wide, and, in moments, Bacchus entered the room followed by other prison guards dragging Tuuwee and Luba Zandi. They brought them to rest in the center of the floor.

Immediately Tuuwee's and Duugawdu's eyes met. For a quick moment, Tuuwee thought he was looking at his father. The resemblance between Muusamali and Duugawdu was striking. Tuuwee found exception in Duugawdu's size. Muusamali was tall and lean. His younger brother, by contrast, was heavier because of too many fatty meals and far less physical activity.

Duugawdu was speechless for a moment, as he looked Tuuwee up and down and immediately noticed his tribal markings. The Cuuzan, as well as the other six tribes, had outlawed the tribal custom of marking their young once the seven kings agreed to become a federation of tribes, one nation under the sun. Only the older Cuuzan males wore the beaded knots across the forehead. And being old scar tissue, they were not readily visible from afar. But Tuuwee's markings were still prominent, causing Duugawdu to stare at them with a certain pride and wonder.

"Unhand him!" Duugawdu snapped. As the guards released their hold on Tuuwee's arm, one of them was a little slow and Tuuwee yanked himself free as he stared angrily into his face.

"A real fighter, I see," Duugawdu said then quickly added, I also see by your markings that my brother Muusamali keeps with the old ways." A soft glint sparkled in his eyes as he said this, but they quickly turned cold again. "But why would he not? He is outcast, out of touch. Why did you come here?"

"This is my home. Now release me from these chains," Tuuwee said with a demanding tone. However, he looked as though he were pleading when he raised his chained hands in the air to emphasize his remarks.

"The chains will stay," Duugawdu said without emotion. "The exiled clan was barred from the homeland and forbidden to ever return. You've broken that law and now you must be dealt with. Rather than punish you, as tribal law dictates, I've decided to banish you once again. This time in chains, and to a place from where you cannot return!"

"You are not King Nuumyu and you don't have the authority to do this to me," Tuuwee shouted while stepping forward to state his case, chains noisily rattling.

Duugawdu sat motionless and unafraid. He had an almost amused expression on his face. The two guards standing just over Duugawdu's shoulder did, however, flinch. So did Bacchus and two of his guards as they took a step toward Tuuwee.

"But that's where you are wrong, son of Muusamali," Duugawdu said. Then, for the first time, he looked over at Luba Zandi. "Who's that?" he demanded to know with a frown on his face.

"Your eminence," Bacchus said, stepping forward just as the warden was leaving his post by the wall.

"The Puma Dorr general!" The warden stepped closer, cutting Captain Bacchus's words short. The two men looked at each other with glaring eyes. Finally, Bacchus submitted to his superior, and the warden continued, "He is the most wanted 'Ikeele' in the whole territory. And it was by the luck of the draw that we were—"

Suddenly, Duugawdu held up a hand bringing the warden to a sudden halt. The room fell quiet. Luba Zandi, though dazed and standing on wobbly legs, was staring and listening with intense interest. "I am less concerned with this man's profile than I am with the whereabouts of the other Cuuzan swamper," Duugawdu said.

"He was a Cuuzan warrior," Tuuwee spoke up. The distress he felt in his heart was evident in his voice. "Kuula was his name, son of Luuka, son of Muututa, your sister. And he is dead! Killed by your very own warriors while he stood defenseless in chains like mine!" Tuuwee yanked on his own chains to emphasize his point. Their sound broke the stillness until he finally dropped his arms to his side.

Duugawdu looked at the warden, who immediately turned to Bacchus. Bacchus swallowed hard then said, "Unfortunately, my prince, he died in one of my cells. But I swear he was already gravely wounded whenever he first arrived."

All eyes just naturally turned to the sergeant as he stood alone against the far wall behind Bacchus and the warden.

When Tuuwee finally turned to look, he saw the man who had clubbed Kuula in the streets of Bawku and promptly came unglued. As fast as the leg irons would allow, Tuuwee rushed toward the sergeant bent on tearing him apart with his bare hands. But two of the prison guards reacted on instinct, as they were trained to keep the inmates in check. They grabbed hold of him before he could reach his mark. "You killed my cousin, you coward!" Tuuwee screamed as he fought with the guards for his freedom.

Duugawdu was on his feet glaring at the sergeant. As the sergeant quickly stepped away from the wall to avoid Tuuwee's wrath, he walked to the side of the desk where Duugawdu was standing.

"Is this true, Sergeant? Did you strike a defenseless man of my blood?" Duugawdu asked. "He spit in my face, your eminence," the sergeant cried in a shaky voice. His nervous eyes scanned the other faces in the room for some sign of sympathy, but he found none and only met cold stares. "I was merely trying to discipline him."

"You," Duugawdu said in a stern voice turning into rage, "you dare to discipline a member of the royal family by striking him when his hands and feet are bound?"

"But I swear, my prince, I had no idea of his identity. I would not have acted so foolishly had I have known."

"It is good you accept responsibility for your mistakes. You can accept your punishment like a man as well," Duugawdu said as he turned to his bodyguards holding out his hands.

Tuuwee stood by watching, now with a subdued interest. The others in the room stood motionless as well. The guards calmly handed over their swords, one in each of Duugawdu's outstretched palms. Duugawdu slowly turned back around to face the sergeant with both swords held out in front of him. The sword in his left hand he extended even further toward the sergeant. The sergeant, in spite of his obvious fear, suddenly showed a sense of calm, ready to accept the inevitable.

"Take it and defend yourself. I am giving you more of a chance than you gave my sister's son."

The sergeant hesitated as he looked once more at the warden and Bacchus. Both men dropped their eyes toward the floor. Finally, the sergeant fixed his gaze on the gleaming steel sword before him. He took a deep breath before taking the sword from Duugawdu's hand. It was his final breath.

Duugawdu quickly drew his sword back with both hands and, before the sergeant could flinch a muscle, he quickly and viciously hit his mark. The impact caught the sergeant between the neck and collarbone, splitting him in two like a ripe melon. In one smooth and deadly motion, he pulled his bloody sword back and before the sergeant's body could hit the floor, he once again had the sword positioned high over his head, gripped with both hands.

With the awesome weapon poised over his head ready to strike again, Duugawdu turned and walked directly to Tuuwee. The two guards at Tuuwee's side promptly stepped away, leaving him alone in the center of the room facing a cold killer.

"If a Cuuzan is to die by the hands of a man, a Cuuzan will act as executioner. It is Cuuzan law," Duugawdu said as he stared into Tuuwee's eyes. Everyone held their breath as they watched the sword hovering over Tuuwee's head like a razor-sharp pendulum ready to drop.

Tuuwee stared at his uncle's face. He showed no fear. Tuuwee had seen more death in twelve hours than he'd seen in a lifetime. Death suddenly meant nothing to him. With Kuula gone and his death swiftly avenged, he saw little or no reason to go on.

Abruptly, Duugawdu brought the sword down from the air and extended it to one of the guards with the handle pointing toward him for an easy grasp. The man stepped forward and took the weapon then stepped back again. "You are brave. And may the gods reward your brave heart with a long life, my nephew," Duugawdu said then nodded his head toward the warden and Bacchus. He added, "But not here in the land of Kongolia."

Surprisingly, Tuuwee didn't bother to fight as the two guards stepped up and gently took hold of his arms. His eyes, however, blazed with animosity as he glared at his uncle. If looks could kill, Duugawdu would have fallen to the floor. Quietly, however, he turned away and headed for the door.

"I am an Ikeele nationalist," Luba Zandi spoke up for the first time. He was still in obvious stomach pain by the way he leaned forward and strained his words. "I demand a proper court hearing with the proper Ikeele authorities!"

Duugawdu, still a bit uneasy from Tuuwee's threatening stance, turned and gave a sideways look at Luba Zandi and said, "I recall, Puma Dorr, a recent high jacking of a merchant caravan. Valuable goods were stolen and several Kongolian soldiers killed. Did you and your band of outlaws permit my soldiers a proper court hearing before you murdered them? I venture to say you did not!" With that, Duugawdu turned his back.

"I'll return, Duugawdu. One day, I will return," Luba Zandi yelled as the guards pulled him out the door behind Tuuwee.

"I don't ever want to see either of them again," Duugawdu said to the warden and Bacchus. "Pass that on to the ambassador. And circulate the word among all those who know of this incident that this is to be the most well-kept secret of their lives. If anyone speaks of this incident to another person, they will pay with their heads." Duugawdu looked over at the bloodied, mangled corpse of the sergeant laying in the corner. "Do I make myself perfectly clear?"

"Yes, your highness," came the warden's response. "Perfectly clear," echoed Bacchus.

A number of large, well-organized tent cities were stamped along the eastern straight of desert bordering the Kongolian territory. These were Arab colonies situated many miles apart, and they were well armed and strictly avoided. Each camp housed hundreds of soldiers and their families, their Arabian steeds, camels, and other livestock.

Khaburahs was the name given to these colonies. It meant "sultan's nest," a name which adequately explained why the Kongolian government allowed these Arab camps to exist on its border like wasp nests littering a tree. In spite of the common knowledge that Khaburahs were Puma Dorr strongholds, the fear of sparking a war with the Muslim Arabs kept the Kongolian forces at bay.

The arrest of Luba Zandi prompted an emergency meeting of the Puma Dorr hierarchy the very next morning. The Oupa Ra was present, as was Zuuox, along with half a dozen other men situated around a long banquet like table.

Several personal bodyguards flanked the walls. Standing among them were the Oupa Ra's daughters Ty and Nala. Ty was armed with a rifle strapped around her shoulders.

Two men in the room were Arabs. One seated at the table was wearing the Arab head garment sporting a gold headband. The other Arab, a darker-complexioned and younger man, stood just behind with a rifle on his back, a holstered pistol on his hip, and an ammunition belt tied across his chest.

Another man at the table, wearing dark African robes, had his face completely hidden behind a veil and head wrap. He kept his hands on his lap underneath the table. Only when he spoke was it obvious that he was an African.

"The important thing for us to realize is that Luba Zandi knew the risk he was taking by entering Bawku." The man behind the veil was addressing the other occupants at the table. "It is highly unlikely that he would wish to see us react hastily to a situation which he created. From Luba Zandi's mistakes, we must exercise wise judgment. Launching a revenge attack now, when our enemy is on the alert for such a move, would only risk losing more men."

"If anyone is to blame for Luba Zandi's capture, it is I," the Oupa Ra said. "I summoned him because I felt strongly that Igun had delivered upon me two long-lost members of the royal family. Luba Zandi, being the brave comrade he is, came to Bawku in good faith."

"We are aware of your noble intentions, Oupa Ra," the Arab with the gold headband said from his place at the head of the table. "And who among us would not have jumped at an opportunity to bring the emperor's own nephews into our fold. No, dear lady, no one is to blame but fate itself. Even fate has disguises. What may seem a tragedy now may open a door of opportunity in the future." The Oupa Ra's expression was one of gratitude as she looked at the Arab.

"I think the veiled one is right," one of the men wearing long, reddish dreadlocks spoke up. "Luba Zandi is more than just a comrade. He is my cousin. But I say we should act wisely by holding back until the enemy drops his guard. Patience is a virtue."

"Sure it is, comrade," another spoke. "We are less than thirty days from executing our larger plan. Why put a strain on our resources and manpower by trying to stage a needless revenge attack?"

"If we were to move against Gorma itself, that wouldn't be a needless attack," another offered to the debate.

"No, that would be suicide," the veiled man said. "Complete, fool hearted suicide! Besides, I'm not sure just where Luba Zandi is being held. The old prison or the new jail facility?"

"Why is that?" one of the younger men asked. He, too, wore long reddish dreadlocks. "You are supposed to be our eyes and ears on the inside. How is it that you do not know the whereabouts of our leader?"

I resent you questioning my efficiency," the man behind the veil said in a sharp tone.

"So be it," the youngster said as he raised back in his chair, a slight grin on his lips as he added, "Must I repeat my question comrade?"

The veiled man sat straight and tall. His voice took on a sharper edge but remained steady. "I've been away from the capital city all night on a mission. I should have the details of Luba Zandi's whereabouts upon my return to Shacuwa. I will relay the information through the usual channels."

"What good will it do us to know Luba Zandi's whereabouts? All of you have apparently made up your minds to let him rot in whatever jail he's in." It was Zuuox who spoke, and as the others sat motionless, he slowly stood up.

"And what do you suggest we do, Zuuox?" one of the men asked. He was a Cuuzan native judging by the old tribal scars lining his forehead. "Give me a dozen men and I'll free Luba Zandi and my prince from any man-made cage on earth!"

A few of the men looked around at each other with disbelieving smiles on their faces. The Arab studied Zuuox with serious interest. So did the man with the Cuuzan tribal scars. Finally, the Cuuzan spoke again, "Zuuox, I know you better than you know yourself. Your heart is bigger than your muscles. It was so when you were a young man, and now that you are old, it appears that your lion's heart has grown foolish. Your intentions are good, but to take you seriously would be an act of madness."

Zuuox placed his big hands on to the table. Leaning forward, he glared across it into the face of his Cuuzan tribesman and said in his deepest of tones, "You may have grown a little older, and a lot uglier, Buukada, but remember . . . you are still the pup that I raised! So mind your manners." Buukada smiled and rolled his eyes but kept quiet for the remainder of the meeting.

"And what will you do if we don't give you leave of twelve men, comrade Zuuox?" the veiled man asked.

Zuuox pried his angry eyes from Buukada and looked up and down the table, pausing a moment at each face. "Either I get the men, or I don't," he said flatly.

A tense few moments passed as some of the men at the table picked at their nails, and others sat casually in their chairs staring at Zuuox.

"I say we take a vote," the Arab spoke up. "The mission would be suicide," the veiled man pleaded. "The security in and around Gorma is too tight. Rethink your position on this matter, Zuuox. Surely there are—"

"That's one vote against me," Zuuox said cutting the veiled man short. Zuuox waived his hand at the others and said, "Who else is against me? Raise your hands."

Immediately hands went up. Only the Oupa Ra and the Arab kept theirs on the table. The Oupa Ra seemed to be studying every move the Arab made. Zuuox didn't have to count the hands; neither did he bother to say another word. Abruptly he turned and headed for the door.

As he stepped outside into the hot sun, he walked several yards down the road between long rows of tents. Someone called out his name. He turned to find the Arab and his darker-skinned companion hurrying toward him.

"You didn't count my vote, comrade. Otherwise you would have counted one in your favor," the Arab said. He had to look up to the taller Zuuox, but it didn't diminish his dignified posture.

"What use is one vote?" Zuuox asked. "Now I must go!" With that, he turned and started off. The two Arabs fell in step beside him.

"I have a business proposition, my friend," the Arab began. Zuuox was all ears but his feet kept moving. "I believe in possibilities, and I see the possibility of you rescuing Luba Zandi and your Cuuzan prince. For obvious reasons, having to do with my country's interest in overthrowing Duugawdu, I am willing to help you in your efforts to free your prince and challenge Duugawdu to the throne."

"Good. Then give me the twelve men I need," Zuuox stopped and faced the Arab.

"It's not quite that simple, my friend," the Arab replied. Zuuox turned to leave again, but the Arab touched him on the arm causing him to stop. "The political ramifications would be too intense if I were to send twelve Arabs to invade the capital city. It would spark a war between my country and Kongolia. And we are not ready for that yet. My orders are to maintain a low profile behind the scenes. I can only offer you my most loyal soldier and friend, Firok, and all the guns and ammunition you require."

Zuuox looked at the dark-skinned Arab called Firok. Likewise, Firok's eyes met Zuuox's with a certain steadiness which revealed an unmistakable strength. But more interesting to Zuuox was the small arsenal of weapons donning the man's young and slender body.

"Take Firok," the Arab pressed on as Zuuox hesitated. "I sense that you have other resources you intend to utilize. But Firok is two men in one. I assure you!"

Finally, Zuuox stepped closer to the Arab and said, "I will take him. Him, along with a rifle for me to replace the one lost. When I return with these other . . . resources . . . I expect them to be given rifles and ammunition as well."

"My esteemed sultan wants nothing more than to see Duugawdu removed from power. Your wish is my command."

As Zuuox and Firok turned to walk away, the Oupa Ra's voice rang out. "Have a safe trip, Zuuox," she said, standing from her place between her daughters. They had been on the side of a tent just yards away . . . unnoticed by anyone. Zuuox stopped and looked at her with suspicion. "I shall await your return so that I may bestow Igun's blessings upon you and my dear childhood friend," she added. The Oupa Ra flashed a smile as Zuuox nodded his head and walked off.

After gathering ample provisions for the trip, Zuuox and Firok headed out across the hot, sandy desert. Zuuox was on foot leading the march, with

Firok riding atop a camel. They headed east toward the Bomu Plains. In actuality, a portion of the Bomu was under their feet at that very moment. About ten feet beneath this stretch of sand lay the grassland which Zuuox and the other exiled clan had traveled over fourteen years earlier on their way out of Cuuzanland.

This was just another tiny fertile corner of Africa which Mother Nature chose to transform into desert. To accomplish this metamorphosis, powerful winds from the north would sweep across the surface of the mighty Sahara, shifting sand like an incoming wave, turning grassland into desert.

Zuuox refused to disclose any details about where they were headed or what his plans were. All he would say was that he was being led by the all-powerful hand of Cuuz and that whenever he and Firok returned to Cuuzanland, he would have a twelve-man army.

Zuuox wore nothing more than his loincloth and had only his spear in hand. He couldn't have been more comfortable . . . being naked and barefoot under the sun, free to walk to the ends of the earth if he so chose.

In spite of being a desert dweller, Firok's head and shoulders, as well as the rest of his body, were well covered with a thin layer of cloth. He guided his camel behind Zuuox, keeping a distance of some fifteen yards behind. Firok was well aware of the Africans' love for walking. Still, it never failed to amaze him how any man could choose to walk rather than ride atop a comfortable camel.

After five straight hours, the two finally cleared the sea of sand and reached the open grassland. They stopped to rest, and this allowed Firok to perform one of his five daily prayers. Within a half-hour, they were on the move again, with Zuuox's long legs setting the pace and Firok on his camel once again, bringing up the rear.

A heavy spring rain dowsed them with a fifteen-minute shower as they crossed a lowland stretch of high grass. The dry earth so welcomed the relief the rain brought that it seemed that the lilies began to blossom and flower before their very eyes.

Zuuox and Firok kept moving on into the late evening. The sun had long faded from the sky like a passing hot breeze, as the nighttime brought with it the cooling calm of a full moon. Zuuox chose to push on until they reached the great canyon. It was even later into the night when they finally reached the canyon's mouth. It was here Zuuox decided to set up camp. It wasn't that he didn't have the stamina to keep moving and the inspiration to do so, but he wanted to be sure not to descend into the canyon's mouth without the light of day. The mouth was more like a pit, sporting poisonous snakes and scorpions requiring good vision and much skill to maneuver along the shoulder of the cliffs. Thus, they would wait until daybreak.

Firok had just concluded his last prayer of the evening. By the light of the full moon and a modest campfire, he neatly folded up his prayer blanket and began unrolling his sleeping gear.

Zuuox was just returning to camp after relieving himself behind the cover of the tall brush which surrounded them. "I don't know how you feel after praying all day," he said to Firok as he dropped to a squatting position in front of the fire. "But one time to the bush for me and I feel like a new man. Ten pounds lighter!"

Firok calmly climbed underneath his blanket and laid back with his head propped up on the gear he'd placed there for that purpose. "As much as you stay on your feet, you should think about losing even more pounds, my friend."

Zuuox stared at him with a certain look of annoyance. "You said that for what purpose, my friend?"

With a smile, Firok answered, "It's of no real importance. Good night." With that, Firok turned on his side and pulled his blanket up to his shoulders.

"Oh, I think it is important," Zuuox pressed. "I can outwalk you into the ground, overweight as I am. You and that strange beast you depend upon so heavily."

"My friend," Firok said as he turned over and looked at Zuuox, "you could never outwalk a camel. And I would beat you in a fair race anytime, anywhere. As Allah is my witness."

Zuuox smiled and looked over at his friend like a cat who had just cornered a mouse. "Fine. Allah can witness your defeat. At first light we'll have a head-up race. Last to reach the finish point will bow before the winner and kiss his feet. Agreed?"

"Agreed," Firok said as he turned on his side once more. "Make ready to eat dirt for breakfast, my friend," he added in a sleepy voice. Zuuox's smile widened as he looked off into the night convinced he could outrun any man who spent the majority of his life riding animals and hiding from the sunlight.

The next morning, Firok was stripped down to his underpants and bare feet. Zuuox, having shed nothing more than his spear, stood at his side ready and eager to take off running.

The sun hadn't quite peaked, but what early morning light streaked across the clear blue-gray sky was just enough for them to chart their course along the road that ran parallel with the steep cliffs of the canyon.

"Do you see that small cactus bush about two hundred yards up the road?" Zuuox asked. His right foot was pivoted behind him ready to spring his 230-pound, 6'2" frame forward.

"Yes, but I have my sights set on that large oak tree further up the road," Firok said, calmly going through his warm-up routine and shaking his arms and legs to get them good and loose. "First man there is the winner!" Firok added as he ceased his warm-up and fell into an intense and ready stance, eyes fixed on his mark.

Meanwhile, Zuuox was straining his eyes to get a fix on the oak tree which was some five hundred yards away. "That's a bit far to be running a race," he said.

"So, you choose to surrender?" Firok asked, maintaining his ready stance.

"Of course not!" came Zuuox's quick reply.

"Then—go!" Firok said and took off running.

Zuuox bit down on his teeth and shot off the starting line in hot pursuit. Running in full stride, it didn't take him more than a few seconds to catch Firok. He raced past him at breakneck speed. It appeared Firok was running at a leisurely pace but, in Zuuox's mind, the Arab was just no match for his superior speed and might. Zuuox's anticipation of winning gave him an instant adrenaline rush which caused him to push his tiring legs faster and faster.

The repetitious thunder of Zuuox's big feet scurrying along the edge of the steep canyon was the only noise heard for miles, along with his heavy breathing which sounded much like a bull snorting every time his fast-flying feet touched the ground.

With the oak tree two hundred long yards away, Zuuox began to show signs of fatigue. The sound of his thundering feet grew softer, the repetitions fewer, and his snorting seemed to ring even louder, almost twice for every step he now took.

Suddenly, the clattering sound of fast-approaching footsteps at his rear caught Zuuox's attention. For the first time, he took his eyes from the oak tree target in the near distance and turned his head to look back. At that instant, the little Arab bolted past him so fast that he left Zuuox's head still turned to the rear. When Zuuox finally turned around, all he saw was Firok's backside racing away from him like a bat out of hell!

Zuuox finally reached the oak tree and fell instantly to the ground in total exhaustion. "You okay, my friend?" Firok asked, breathing heavily but still standing on his feet with one hand resting against the oak and the other on his hip. "I'm fine," Zuuox managed between beaten breaths.

After a few moments, Zuuox looked up at Firok, waved his hand, and said, "Come, give me your little lightning-quick feet that I may pay my debt." Firok smiled as he walked over to him. Instead of giving Zuuox a foot, he reached out his hand saying, "You owe me nothing but your friendship, Cuuzan."

Zuuox hesitated a moment and then accepted Firok's hand as he pulled the big African easily to his feet. "I could have beaten you in a shorter race," Zuuox said. "Perhaps," Firok answered as he turned to head back to camp and Zuuox fell in step beside him. "Or perhaps not," he added and then pointed up ahead and said, "Care to try it now?"

Zuuox thought about it for just a minute. His aching legs felt like heavy logs. "I will spare you for the moment, little Arab. But beware of the future."

By nightfall that same day, the two had reached the point along the canyon road where Tuuwee had met with the nest of scorpions.

With Zuuox's legs still aching, it didn't take much discussion for Firok to convince him to take his place on the camel's back for a while. They pushed on deep into the night, finally bedding down when they reached the skeleton jungle that was once the Kinshasa paradise.

By midafternoon the following day, they were watering the camel and filling their skins at Lake Runyum. The lake was serene and beautiful, surrounded by banks which were mostly deserted except for a few winged creatures and, on the far opposite shore, where a small band of spotted hyenas refreshed themselves.

Zuuox found the quiet on their side of the lake a bit unnerving. He sensed the presence of someone watching them from a dense cluster of tall brush not far from the lake's edge. As Firok was tying the water bags to the camel,

Zuuox stepped slowly toward him and said, "Pass me a rifle, Firok. Slowly and carefully."

Without a word, Firok slipped the rifle from its pocket pouch and handed it to Zuuox. Once in hand, Zuuox quickly cocked the hammer back, aimed it in the air, and fired off a round.

At that instant, the bushes started to move as half a dozen Foliose warriors, in camouflage headdress made from twigs and leaves, stood up from their hiding place and ran in the opposite direction.

Zuuox led Firok and his camel across the stretch of grassland separating Kinshasa and the Sudd Swamp in record time. The closer he got to his destination, the more determined he became.

Remembering Firok's implication that the camel was a superior walker, Zuuox decided to put the animal to the test. The camel didn't drop from exhausting, but neither did Zuuox. At least not until he had crossed thirty miles of grassland nonstop.

After a night's rest, Zuuox led Firok, minus the camel which they'd left behind, into the dark and wet recesses of the Sudd swampland. Firok, being a desert dweller, had never ventured beyond its outskirts into swampland before. His encounter with the gloomy wet interior of the Sudd was an uneasy experience, even for a hardened soldier like himself.

As he followed Zuuox through the murky maze of rotten vegetation and twisted vines, Firok was glad Zuuox had insisted they leave the camel hidden near the dry meadow by the mouth of the swamp.

Three hours into their trek, with Firok fighting off giant mosquitos the size of wasps, they passed along the banks of a swamp lake littered with floating twigs and a scumlike moss. Zuuox asked if Firok wished to take a short break. Having already seen several alligators, and a huge boa constrictor hanging from a tree, as Firok contemplated Zuuox's offer, he looked out across the murky haze and spotted a water moccasin slowly making its way across the lake.

"My friend, if you are truly leading me to the devil's house, then let's not waste any time getting there. I'd much rather meet him alive than dead."

Zuuox smiled at his little companion, turned, and headed on through the tangled brush.

Several hours later, they reached a narrow strip of land that bridged the tiny dryland enclave. One of the few elevated enclaves in the swamp, the land bridge was flanked by deep water, and alligators swam along as if following Zuuox and Firok as they walked up the banks and finally reached the little island with its sloping hills and green meadows.

Firok was amazed at the way the sunlight suddenly cascaded down upon them through a huge opening in the treetops. It was as if someone had rolled back the roof from a portion of a giant sky-dome. Off to one side of the trail, Firok noticed a large cornfield and an orchard of nut trees. Fruit loomed in the distance on the other side. They passed numerous vegetable gardens, and Zuuox noticed baskets of half-filled vegetables lining the fields. Obviously, some of the Cuuzan women had been in the gardens working when they spotted the two travelers crossing the land bridge.

Zuuox had chosen to enter the village from the rear rather than come in by boat on the front side so as to not spook the whole village by his sudden return from the grave.

Soon the two could see the rooftops of the huts sitting on the slope just beyond a group of trees. Zuuox decided to pull up and wait at the base of the hill. They helped themselves to freshwater from a man-made lake. Within several minutes, four Cuuzan warriors armed with spears and shields appeared on the trail just as Zuuox had anticipated.

Zuuox adjusted his rifle where it rested across his back, and he placed the butt end of his spear to the ground with the point aimed skyward. "I am Zuuox. I have returned with a friend," he yelled at the men. The four warriors looked at each other in disbelief. "We come in peace," Zuuox quickly added.

One of the men, however, was already in motion as he broke away from the others and ran back up the hill into the village.

"Come forward, Zuuox, if it's truly you," one of the warriors shouted. "But if you lie, I warn you—do not approach."

Zuuox didn't hesitate as he marched up the trail. Firok, with his rifle strapped across his back in similar fashion to Zuuox, fell in step and followed his friend up the path.

As Zuuox came within clear view, the three men stepped up to meet him. A broad smile, mixed with sudden surprise and joy, crossed their faces. Zuuox was the favorite among all the Cuuzan warriors, save one perhaps—Suubala.

Zuuox and Firok were surrounded by the warriors and a host of small children who had gathered to witness the event as they walked into the village square.

Muusamali, with Suubala and Ruuski at his side, stood in the village square waiting. A host of other warriors surrounded King Muusamali. His two top aides along with the village women and children milled about throughout the square.

Zuuox looked into the face of one man only—Muusamali—as he stepped into the center of the horde of black, shiny bodies. Muusamali, dressed in his catskins and tall leopard headdress, held his stare for several moments. "So you are not dead after all!" Muusamali said.

"No, my king. I still live. But I bring sad news about Tuuwee and Kuula and the uncertain fate they face in the land of our ancestors."

"My son and his cousin choose to risk having their fates cursed by going into the Forbidden Zone. What concern is it of mine if they meet with the results of their own doing?"

"Family concern, my king," Zuuox answered with as much restraint as he could muster. "The concern of a father for his son. A son who I witnessed being chained at the hands and feet like a captured animal. Thrown into animal's cage to likely die an early death—or worse, to rot away into old age never to see freedom again. And the one responsible is not the gods, mind you!" Zuuox paused to look over at the oldest and reputed wisest of the Huzza in the tribe, Ruuski. Ruuski didn't blink an eye as he stared at Zuuox with intense interest. Somehow, Zuuox picked up a positive vibe from the old Huzza and he turned back to Muusamali with renewed vigor.

"The gods do not use family to torment or kill family. Your own brother, Duugawdu, has not only imprisoned your son and nephew, but King Nuumyu himself is a prisoner in his own house as well!"

A murmur of disbelief buzzed through the crowd at the mention of the king being held a prisoner. The crowd had grown considerably from when they first arrived. Men women and children peered over each other's shoulders trying to hear what was said and catch a glimpse of Zuuox whom they thought had actually risen from the grave.

The realization of Zuuox's presence, coupled with the startling news he brought, was the single most crucial event to befall the exiled clan since they were first chosen by King Nuumyu to leave the homeland twenty-two years earlier to establish their present home away from home.

Among the late arrivals to the gathering in the square were Luuka, Kuula's father; Muututa, Kuula's mother; and Puulu, Tuuwee's mother. Slowly, these three worked their way toward the center of the sea of black bodies, as the crowd moved to one side to give them passage.

"And who is this stranger you bring to our village?" Muusamali asked, looking at Firok. Puulu had posted herself at Muusamali's side while Luuka and Muututa stood next to several tribespeople who brought them up to date on what Zuuox had said.

"He goes by the name of Firok," Zuuox said as he placed a hand on his friend's shoulder and added, "He is a trusted friend who has sworn to help me rescue Tuuwee, Kuula, and King Nuumyu."

"Rescue Tuuwee?" Puulu cried. "Where is my son that he needs rescuing?"

"Duugawdu is holding him and Kuula prisoner. They are in chains and locked away in animal cages." Zuuox paused to look from Puulu's terrified face and over to Luuka and Muututa, whose expressions were equally tormented. In so doing, Zuuox's eyes fell upon Suubala. Surprisingly, he looked back at Zuuox with an expression marked by compassion. Zuuox wasn't sure whether or not his eyes were playing tricks on him. But he somehow drew strength from Suubala's expression. He was the one person in the entire village Zuuox didn't expect to get a warm welcome from. In Zuuox's absence, Suubala became chief warrior, a position Zuuox was sure Suubala enjoyed and wouldn't care to relinquish.

Turning back to Muusamali, Zuuox continued his message to the king and his people. "My king. The lives of Tuuwee and Kuula are in grave danger because of Duugawdu's fear that Tuuwee came to the homeland in order to take Duugawdu's place as heir to King Nuumyu's throne. King Nuumyu is on his sickbed, unable to exert any authority in the land because of Duugawdu's evil influence over the elders on the counsel. White men are Duugawdu's closest companions. He allows them access to our homeland against King Nuumyu's stern disapproval, the very same white invaders who killed a great number of our fallen brothers during the war. A war that was fought to keep the whites from the land, a war that our brave brothers won on the battlefield at a terribly bloody price, only to have Duugawdu spit on their blood. He has betrayed the ancestors, King Nuumyu and the souls of our fallen Cuuzan comrades.

"And now, your son . . . and your son, Luuka"—Zuuox pointed at Luuka and Muututa—"are at the mercy of this traitor who will stop at nothing to secure his rise to the throne. Even if it means killing two members of the royal family!" Zuuox paused again and stepped even closer to Muusamali. They were the same height except for the tall headdress which Muusamali was so accustomed to wearing, and it made him appear taller than any man in his tribe.

The entire Cuuzan population was present now. Every eye and ear were focused on the king and Zuuox. It was clear that Zuuox was getting his point across. Not ordinarily a man of many words, Zuuox was not only surprising the king and the villagers, but he was also amazing himself.

Muusamali's silence was Zuuox's clue to press on. In fact, Muusamali's subdued expression almost screamed for Zuuox to continue. "I know all about the secret covenant between you and King Nuumyu. Had I been able to speak with the old king before coming here, I know he would have sent you an urgent message to abandon the covenant you and he made some twenty-two years ago! The purebred clan of Cuuzan he sent to live abroad is needed at home in order to save our homeland. We were forced to miss the first war against the white men as they invaded our homeland twenty-two years ago. Now there is a new war waging against the same old enemy who happens to be using a different tactic—Duugawdu's greed for power! Your brother is on the verge of single-handedly destroying our homeland and our people. Only your immediate return, my king, will preserve the land and keep the ancestral dream from dying!"

Muusamali stared at Zuuox long and hard. All eyes were on the king, waiting for his response. Puulu looked around anxiously, as did Muututa. The two mothers were filled with questions about their sons, but they knew to hold their tongues, as did the rest of the onlookers, until the king had spoken.

It was a long and tense wait as Luuka's patience was wearing thin, and he shifted positions with his wife, moving closer to Muusamali. Luuka stared openly at the king, as he fought the urge to speak.

Finally, Muusamali said to Zuuox, "If what you are saying is accurate, then perhaps my brother, the king, does now require my presence in the homeland?"

The crowds' instant reaction was that of muffled joy as the listeners quickly passed on, in soft whispers, to the ones behind what their king had said.

Puulu's pretty black face lit up as did Muututa's and excitement radiated from her being.

Zuuox and Luuka, along with Suubala and Ruuski, kept stern expressions on their already hardened faces. Whatever joy they felt about the idea of going home, these elder leaders would never reveal inappropriate emotions in front of younger warriors and the boys of the tribe who were yet to become men. The king had just made a most crucial decision. Tribal history was right now being written. The elders would have to be very careful to play out their roles like the wisest and bravest of men because tomorrow's elders were watching and studying every move the king and his aides were about to make.

Ruuski took a step closer to Muusamali and said in a clear voice, "A situation as grave as this, involving the homeland, need not be brought before the full body of elders for a vote Muusamali. Obviously, you understood this without my mentioning it." Ruuski smiled a toothless grin as he cut his eyes to look into Muusamali's cold stare.

"So I take it I have your blessing to act without any further delay?"

"In a situation such as this, you alone are king and counsel. Until the crisis is over. But it's my hope that the ending of this particular set of circumstances will bring us all back home to Cuuzanland."

"Apparently the gods are touching us both with the same hope and inspiration, Ruuski," Muusamali whispered in response.

With that said, Ruuski calmly stepped back as quietly and discreetly as he had stepped forward.

"I wish to make the trip with you," Luuka turned and said to Muusamali. Luuka was short compared to the average Cuuzan male. Muscular and smaller in stature, he stood about four inches shorter than his wife Muututa. She stood by his side while he appealed to her twin brother. "I know that under normal circumstances you would choose a younger man over me. But remember, I am only five years above you in age and I insist on being one of the chosen to go in search of my own son, my king."

"Let me make one thing clear," Muusamali said as he held up his hand for silence. He looked into Luuka's eyes and then at his sister before turning to address the entire Cuuzan populace. "I do not condone breaking tribal laws under any circumstances short of life-or-death situations. Laws and customs are the glue which holds a tribal community together like bee's honey to the hive. There will be a punishment handed out to Tuuwee and Kuula for their lawless behavior." Muusamali then paused and looked back to Luuka. As he continued, he and Luuka held each other's eyes. "Your age is not a factor in my mind, Cuuzan. Your heart and courage make you an automatic pick to accompany me anywhere for any purpose. If you accompany me this day, however, you must keep in mind that this is not a rescue mission. I am going in search of our sons. But when I find them, I am going to punish them!" Muusamali then turned back to Zuuox and said, "I agree to go with you Zuuox . . . back to our homeland."

Cheers and shouts of joy went up as the clan of Cuuzans began jumping up and down with excitement. Men and women milled around Firok, shaking his hand, touching his rifle and ammunition belt. Warriors, young and old, began approaching Muusamali, pleading their case, asking to be chosen. Puulu and Muututa sandwiched Zuuox as they showered him with a barrage of questions concerning their sons.

Sometime later, Muusamali, along with two of his younger wives, busied themselves putting provisions together for his trip. Ruuski was present in the room. The old Huzza priest stood silently against a far wall with his arms crossing his chest watching everything that was taking place. Obviously, Ruuski was on site to make sure that the king was properly equipped for his trip, down to the smallest detail.

Muusamali discarded his heavy catskin outfit. His wives smeared his body with a light blue chalk. The curing process to make the chalk was mystical in nature in that the war god, Cuu-ba, blessed the chalk which covers the warrior's body, and it's thought to be a coat of protective armor.

In addition to the blue chalk, Muusamali donned himself in a lighter outfit consisting of a thin cloth wraparound which covered his upper body. Unlike the other Cuuzan males, Muusamali wore a short skirt made of a very thin weave, over his loincloth. His headdress was considerably lighter as well, sitting not quite as tall as his many leopard-skin hats.

Puulu entered the hut carrying a waterskin filled with freshwater. She walked over to Muusamali wearing an endearing expression marked with a certain apologetic sparkle in her eyes. Holding the waterskin close to her breast in both hands, she rolled her eyes up at him and said, "Allow me, my husband, to offer you my skin pouch filled with water from my well."

Muusamali looked at her with questioning eyes. His two other wives had already filled his own waterskin, and they were making rude and distracting noises in the background to emphasize that fact. But Muusamali ignored their childish behavior, and his undivided attention rested on Puulu. "Why would I not accept your traveling gift, first wife?" he said as he quietly took the water pouch from Puulu's nervous hands.

Puulu waited until Muusamali had secured the pouch across his shoulders and said, "After what I'm about to tell you, you may not want to accept my token."

Muusamali gazed into her eyes for several moments. Puulu, although nervous, managed to hold his disarming stare. "Leave us," Muusamali said, neither turning nor taking his eyes from Puulu.

Ruuski, at that point, came off the wall as he waved the other two women to the door. With pouting expressions, the other two wives marched to the door without making a sound. Ruuski followed them and, just before stepping outside, threw the king and his first wife a suspicious glance and then left.

"The night before Tuuwee left, he confided in me that he and Kuula were going to run away to the homeland," Puulu began. Suddenly, the nervousness seemed to leave her. It was as if she had put her head into the lion's mouth and was ready to accept her fate. "Essentially, I gave Tuuwee my blessing. If there is to be any punishment leveled against our son, then I must bare most of it myself. Had I not given him my blessing, or had I simply come and told you of his plans, Tuuwee would be here now, and you would not be going in search of him for the purpose of administering punishment."

No one could touch Muusamali's heart like Puulu. His stony face suddenly went flush, and his otherwise hardened eyes softened as they looked upon her. Finally, he said, "Don't fret, my wife. Had you told me of Tuuwee's intentions, I may have prevented him from leaving that day. But I was never fooled into thinking that our son would spend his life here in these swamps. He would have been less than my son had he not dreamed dreams of being king of Cuuzanland." Muusamali's face then took on a smile, which Puula revered with delight. He continued, "I did my part in keeping my word to my brother Nuumyu. But nothing short of cutting off Tuuwee's feet would have kept him here."

Puula had a look of astonishment on her face which brought an even broader smile to Muusamali's. "You mean you knew all the time that you would eventually turn your back and let Tuuwee go as I did?"

"Well, I would have preferred him to wait until he was a bit older and a lot wiser. But according to Zuuox, my brother Nuumyu needs Tuuwee and Tuuwee now needs me. And so . . ."

Puulu suddenly rushed into Muusamali's arms, catching him by surprise. As she held him tightly with tears in her eyes, he wrapped his long arms around her shoulders in a gentle bear-hug.

"I knew all along that you loved our son as much as I do," Puulu said between sobs. Then, as she pulled back just a little, she gazed once more into Muusamali's eyes and added, "But you had such a cold way of showing it."

Muusamali held her tender look for several moments. Suddenly his expression turned stern and hard once more and he said, "It was my way of keeping our son strong. Strong like his dreams."

The entire village of Cuuzan exiles turned out to see the king and ten chosen warriors off on their journey. Muusamali and Puulu left the hut and walked, side by side, the short distance into the village square with Puulu carrying his spear and shield.

With their bodies smeared in light blue chalk, ten fully armed warriors, along with Zuuox and Firok, Ruuski, and four other elder members of Muusamali's counsel, stood in the center of the large crowd of spectators. The ten warriors and Zuuox promptly raised their spears and shields in the air as Muusamali pulled up and stood before them. The crowd fell silent. The moment was meant for the king to inspect his warriors and their weapons. Suubala was out in front wearing the traditional leopard headband with the two matching armbands fitted around his biceps which distinguished him as the commander, second only to the king.

Surprisingly to Zuuox, Suubala had offered to pass the leopard headband to Zuuox. But Zuuox had politely refused, accepting instead the single leopard armband which was the traditional dress attire for nonranking warriors going into battle.

Luuka stood at Suubala's side with his chest out and chin held high. He looked fit and ready for the task at hand.

As Muusamali stood before Luuka, he gave the old warrior a rare pat on the shoulders, a special gesture reserved for warriors whom the king held in high esteem.

When Muusamali turned to Suubala, he gave his trusted commander a mere nod of the head. In that brief moment, Muusamali's eyes revealed his utter faith and confidence in this big bull of a man.

To Suubala's right stood the youngest warrior in the group. He was a mere nineteen years old, and his name was Guuramas. His chosen destiny was to someday wear the leopard headband and lead the next, up-and-coming generation of Cuuzan warriors like Zuuox and Suubala before him and those countless other mighty Cuuzan commanders of generations past.

Muusamali nodded his head in approval of Guuramas's bold appearance and the excellent condition of his spear and shield. This time, however, Muusamali lingered briefly to emphasize his satisfaction with the young warrior and future commander.

Zuuox, with Firok at his side, stood next to Guuramas. Muusamali looked past the spear in Zuuox's hand and stared at the rifle strapped across his shoulder. Calmly, Zuuox passed his spear to Firok and then slipped the rifle from his shoulder and held it out to Muusamali for his inspection. "A most effective weapon, my king. Like none you've ever known." Zuuox said. But Muusamali didn't look the least bit impressed. Without comment, he turned his gaze to Firok.

Muusamali looked puzzled by Firok's dark-skinned complexion and sharp European features as if he wanted to reach out and touch his face. But just as abruptly as he turned toward him, he turned away and began working his way in and around the group of warriors. As he went, he glanced at weapons and nodded his head every now and then.

Each of the ten warriors chosen, with the exception of young Guuramas, were original warriors who had left Cuuzanland along with Muusamali when he was forced into exile so many years ago. They were all close to Muusamali's age, give or take a few years. All were excited about returning home. But they also understood that they faced many uncertainties. They had been chosen by King Nuumyu to accompany Muusamali into exile and had sworn never to return to the homeland, no matter what the circumstances. They were now being chosen by their king in exile to break the sacred decree of the homeland king and true ruler of the Cuuzan tribe.

This was a dilemma none of them had ever before faced. But it took little soul-searching to resolve the conflict. Muusamali was their king and their only king for the time being. They would follow him anywhere, bravely so, and not think twice about laying down their lives for his—whatever the cause or cost might be.

As Muusamali and the other men headed out from the village square, the crowd chanted softly and stomped their feet to the beat of the march. This gave the warriors a soulful escort and the villagers followed along as far as the clearing where the shrine of Cuu-ba overlooked the freshwater lake.

Here, the singing and foot-stomping ceased as everyone began saying their goodbyes. Wives and children began hugging husbands and fathers, while young and old warriors who were left behind shook hands with the fortunate few departees.

Puulu, with a look of sadness yet high-spirited expression, handed Muusamali his spear and shield and said her goodbyes. Muusamali's other two wives, along with several of his sons and daughters, paraded before him as they, too, voiced their farewells.

Muututa asked Luuka to promise that he would return with Kuula and he did so without hesitation. Guumal stepped up from out of nowhere and stuck out his hand for Luuka to shake. But Luuka left it suspended in midair as he looked into Guumal's sad face. "Son, don't you know if it were my decision, I would take you along?"

Guumal let his hand drop to his side. He looked off for just a moment, lips tightened with anger, but eyes revealing a certain understanding as he turned once more to look at his father. He asked, "Do you mean that, Father?"

"I do," Luuka answered with an expression marked by sincerity. "And I shall be sure to let your brother know that you desperately wanted to come."

Guumal nodded and then once more offered his hand to his father. Luuka smiled as did Muututa. As Luuka took his son's hand and shook it, Muututa came around, placed her hand on the boy's shoulder, and said to Luuka, "We shall await your and Kuula's speedy return."

Suubala held his infant son for a brief minute then handed him back to his wife as he, too, said his goodbyes.

Zuuox and Firok shook hands with any and all comers, and there were many who stepped up to wish them well.

From there, Muusamali led the way off the main road and into the clearing where Cuu-ba's shrine sat like a giant, holy monument against a backdrop of thick jungle brush.

The Cuuzan population turned around to leave the king and his warriors to their prayers and headed back to their homes in the village.

Zuuox and Suubala stood flanking Muusamali as they faced the monument of giant spears surrounding the huge, oval-shaped shield with the life-sized lion's head carved in the center. The other warriors, along with Firok, took up the rear. As Muusamali led the others in prayer, Firok took this occasion to get down on his knees and pray to his god Allah, since they were already facing eastward.

"Oh great Cuu-ba," Muusamali began in a loud, clear voice, "we come before you as humble warriors to ask that you give us the strength to succeed in our mission to find Tuuwee and Kuula and to restore my brother Nuumyu to his rightful position of power. In the name of all the other brave and noble Cuuzan warriors and their mighty deeds done before our time, we swear to also be brave and noble in all our deeds. We pledge allegiance to you this day and honor the souls of our dead brothers who dwell in heaven with you. Bless us this day as in yesterday and every day still yet to come."

Muusamali stepped forward and entered the circle of giant spears. He touched the statue of the lion's head then turned and walked off.

Suubala followed suit, as did Zuuox and all the others as they fell in line to repeat the act of touching the shield then following Muusamali out to the trail.

The march for Cuuzanland was on.

As the last of the warriors went up the trail and disappeared into a grove of evergreen trees, a tiny figure emerged from the wall of thick brush behind

Cuu-ba's shrine. Guumal stepped into the circle of spears and, just as the others had done, he too touched the lion's head with the palm of his hand. All the while keeping a sharp eye, scanning his surroundings making sure he was completely alone.

Then, with his knapsack and waterskin hanging under his arm, and his miniature spear and shield in hand, he headed toward the trail. Once there, he started out on his own personal march to Cuuzanland, following the tracks of those just ahead of him. He kept a safe distance back so that no one would notice.

It was in the predawn hours, just as the sun was about to clear the horizon that the ambassador knocked on the backdoor of the main Christian mission house just outside the town called Tacra. A white priest named Father Poe climbed from his bed to answer the knock. Father Poe hurriedly dressed and snapped on his priest's collar and slipped a large silver cross and chain around his neck. "Coming . . . coming," he said as he crossed the floor in his bare feet. He was halfway to the door when he looked down and realized he'd forgotten his house shoes. As he started to turn and go back, the knock at the door impatiently thundered once more throughout the house. "I'm coming, I'm coming" he yelled with an irritated edge to his voice and discarded any further thought of warm feet.

As Father Poe opened the door, the ambassador hurriedly slipped inside before Father Poe could clearly identify him. "Father, I'm in a hurry. I must ask a favor of you," the ambassador said, standing behind the priest who was still facing the open doorway. "I'm in need of money and food supplies."

Father Poe didn't have to turn and look at the ambassador. He knew perfectly well who had entered his home like a thief in the night. He was more interested in what he saw on the road outside. He rubbed the sleep from his startled eyes, and still he found it hard to believe what he was seeing.

A half-dozen naked Africans were lined up in single file with several other black soldiers on horseback surrounding them. The Africans on foot were bound in chains at the wrist, ankle, and neck. Their shackles resembled the harnesses worn by mules and oxen for plowing the fields. A single chain about four feet long was connected to their wooden collars binding the six men together in a chain gang.

A horse-drawn carriage was also on the road, posted just in front of the chain gang. Father Poe recognized the driver as Dunbar, the black European interpreter. "What's the meaning of this?" Father Poe asked in an alarming, angry voice.

The ambassador didn't immediately answer. Instead, he calmly stepped around the priest and slammed the door shut. The loud bang and suddenness of his move startled the priest, causing him to jump.

"Father, I am acting on official, diplomatic business that is of no concern to the church," the ambassador said as he glared into Father Poe's face.

Though frightened, Father Poe managed to keep a steady voice. "This is not the reason we are here. My superiors distinctly told me that our mission is to educate, heal the sick, and offer these people salvation through Jesus Christ. What you are engaging in is an immoral act and goes against all the—"

"Father," the ambassador interrupted, "I haven't time to debate issues of morality or religion with you. I need money and some decent food. Enough for myself and Mr. Dunbar for our trip to Benin."

"This is an outrage! I demand you release those poor souls immediately," Father Poe said as he reached around the ambassador and grabbed the doorknob. But the ambassador was quicker and stronger as he slammed the door shut and pushed the priest away. Father Poe stumbled backward a few steps. When he finally gathered himself, he noticed that the ambassador had one hand inside his coat. The priest knew the ambassador wore a holstered pistol on his waist belt.

274

"I won't allow you to foul up this operation, Father," the ambassador hissed. His eyes took on a possessed look marked with rage, but yet still subdued—at least for the moment. "My mission in this godforsaken place is to make sure Duugawdu takes the throne. If he doesn't, do you know where that will leave you and every other white man in this land? Uprooted! Uprooted by the opposition forces which are supported by Muslims. All traces of Christianity and European commerce will disappear before you could say 'hail Mary.' Now get a hold of yourself, Father. There is a perfectly good reason why Duugawdu wants these particular six heathens out of the country. A crucial reason which I am not at liberty to discuss in detail."

As the ambassador finished his sentence, he eased his empty hand from under his coat and placed it on his hip. He was anxious to get what he came for and be gone. Compelled by a sympathetic spirit not to hurt the priest, he remained patient but watchful and ready to defend his cause by whatever means necessary.

Father Poe apparently sensed how desperate the ambassador was, and the priest's face turned from anger to one of somber helplessness. For a moment, words eluded him as he stared into the ambassador's face, the face of a man he once trusted and respected but now perceived to be just another of Satan's henchmen.

"Lord, Lord, what shall your humble, powerless servant do?" Father Poe whispered toward the heavens.

"There's only one thing for you to do, Father," the ambassador said as the priest lowered his eyes and fixed them on this man whom he now deemed an enemy of God and everything holy. "And that's stay out of the way. The future of Christianity and democratic rule in this land depends upon Duugawdu's succession to the throne. My mission, right now, will ensure it!"

"Perhaps you're right," Father Poe replied. "I feel the spirit of the Lord moving me to cooperate for the sake of the church . . . and the church's mission here, of course."

"Of course," the ambassador repeated. "Saving souls and converting savage infidels into civilized Christians is the noblest of missions. But it would be an impossible task to perform if you and the church were to be barred from the Kongolian territory. That will eventually happen if my mission is not successful."

"I understand," Father Poe said. Then he turned and headed toward another room down the corridor. "Come, and I will equip you with the necessary money and supplies you need."

The ambassador fell into step behind the barefoot clergy. A grin played on the ambassador's lips, revealing the sinister sense of victory he was feeling.

As the priest entered the kitchen, one of his black aides came in through a side door wiping sleep from his eyes. "Father, is everything all right? Is there anything I can do?" the African assistant asked.

"No, no," Father Poe said as he stepped over to the man. "Everything is fine. Now go back to your room and don't come out again until I personally come for you. Understand?"

"Yes, Father, but—"

"Just do as I say! Now go!" Father Poe pushed the man back through the door from which he came.

The priest then turned around and approached another door which led to a large walk-in storage room. He threw back a latch and swung the door open wide. "You'll find any foodstuffs you need here," he said and then turned and walked away. "I will fetch you some money from our cookie jar."

"I won't need much, Father. Whatever you give me will be considered a loan," the ambassador said as he entered the storage room. "And I will be sure to inform my distinguished colleagues back home, as well as your archbishop in Benin, of your kind cooperation."

Immediately the priest sprang into action. He rushed over and slammed the door shut behind the ambassador. As he threw the latch into a locking position, he leaned on the door and said, "Inform them of my devotion to God Almighty, you devil!"

Father Poe then turned and rushed from the room, leaving the ambassador screaming obscenities and pounding on the locked door with his fist.

Father Poe hurried through the outer room and out the backdoor. With no thought of being barefoot, he rushed across the yard and up to the carriage where Dunbar sat waiting in the driver's seat. A ranking soldier on horseback was situated next to the carriage, and he was talking with Dunbar when the priest approached. "There has been a change of plans," Father Poe barked. "You are to hand over the keys to those shackles to me immediately."

Dunbar stared at the deep frown crossing the priest's brow. Then he looked at the officer, who returned his own puzzling expression. Finally, Dunbar looked back to Father Poe and asked, "Where is the ambassador?"

"Did you not hear me, Mr. Dunbar?" Father Poe held out his hand, palms up. "The keys to the shackles. Now!"

Inadvertently, Dunbar's eyes shifted and stared at a ring of keys fastened to the officer's belt. Without a thought and showing considerable speed and determination. Father Poe reached up and snatched the keys from the officer's waist. The priest ran toward the rear of the carriage where the shackled Africans were lined up in single file.

Leaping from the carriage, Dunbar shouted, "Stop him!" to the soldiers guarding the chain gang as he began running to the mission house.

"Son, when I take these irons off, I want you to run for your life," Father Poe instructed in Bantu as he approached the first African in line. It was Tuuwee.

Tuuwee's heart pounded as he watched the priest frantically fumble with the keys, trying to find the one which would open the iron braces holding Tuuwee captive.

Tuuwee was staring into the face of the white priest, eyes wide with wonder more than fear. The face Tuuwee was looking upon didn't have fangs protruding from the mouth. No long, shoulder-length wild hair. This face was anything but evil. While white in color, Father Poe's face revealed compassion, and his eyes were no less benign than those of a black village elder whom Tuuwee had been taught to trust and respect.

Before Father Poe could unlock Tuuwee's shackles, two black soldiers came up from the rear and grabbed him by the arms. "Unhand me," Father Poe demanded, pulling them backward with the force of his resistance. A third soldier came and wrestled the keys from his grip.

Unlike Tuuwee, Luba Zandi and the other chain gang prisoners took in the scene rather nonchalantly. Most were veterans of the Puma War and had experienced firsthand encounters with white soldiers on the battlefield. They had also handled white prisoners of war, in much the same way that they were now being treated themselves.

Tuuwee, on the other hand, was deeply engrossed in what he was watching. His young, virgin mind was recording every aspect of the incident with curiosity and a certain amazement. Unbeknownst to him, the strange scene being played out before his eyes would have a profound future influence on his conscious perception of a new world and people so foreign and complex that it would boggle his imagination as long as he lived.

Tuuwee looked on, completely bewildered by the priest's effort to free him. But what he was about to witness next was equally confusing and difficult to understand.

The ambassador, with his top hat leaning in disarray to one side of his head, burst from the backdoor of the mission house and stormed across the yard. Dunbar was trailing behind him. The ambassador's face was flushed with rage as he rushed up to the guards holding on to Father Poe. The priest's efforts to wrestle free from the larger and stronger men were useless.

The ambassador screamed into Father Poe's face, and Tuuwee couldn't begin to understand his words. But the ambassador's actions needed no translation, and they would leave an imprint on Tuuwee's mind forever. White men, especially those wearing tall hats similar to that of his father's tall headdress, came to symbolize dominance over those around them.

Tuuwee watched as the hat wearing ambassador stood boldly before the helpless priest, drew back his hand, and, with considerable force, slapped him across the face with open palm.

The ambassador then ordered the soldiers to take Father Poe and lock him up inside the same storage closet where he had been held just before Dunbar freed him.

As much as the heavy wooden collar would allow, Tuuwee turned his head to catch a glimpse of Luba Zandi and ask a question. "Why did that white man try to free me?"

Luba Zandi stared in silence for a moment as he watched the guards drag a stumbling Father Poe toward the house. The ambassador and Dunbar followed as two of the guards, with rifles at the ready, remained outside the backdoor watching over the chain gang from a distance.

Finally, Luba Zandi answered, "The priest stands alone, acting according to the wishes of some god he calls Jesus. The priest is known to have freed a lot of Africans from diseases which tribal healers could not cure. All in the name of this Jesus. Perhaps freeing us from these chains is as difficult a task for Jesus as it is for our own gods?"

"No task is too great for my god, Cuuz," Tuuwee said with total confidence. Then he turned his gaze back toward the rising sun as it peaked over the far horizon. Talking more to himself than to those around him, he muttered, "I dare not try to second-guess my god. In time, when Cuuz is ready, these chains will fall from me, and I shall be free again."

"With all due respect to your god, Cuuzan," one of the men behind Luba Zandi said, "I would not look for those chains to simply fall off. My own god is a mighty god too. I am of the Kodok tribe, and we believe that prayer and faith without action is worthless in most situations."

"He's right, young Tuuwee," Luba Zandi leaned forward and whispered. "This is one of those situations which calls for quick and forceful action if, and whenever, the opportunity arises. Throw off those chains yourself and fight for your freedom as if you were fighting for your very life. Do you understand?"

Tuuwee thought for a moment as he noticed the ambassador and Dunbar exit the mission house. This time, the ambassador's top hat was sitting straight and tall upon his head. Dunbar carried items of food supplies, and they were followed by soldiers doing the same. The ambassador walked with an arrogant, boastful strut. Tuuwee noticed a grin playing on his lips as he spoke with the strangely dressed African at his side.

Tuuwee tried to understand how a man could find anything amusing after all that had taken place over the past twelve hours. But he reasoned when one is the perpetrator and not the victim of calamity and terrible human misery, such as his heart-wrenching loss of Kuula, then perhaps such a person existed out of the realm of feelings and could find amusement in such things.

"I understand perfectly well," Tuuwee said to Luba Zandi. Somehow, Luba Zandi sensed in Tuuwee that, if given half a chance, the young Cuuzan would indeed risk all for freedom. Even his very life.

The native warrior tribes living in the region surrounding Lake Runyum were used to seeing all manner of travelers stopping at the lake to stock up on water. These tribes would harass any of them, few in number, who weren't armed and equipped to defend themselves.

The Cuuzan marchers were more than just a few. They were armed to the teeth and fierce in appearance. Muusamali led his small army across the open plains. Their thundering pace left no doubt of their mission's urgency or the dire consequences any would face who tried to stand in their way.

As Muusamali brought his party to the bank of the lake, all was still and quiet. But the feeling—the presence of eyes watching them from a nearby cluster of thickets—was strong. Muusamali had two warriors posted as lookouts, while the others filled their bellies and their waterskins. Firok and his camel took their business down to the lower end of the lake where it was more accessible for the four-legged beast.

Muusamali hastened the others to finish, not out of fear but simply because he intended for them to reach a certain point inside the skeleton jungle where they would be down for the night. Darkness was near, and he didn't want to linger.

As the Cuuzan marchers and Firok left the lake and walked some five hundred yards to the base of the forest wall, Muusamali brought the group to a stop. This was the point where the Forbidden Zone began. Zuuox and the others thought their king was going to conduct a ritual of some kind, asking the gods to suspend or remove the curse so they could have safe passage to the other side where the great canyon lay. But instead of appealing to the gods, Muusamali handed his weapons to Zuuox and cupped his hands to his mouth and sent out a loud bird call that echoed through the graveyard of barren and fallen trees.

After several minutes, no answer came. So Muusamali repeated his call. Again, no answer, and they stood staring into the dark forest waiting—all for naught.

None of the Cuuzan present, except Zuuox, had come this far south since the exiles first traveled through here on their way to the Sudd Swamp. Not even Muusamali had ventured this close to the forest which he had cursed.

Muusamali was hoping to get a response from his little friends, the Gatooma pygmies. He decided against pressing any further for a response. However, it had been a long time. Perhaps the old Gatoomas he'd known and befriended had passed on? Perhaps they'd forgotten about their friendship? he thought to himself. Maybe they just didn't want to be bothered, he continued to muse, and he suddenly felt as if he were intruding on their right to privacy.

"We will go forward in silence"—Muusamali turned toward the others and continued—"for however long we have until night fall, and then we'll bed down."

The others fell into step behind him, and they marched on out. They penetrated deep into the skeleton jungle before a starless night blanketed the whole Kinshasa under total darkness.

The Cuuzan party along with Firok and his camel were situated around a large campfire. They were grouped off in twos and threes, some lying down, some propped up against the trees, and others seated listening to Luuka recite old folktales passed down through countless generations of Cuuzan.

Firok was among the storytelling group. Wide-eyed and all ears, he was never so happy about conversing in the Bantu language than he was right then as he listened to the fascinating stories being told.

Muusamali and Zuuox sat apart from the others and were engaged in a private conversation. Zuuox informed Muusamali of everything he knew regarding the conflict between his two royal brothers, Nuumyu and Duugawdu. He also explained the merger of the seven tribes into the Kongolian Empire and gave him a brief account of the Puma Wars. He told of the struggle being waged by the Puma Dorrs to keep a power-hungry Duugawdu and his white associates in check. Muusamali was surprised and fascinated by the information Zuuox had stored in his brain. He was even more amazed at what Zuuox had to say about the Oupa Ra and the unusual power and influence she held over the land.

Muusamali was grateful to Zuuox. He'd always been a man he'd mistrusted, in spite of the fact that Zuuox always displayed loyalty and respect toward him.

The hardest thing for Zuuox to tell Muusamali was that he had eavesdropped on his conversation with King Nuumyu that morning years ago when Nuumyu had first instructed Muusamali to go into self-exile with a third of the tribe and the clandestine purpose for doing so.

Unbeknownst to Zuuox, Muusamali actually felt glad that Zuuox had overheard the conversation. It meant that he didn't really believe that Muusamali had been a coward and ran to avoid going to war with the white invaders.

Muusamali was thankful, too, that Zuuox had placed Tuuwee on such a high pedestal and that he'd helped to make Tuuwee the man he'd grown into. Zuuox and his information had suddenly freed Muusamali's keen mind from years of lying dormant in that remote and simplistic world of the Sudd Swamp. His mind whirled with all sorts of enlightening thoughts. One thought, however, dominated his mind, and that was the belief that Zuuox had been a godsend all along! Everything that had taken place in the past and present, and would take place in the future, were events happening according to some divine plan.

Muusamali and Zuuox fell silent for a long while as they passed a corncob smoking pipe between them. They watched the others as they entertained themselves laughing, telling stories, and passing a pipe of their own.

Zuuox was satisfied that he had sufficiently brought Muusamali up to date on everything he needed to know about the present state of the Kongolian Empire, formerly known as Cuuzanland.

Now Zuuox felt as if a heavy burden had been lifted from his shoulders. Muusamali was king of the exiled clan, and Zuuox would view him this way until the homeland king, Nuumyu, said otherwise. It was a king's duty to make decisions and take on the responsibilities of directing the troops. Zuuox could now assume the role of a battlefield general, alongside

Suubala—a role more comfortable for him and one which he felt better suited.

For the first time since the exodus from the homeland, Muusamali felt Zuuox's true worth. He felt almost invincible when Zuuox was near, not to diminish the strength and confidence he felt being in the company of Suubala and the other Cuuzan warriors. But somehow, Muusamali sensed that Zuuox was an instrument of the gods, a messenger of sorts, meant to inspire and direct him on some path which the gods had laid out. To what end this path would lead, he was uncertain. He was simply convinced that he was being called on this mission. With the gods' messenger at his side, no man, beast, or evil force could prevent him from accomplishing whatever he set about doing.

"My brother, Duugawdu, was always ambitious," Muusamali finally broke the silence by saying. "But I would never have imagined that he would become so consumed with ambition that he would totally ignore ancestral traditions and seek to destroy the Cuuzan constitution for personal gain."

"He is bewitched by the white men he allows to freely walk our land and even tend to our sick."

Muusamali fell quiet again. As he pulled on the smoking pipe, his eyes fixed on Firok. As he watched him, he asked, "What motivates these Arabs to help you and your Puma Dorr friends, Zuuox?"

"If you believe them, they do it out of compassion for the men of color who are struggling to keep the white man from dominating the lands," Zuuox answered as he stared fondly at the pipe in his hands.

"I take it you do not entirely believe that. So tell me, what do you believe?" Muusamali questioned, turning his eyes back to Zuuox.

"That the Arabs are after the same thing as are the White Dragons: the diamond mines atop the Ikeele Mountains."

Muusamali hesitated a second as he accepted the pipe from Zuuox. "And so you think it's more practical to lay with snakes than swim with sharks? Both their purposes are the same: to rob our land of its wealth."

"Well, my king," Zuuox said in a sleepy tone, "I'm just a man of simple understanding. But I think it is better to fight one enemy with the help of the other rather than fight both enemies at the same time. The snake, I believe, will respect and preserve the land more than the one who comes from the sea by boat and can return to the sea at will, disappearing forever with our wealth.

"Is this my brother Nuumyu's way of thinking as well?"

"I wouldn't know," Zuuox answered. "But I am certain of one thing. Whatever King Nuumyu's feelings are, Duugawdu finds ways of keeping them from the public.

Just then, one of the warriors stood up as he peered out into the darkness and said, "Someone's coming." Everyone began scrambling to their feet, reaching for their weapons as they rose.

Three small figures came into view out of the darkness. As they stepped into the light of the campfire, mouths dropped open, and spears and shields instantly lowered.

"Guumal!" came Luuka's surprised voice.

Guumal and two Gatooma pygmies were greeted with mixed emotions. Luuka was visibly embarrassed and somewhat upset that Guumal would pull such a stunt. But on the other hand, he was proud as any Cuuzan father would be at his son's bravery and loyalty for his brother Kuula.

Muusamali and the others were amused, especially after hearing how Guumal was apprehended by Foliose warriors and brought to the Gatooma kicking and screaming obscenities.

The Gatooma kept straight faces while telling the story because, in their minds, Guumal was lucky that the bully warriors hadn't taken him to their village and used him as a practice dummy to train their youngsters in the art of combat. The Foliose were known for such things.

"Had they not surprised me while my weapons lay on the ground and my face was in the lake drinking," Guumal told the others, "I would have taken down two of them for sure!"

A few muffled snickers went through the group. Suubala, however, pretended to be serious as he raised his hands for everyone to lend an ear. He said, "I bare witness that this little one is, indeed, brave and greatly feared by the Foliose. In fact, the last time we were on the lake together with Tuuwee and Kuula, the little one put several Foliose to flight! He and I gave chase to them for a great distance. Did we not, young Guumal?"

"Indeed we did, Cuuzan!" Guumal boasted with his chest out and head high. Then he added matter-of-factly, "It was while we gave chase that Tuuwee and my brother disappeared into the Forbidden Zone."

Everyone suddenly fell silent. A few eyes shifted Muusamali's way, while others fought to keep a straight face.

Muusamali, however, was being entertained by the whole episode. He was especially delighted to see his old friends the Gatoomas.

Muusamali broke the tension by addressing the two Gatoomas who sat like tiny statues at his side. "These Foliose must have thought our Guumal was one of your people, my friends." Muusamali was smiling and everyone else followed his lead and smiled too.

"I am certain they did not," the eldest Gatooma said. He was the old man who had seen to it that Tuuwee and Kuula made it out of Kinshasa alive. But the old Gatooma chose not to mention Tuuwee and Kuula. Neither Muusamali nor the others brought it up. "I believe the Foliose knew who the youngster was Cuuzan when they captured him. Perhaps they feared serious reprisal had they done anything except turn him over to us."

The next morning, the party of Cuuzan warriors, with Firok bringing up the rear on his camel, set out once more for Cuuzanland.

The Gatooma pygmies had left for their village in the wee hours of the morning after they and Muusamali reminisced about the good old days when Kinshasa was a paradise fit for the gods.

For the next two days they pushed on in a desperate march. They passed the great canyon region and went into the open plains of the Bomu desert. Eventually, the march took its toll on Guumal's young legs, forcing him to share the camel with Firok for the final eight hours of the journey.

Finally, they reached the number one Khaburah colony on the southern fringes of the Kongolian territory. Lookouts posted in the desert had spied their approach and rode their fast Arabian steeds back to the Khaburah and informed their superiors that Firok and Zuuox had returned.

A welcoming party was already in place when Firok, now out in front, led Muusamali and the others into the tent city. The Khaburah commander, wearing his kaffiyeh with the gold headband, stood with the Oupa Ra and her two daughters. The other members of the Puma Dorr hierarchy, who were present at the last meeting from which Zuuox had stormed out, were also present with one notable exception. The "veiled one" was elsewhere . . . leading the other half of his double life.

No one could hide the surprised expressions on their faces as they watched Firok lead the Cuuzan warriors past the entrance gates and into the center of the tent city. Arab women and children all flocked to get a glimpse of the crude-looking swamp warriors.

By present-day standards, the returning clan of Cuuzan tribesmen were aboriginal. The Cuuzan dress code, especially among Kongolian Cuuzans, had changed considerably since Muusamali's departure. To look upon the returning exiles was to witness time at a standstill.

Buuk, the only Cuuzan among the Puma Dorrs present, looked at his long-lost returning fellow tribesmen. He had a proud smile on his face and an anxious sparkle in his eye. From where he stood, he had been able to recognize Muusamali and Suubala. His eyes continued to scan the dusty faces as if searching for one in particular.

The Oupa Ra, on the other hand, wasted little time gawking. Once she spotted Muusamali in the crowd, she took two steps forward as she opened her arms and said, "Pinch me where it hurts the most if my eyes don't behold Muusamali!"

"I am Muusamali," he answered as he stopped just short of the Oupa Ra. "And what I have for you, Nomaa, is a big hug and not a pinch." Muusamali spread his long arms like the wings of an eagle, spear and shield still in hand. The Oupa Ra stepped lively into his embrace and he held her small frame in a smothering bear-hug.

Zuuox stepped around Muusamali and the Oupa Ra and approached the Arab commander. "My assessment of you, comrade Zuuox, was correct, I see," the Arab said as he and Zuuox shook hands. "You are a man of your word."

"My word is still unfulfilled until my prince, his cousin, and Luba Zandi are free."

"Well, I am prepared to fulfill my word by providing you and your people with all the necessary guns and ammunition you'll need. But I am afraid I have a bit of bad news regarding your prince's cousin."

At that moment, Buuk suddenly came unglued as he shouted out a name—"Duuyard"—and raced past Zuuox and the Arab and headed toward the group of Cuuzan warriors. Instantly, one of the warriors raised his hands in jubilation as he rushed forward to meet Buuk. "My brother, my brother!" he yelled as they embraced. When they parted, Buuk turned and shook Suubala's hands then another hand caught Buuk on his shoulder and spun him around.

"Luuka," he shouted as he stared him in the face followed by another embrace.

"Commander Mustafa, I present to you King Muusamali, brother of Emperor Nuumyu," Zuuox announced as he led the gold-wearing Arab over to Muusamali. By this time, Firok and Guumal had dismounted the camel, and Firok stood just over the Arab's shoulder looking on.

Surprisingly, Muusamali did not readily accept Mustafa's hand. He stared at the little Arab commander with an expression of deep interest, marked with a look of distrust. Everyone fell silent as more and more eyes began to turn and focus on the two leaders.

Mustafa's outstretched hand was left lingering in midair. Suddenly, the Oupa Ra stepped forward and touched Muusamali on the sleeve. She said, "Never was there a man born in our land more devoted to our cause than this man who stands before you, Muusamali!"

Muusamali still ignored the hand as he glanced at Zuuox. Zuuox held his stone-faced expression. He had thoroughly briefed Muusamali regarding everything, including his own feelings. Zuuox felt there was nothing more for him to say or do except observe and follow the king's lead.

Mustafa was neither a shortsighted man nor a man short on patience. Calmly, he lowered his hand and allowed himself a subtle smile. Muusamali looked at him with his piercing eyes and said, "Before I accept your hand in friendship, there is one other you must first befriend—my brother and true king of the Cuuzan, Nuumyu." Muusamali's expression softened as he paused and then quickly added, "So come with us now and we will meet with my esteemed brother." With that, he turned and motioned for the Oupa Ra to join him.

The Oupa Ra's expression was one of astonishment, as were those of the others as they looked on in silence. Zuuox appeared to be the only person who wasn't the least bit surprised by anything Muusamali said or did.

Finally, Buuk stepped forward from the crowd and said, "King Muusamali. I am Buuk, son of Muuel, brother of Duuyard." Buuk paused and pointed at Duuyard with a proud smile. Then he turned back to Muusamali with a sad look in his eyes and said, "It pains me to inform you, King Muusamali, that access to the Emperor Nuumyu is restricted to a chosen few. You would never get past the border guards, let alone inside the palace where the emperor is said to be bedridden."

Muusamali looked at Buuk with an equally sad expression and said, "Buuk, son of Muuel, brother of Duuyard, it pains me to tell you that your poor brain is touched with the fever if you think that border guards will keep me from seeing my brother."

Buuk was visibly shaken as he fought to keep his posture. Inadvertently, his eyes shifted and fell on Zuuox. Zuuox rolled his eyes upward with a slight grin to his lips which reminded Buuk of the last time his foot got caught in his own mouth.

"Since you give the appearance of being in the know," Muusamali said, snapping Buuk back from the painful past to the painful present, "tell me: where is my son Tuuwee and my nephew Kuula?"

By this time, Duuyard had worked his way forward and now stood at his younger brother's side. Buuk and Duuyard's eyes met briefly, as Duuyard nodded his head, giving Buuk a sense of confidence.

"Our source inside the capital city tells us that your son is being kept in a secret location known only to Duugawdu and his closest aides," Buuk said with a steady voice. As he paused, he looked over at Luuka. "I assume Kuula was your son by King Muusamali's sister?"

Luuka stepped closer with Guumal following at his side, and said, "Kuula is my son. Yes."

"And my brother," came Guumal.

Buuk avoided all eyes except Luuka's as he swallowed and said, "Our sources inform us that Kuula died in Gorma prison three days ago.

Luuka's lips began to tremble, and his eyes took on a faraway look. Had not Guumal been at his side, his knees might have given out completely.

As it was, he leaned on Guumal's shoulder as the boy caught his father around the waist and held him from falling.

Just then, Suubala stepped up, stood at Luuka's other side, and said, "Are you sure about his, Buuk? Couldn't your sources be wrong?"

"I wish they were," Buuk answered as he looked up at the giant of a man known by all as the "Raging Bull." "And the one responsible for Kuula's death, I take it, is Duugawdu?" Muusamali asked with shock and sorrow.

Again, Buuk searched carefully for just the right words before finally saying, "The soldier who actually wounded Kuula was later beheaded by Duugawdu himself. However, it was by Duugawdu's order that Kuula and your son were thrown into prison." Buuk paused for a moment then, with a stiff upper lip, added, "I am as brave as I am naïve, King Muusamali. It would be an honor if you would count me as your twelfth warrior. I will fight to the death for your cause, at my brother's side."

Muusamali didn't have to give Buuk's request much thought. As he stared into his eyes, he sensed a strong resolve about the young man. Very gently, Muusamali touched his shoulder with his spear and nodded his head.

"I will join you also," Firok said as he stepped over and stood next to Zuuox. The two of them looked at each other for a moment then Firok looked toward his commander.

Mustafa acknowledged the look by turning to Muusamali and saying, "I could never allow one of my soldiers to go on a suicide mission that I, myself, would not go on. Because of political reasons, I cannot give you any more men than Firok. However, I can offer myself and all the guns and ammunition you'll need."

Muusamali looked at the little Arab with studying eyes. He didn't quite know what to think about this non-African who seemed to be willing to put his life on the line for African tribesmen. Were the diamonds of Ikeele Mountain worth more than life itself? Or were these Arabs truly acting out of a sense of friendship and caring? Muusamali was uncertain and until he heard his older brother Nuumyu's views on the subject, he would remain skeptical.

"Your weapons we do not need," Muusamali said after much thought. "Neither do we need you to fight our cause. But you may accompany us if you wish to make my brother's acquaintance. I'm sure my brother, king of the Cuuzan, will be interested in meeting you."

Muusamali then turned and addressed the Cuuzan warriors surrounding him. "Cuuzans," he said in a loud voice, "we march on the border. Then on to this place called 'The Palace' where my brother is said to be." Muusamali looked at Luuka standing next to the giant Suubala, and suddenly he saw a frail old man and not the same feisty warrior he appeared to be just moments before. He put out his hand, not on Luuka's shoulder, but on the person of Guumal. When Muusamali spoke he looked into Luuka's eyes and said, "If I find that my brother, Duugawdu, was responsible for Kuula's death, I will not spare him my wrath. Of this you can be certain!"

Luuka still had a blank look in his eyes, but his shoulders stiffened as his head rose, chin up. Guumal looked at his father and he stepped closer to him, as his father's arm cradled his shoulder. "My faith and that of Guumal is in you, my king," Luuka said.

Muusamali then stepped over to the Oupa Ra, and he looked at her affectionately. Before he could speak, she said "You know I haven't seen Nuumyu in years. I think it's time I pay the old man a little visit and show off my two beautiful daughters whom he has never met."

Muusamali followed her stare and beheld Ty and Nala as they smiled back at their mother. Muusamali understood why the Oupa Ra wanted to showcase the two lovelies. "Nuumyu will be delighted to see you," he said as the Oupa Ra walked to his side and they led the others from the tent city.

Zuuox stepped up to Muusamali's other side, and the march was on once again as they headed toward the Kongolian border.

The main border station on the eastern front of the Kongolian territory was heavily guarded—round the clock. A five-mile stretch of brick wall separated the town of Bawku from the capital city. The wall was sixty feet high with a fifteen-foot-wide catwalk on top where at least fifty European cannons were mounted and manned at all times.

The canon lookout atop the guard shack spotted the group on the road as they marched strong toward the main gate. He called down to his superior informing him of an unusual crowd fast approaching. The sergeant of the guards, a bold Kodok tribesman about thirty years old, sat at a table with several other guards engaged in a game of gambling said, "Damn peasants looking for work." As the sergeant got up from the table, he scooped up a handful of gold coins and stuffed them into his pocket as he left the shack.

Outside, the sergeant peered through the giant gate. It was twelve feet tall and wide enough for two wagons to pass through at once. It was made of steel crossbars, an inch thick, with square openings allowing for see-through visibility. From his position, the sergeant could see the marchers coming up the road, and, immediately, he knew they were no mere peasants looking for employment. The sight of spears and shields in the hands of so many warriors struck an instant alarm in his head.

"All of you, get out here now!" the sergeant yelled. In seconds, a half-dozen guards with rifles in hand streamed from the shack and positioned themselves in front of the gate.

In a short while, Muusamali and his mixed entourage came to a stop in front of the giant gate. It was not hard for the sergeant to recognize the leader of the march. Muusamali's headdress stood taller than the others, and he stood in the middle of the two biggest warriors in the group, Zuuox and Suubala.

By the same token, Muusamali's senses told him who the leader was on the inside of the gate. As he stared into the sergeant's eyes, the sergeant returned his gaze and yelled out, "State your business!"

"I am Muusamali, son of Fuuru, brother of King Nuumyu. Open this gate that I may pass through to the palace where my brother is said to be."

"By god, it's him," one of the guards whispered. "Quiet, soldier," the sergeant warned as he looked at the guard who'd spoken. The guard's forehead bore the tribal markings of the Cuuzan. Even though the younger man standing next to him didn't wear the tribal scars, he bore all other physical characteristics of a Cuuzan tribesman. As he and the older Cuuzan stared at each other, their peculiar exchange made it evident they represented both the old and the new Cuuzan generation.

"I don't care who you are," the sergeant yelled through the gate at Muusamali. "If you don't have the palace's seal of approval, you don't enter. I will dispatch a runner to the palace to relay your claim to my superiors. In the meantime, there's a clearing over there—among the trees—where you and your group can wait until I summon you."

"You summon me!" Muusamali said to the bald-headed sergeant with astonishment. "A lowlife Kodok telling a Cuuzan king when to come and when to go on Cuuzanland?" Muusamali took several steps forward with Zuuox and Suubala glued to his side. The entourage behind him moved forward as well.

"Stop where you are. I warn you not to approach the gate!" the sergeant bellowed as he raised one hand high in the air. The guards shifted nervously and one, on instinct, brought his rifle to the ready and aimed it squarely at Muusamali. Also on instinct, the guard bearing the Cuuzan markings reached out and grabbed hold of the rifle's barrel. The one aiming the rifle cut his eyes toward the Cuuzan who stared back at him threateningly as he shook his head slowly from side to side. Finally, the guard relaxed his grip and placed the rifle back at his side.

Zuuox caught sight of this and took another three steps forward, straining his eyes to get a better view of the guards behind the gate. He yelled at the one who had thwarted potential disaster saying, "Buujinka, is that you, old friend?"

"Yes, it is I, Zuuox," the man called back. He dropped his gaze from the sergeant as if he were embarrassed at the exchange. The sergeant, however, glared at him with an angry, almost fearful, expression.

"Ah, but you've grown skinny to where I hardly recognize you," Zuuox said. Then, as a sudden afterthought, Zuuox pointed around Muusamali toward Suubala. "Here's your cousin, Suubala, still as large as an elephant! Suubala look—it's Buujinka!"

All the while, Suubala stared at his cousin with a look absent any enthusiasm. Buujinka made it obvious why when he shouted. "Hello, cousin. So how is my wife these days?" "She's fine," Suubala shot back then added, "having my children and enjoying being my wife."

Suddenly, the sergeant yelled at the two guards manning the overhead cannon. "Send out a stage-two alarm and stand by to fire on my order."

One of the guards immediately turned the cannon down, aiming it directly at the crowd below. The other began beating out a message on his giant drum. The sergeant's back was turned toward the gate, and he was facing his troops on the ground. He raised his hand high in the air and yelled, "Ready!" Only half of the eight soldiers snapped to attention, their rifles at their hips. The others, along with the two Cuuzans, hesitated.

Muusamali, meanwhile, didn't hesitate for a second as he marched toward the gate. Zuuox and Suubala rushed to his side, followed by Luuka, Buuk, Duuyard, Guuramas, the two Arabs, and the other Cuuzan warriors. The Oupa Ra, along with her daughters, followed Muusamali's lead and all who could squeeze in grabbed hold of the gate.

"Aim," the sergeant ordered. Instantly the four soldiers brought up their rifles and trained their sights on the easy targets.

Muusamali and the others yanked on the gate to test its strength. It held—but barely—giving just enough to reveal some weakness. With the manpower they had, and enough time, they were confident they could eventually pull it down and gain access.

Buujinka was poised to do something to stop the sure massacre of his people. But he was at a loss to know precisely just what that was. His young counterpart stared at him, as did the other two soldiers who chose not to follow the sergeant's order.

"Sir, I caution you not to fire on my people," Buujinka said as he took a step closer to his commander. "The emperor's own brother is among them!"

"Stay put, soldier," the sergeant warned, pointing a bony finger at Buujinka's nose. Buujinka knew if the sergeant dropped his hand, and even if he were to stop the guards on the ground, the ones on the wall above him would surely fire.

"Buujinka," Zuuox called out, "remember the spider we used to feed live insects to in its web?"

Buujinka's eyes widened as he recalled their childhood exploits with the spider in the old tree. Suddenly, he realized what Zuuox meant, what he wanted him to do. Without hesitation, he moved with lightning speed. Dropping his rifle, he lunged forward and caught the sergeant by the arm with one hand, and with the other, he collared him by his shirt. Buujinka back slammed him hard against the gate.

Instantly, Suubala reached through the square opening in the gate. Like an elephant's trunk, he wrapped his arm around the sergeant's neck pinning him against the gate in a deadly choke hold.

"Drop your rifles or my comrade will break his neck like a twig," Buujinka warned as he turned toward the guards. The men watched in horror as Suubala slipped his free arm inside another one of the gate's openings and pressed the palm of his hand against one side of the sergeant's head while maintaining the hold he had around his throat. Slowly, Suubala lifted the sergeant off the ground, twisting his head one way and, with his powerful grip, squeezing his neck the other direction until the sergeant's feet were dangling in midair like those of a rag doll.

"Don't fire" were the only two words the sergeant could manage to muster.

As the guards lowered their rifles, the young Cuuzan guard raced to the gate and unlocked it. As it swung open, the throng of Cuuzan warriors rushed inside led by Muusamali, Zuuox, and Suubala.

Luuka, Buuk, Guuramus, and Duuyard hurried over to the guards and snatched away their rifles, as the other Cuuzan warriors swarmed on the two remaining guards. Other than taking their weapons away, the Cuuzans left them and their sergeant unharmed, except for their shame and embarrassment. They stood silently watching this small Cuuzan aboriginal army head up the road toward the capital city.

"What are your orders, Sergeant?" one of the guards manning the overhead cannon yelled down. The sergeant's face was twisted with anger as he stared at the departing army massaging his neck. "Shut up! Do you hear me? Just shut up!"

Although the two fell in step behind him on their march to the capital city, Muusamali barely looked at Buujinka and the young Cuuzan wearing the guard uniform. He was preoccupied with the surprising sights looming before him. Where straw huts, cornfields, animals, and corrals had once stood, there were now strange buildings—magnificent structures which defied his imagination. Although Muusamali had no idea where to look for his brother or his son, he followed his nose, which instinctively pointed him toward where King Nuumyu's hut used to sit.

The marchers blindly followed Muusamali's lead. They had no idea where they were headed or what they would find once they got there. Their eyes, however, like Muusamali's, were wide with amazement. They took in their first-ever sight of a modern city spread out before them.

The city was nothing new to Mustafa and Firok, who had traveled throughout Africa and had witnessed such wonders on an even greater scale.

The Oupa Ra and her daughters used to visit the city frequently some years ago before Duugawdu tightened restrictions on visa eligibility. "The palace is straight ahead, Muusamali," the Oupa Ra called out from her place on the far side of Zuuox. It's there you should find Emperor Nuumyu."

As they rounded a bend in the road, an army of horse soldiers suddenly appeared, galloping straight for the marchers. In a matter of seconds, they brought their mounts to a halt some thirty yards in front of the advancing group.

Muusamali raised his spear in the air, bringing his people to rest in the center of the road.

On command and in perfect unison, the horse soldiers slowly worked their mounts into a spread formation. They formed a wall blocking the road, extending several yards into the surrounding field to the right and to the left of the road. Another order was sounded, and they pulled their rifles from their saddle straps, positioning them at the group before them.

From the center of this wall of horsemen, the officer who had been barking orders spurred his horse forward. As he neared the marchers, Muusamali moved to meet him, but Zuuox spoke, freezing him in his tracks. "Wuuta," Zuuox said with a touch of zeal to his voice. "It's my brother!" Zuuox turned to Muusamali and added, "You remember Wuuta. 'The caterpillar with teeth' is what you used to call him when we were children." Muusamali may have remembered, but he gave no indication as he stared at Wuuta with cold untrusting eyes.

Wuuta dismounted and walked toward Muusamali. "Prince Muusamali, I am Wuuta, captain of the Royal Guards, son of Zuucar, brother of Zuuox."

For the first time, Wuuta and Zuuox's eyes met as Wuuta looked over at his older brother. It was a brief but emotional exchange, and Wuuta quickly turned back to Muusamali.

"Wuuta," Muusamali announced, "son of Zuucar, brother of Zuuox. I acknowledge you with respect. Now stand aside, you and your warriors. My people and I must go to the palace and meet with my brother, King Nuumyu."

"One moment please," Wuuta said as he held up a hand. "It's absolutely amazing that you somehow managed to get past my trigger-happy Kodok sergeant without a shot being fired, let alone coming through such an encounter alive." Wuuta paused and glanced at Buujinka and the young Cuuzan border guard. Buujinka, in turn, cut his eyes toward Zuuox and Suubala, and the three old friends smiled at each other. "But don't count on getting inside the palace without a fight. A fight you cannot possibly win."

"I don't agree. And unless I try to get inside your palace, then we shall never know for sure," Muusamali said then paused and stared at Wuuta. Wuuta had such a sad expression on his face that Muusamali's turned from a cold glare to one of comforting warmth. "Wuuta," he said as he looked into the man's eyes, "I remember you as a careful person even in your youth. Like a wise caterpillar, you always seemed so secure in your thinking and actions. So tell me, wise caterpillar, how can I possibly accept not being able to see my own brother in my own land?"

Wuuta looked at Zuuox, then at the Oupa Ra. Finally, his eyes settled on Mustafa and Firok. Each face revealed an unyielding resolve. Even when he looked down at little Guumal, who glared back up at him, Wuuta saw nothing to indicate that they were afraid to die for what Muusamali believed was his right.

"All right," Wuuta said, "I will get you inside. Hopefully. However, allow me to lead the march from this point forward. No one, and I mean no one, is to raise their rifle or their spear or we shall all be killed. We may all die anyway," Wuuta added as an afterthought then quickly said, "Now do I make myself clear? You must do nothing to provoke a fight."

"I didn't come home for a fight. But I didn't come all this way to run from one either," Muusamali said with conviction.

Wuuta looked at Muusamali with a certain admiration. He had no doubt about his seriousness. In fact, that was what caused him to put aside his own fears and allowed him to draw upon the strength he was witnessing from Muusamali and his followers.

"Just one moment more, Prince Muusamali," Wuuta said as he spun around to walk back to his men. "Lieutenant," Wuuta said to his young officer sitting in the saddle holding the reigns to Wuuta's empty horse. It was the same young officer who participated in the raid on the Oupa Ra's house.

"Yes, Captain?"

"Lieutenant, I am going to lead these people to the palace. They are returning Cuuzan exiles. Among them is the emperor's brother, Muusamali, who also happens to be a king in his own right. King of the exiled Cuuzan clan." Wuuta paused to allow his words to sink into the minds of everyone listening. As he looked away from the lieutenant, he allowed himself a moment to scan the faces of these Cuuzan tribesmen and to stare at Zuuox, who was standing in the very first row of the marchers.

"I want you and the rest of these soldiers to ride back to the palace and inform the palace guards that no one is to stand between us and the emperor's chambers. Is that clear, Lieutenant?"

The lieutenant pried his eyes away from Zuuox and looked down at Wuuta with a peculiar grin on his lips. It was the same kind of grin he threw Wuuta and Zuuox just before leaving the Oupa Ra's house that day when they were standing alone in the front room, and sometime later, Zuuox was said to have escaped.

Before the lieutenant could speak, however, one of the Cuuzan horsemen suddenly climbed down from his saddle. All eyes turned in his direction as he approached Wuuta and said, "I wish to join you and the returning exiles, Captain." The soldier bore the older tribal markings of the Cuuzan clan.

Wuuta thought for a moment, reflecting on the graveness of his own actions. Wuuta understood that life, as he'd known it, was going to drastically change . . . if not end in his sudden death. "Do you realize that if you join us, you risk dying or being thrown into the Gorma prison for life?" Wuuta asked.

The soldier peered over Wuuta's shoulder at the marchers standing several yards away. "Unless my eyes and ears deceive me, that is Prince Muusamali and General Zuuox!"

"It is," Wuuta replied.

"Then I'm willing to take the same risk as you, for the same reasons as you. Duugawdu must be dealt with."

Just then, another soldier dismounted and walked toward Wuuta. He too bore the old and original tribal markings of the Cuuzan. "Do you know what you are getting into?" Wuuta asked the man.

"I know that Emperor Nuumyu's greatest wish is to live to see his brother Muusamali return. I've heard this from his personal cook who is my wife," the soldier said then added, "I am willing to help see that the emperor gets his dying wish."

When Wuuta looked up, he was surprised to see the three remaining Cuuzan soldiers had dismounted and stood behind their two comrades. These last three were young men were born after the practice of marking male children had been laid to rest by the federation of tribes.

"Lieutenant," Wuuta called out with renewed vigor in his voice, "you've been given your orders. Carry them out as you see fit. My people and I will do what we think is best. We are coming in to see our homeland king."

The young lieutenant, as he stared back at Wuuta, raised his right hand in the air. With his two middle fingers, he made an Ikeele sign that meant more than words could have conveyed. It was the Ikeele display of respect and admiration. In turn, Wuuta threw up a hand sign that veterans of the Puma War had used to acknowledge loyalty toward a mutual cause: overcome the enemy.

With that, the lieutenant and the horse soldiers turned their mounts around and headed back toward the city taking with them the six extra horses with empty saddles.

Duugawdu was seated at the head of a long table in the business room of his well-appointed mansion house located a half-mile from the palace at the southern end of the city. Three distinguished guests were seated at the table with him: King Mwanza of the Warri, King Kweisi of the Owada, and Prince Jammu standing in for his bedridden father, King Ditiro of the Ikeele.

Of the seven members who made up the Imperial Council, these were the only three who didn't dance to every beat Duugawdu played on his political drum. Such was evidenced by the surprise visit to Duugawdu's home that evening regarding a rumor circulating on the gossip mill which had reached the ears of these three liberal council members.

King Mwanza had the floor and was saying, "I stand with Kweisi in that you should have informed us of this new 'labor transfer system' before you actually put it into operation Duugawdu." King Mwanza had thick bushy eyebrows which met in a V at the bridge of his nose. He sat upright in his chair resting on his elbows and staring at Duugawdu.

"What operation?" Duugawdu asked as he stared back at the three men seated before him. He reared back in his high-back chair with a look of complete ease on his face. Yet his eyes would shift then fix again on a target like a cornered cat. "The seven Puma Dorrs I transferred to overseas work camps were merely test pigs. I had to convince myself that the system was sound and worthwhile before I brought the idea before the full council for further evaluation."

"But why did you have to use one of my tribespeople as one of your 'test pigs' as you say?" The young prince who spoke was unmistakably an Ikeele, with long reddish dreadlocks hanging from his shoulders like thick pieces of braided rope.

"With all due respect, Jammu. The Ikeele Puma Dorr you speak of is a major shot caller," Duugawdu said in a sharp tone as he fixed his gaze on the young Ikeele Prince and added, "Luba Zandi is nothing more than a disgrace to your people. In fact, he has been responsible for the murder of just as many Ikeele soldiers as any other of the federation law enforcement personnel. Without a doubt, a Puma Dorr shot caller of Luba Zandi's caliber would have continued to control that murdering organization from the Gorma prison. It was necessary to remove him from the territory completely. I'll have you all know that I did not discriminate one bit! I contributed one of my own tribespeople along with several other convicted murderers from five different federation tribes."

"My father sends his utter disapproval," Jammu said. His look was that of contempt. "He says he will not tolerate Ikeeles being transferred overseas to work camps because the system stinks of slavery."

All eyes shifted to Duugawdu.

"Are you flirting with the slave trade, Duugawdu?" King Kweisi asked.

Just then, a soldier burst into the room. "Your Eminence, excuse my interruption, but there's a grave situation occurring of which you should be aware."

"What could be so important that you barge in here like a mad man?"

"Your brother, Muusamali, has returned!"

Duugawdu's face remained fixed and unreadable. However, his eyes blinked revealing a certain anxiety which his voice further confirmed. "But he is forbidden to do so by Cuuzan law and the king's decree," he said. Then he pointed a finger at the messenger and added, "He must not cross the border, do you understand?"

"But your greatness," the soldier began with a certain reservation, "he and a small army of Cuuzan warriors have already entered the city and should be reaching the palace steps as we speak."

Without hesitation, Duugawdu got to his feet. "This meeting is over!" he announced angrily as if the men at the table were somehow responsible for his troubles. As he stepped toward the door, the young Ikeele Prince called to him from behind. "This meeting is far from over, Duugawdu. Momentarily placed on hold, yes. But over, no!"

Duugawdu paused briefly at the door without turning. He had the urge to respond but decided against it. Why waste time with a matter now frivolous compared to the startling news of Muusamali's return? He mused to himself. Without as much as another backward glance, he bolted from the door.

"You know, it's going to be interesting to see how events unfold now that Nuumyu's brother, Muusamali, is back on the scene," King Mwanza said to the others remaining at the table.

"I'm curious to see how Duugawdu will handle this sudden and unexpected turn of events," King Kweisi added.

"So am I," Prince Jammu offered as he stood up from the table. "Why don't we follow Duugawdu and see this situation unravel for ourselves?"

"Good idea," King Mwanza said, and all three headed from the room in search of Duugawdu.

Wuuta led Muusamali and the others down the middle of the busy commercial street headed for the heart of the city referred to as the Grand Square. Evening shoppers dotted the tree-lined streets, browsing through the farmer's markets which occupied half of the main road and stretched for a half-mile. Horse-drawn carriages and wagons pulled off to one side of the wide street to allow the marchers to pass. Word spread like wildfire that the emperor's exiled brother had returned to claim his birthright as crown prince of the Cuuzan.

Many of those standing along the wayside were Cuuzan nationalist themselves. They looked in awe as the band of aboriginal Cuuzan warriors marched past. Both young and old were amazed at what they were witnessing. Older Cuuzans, upon spotting friends and relatives among the marchers, ran out into the street shouting their names and throwing up their hands in jubilation.

The returning exiles replied with glad smiles, vigorous handshakes, and hearty embraces. All the while, however, they kept moving in a forward advance toward their destination—the Grand Square. As they filed past, the sidewalks emptied behind them as men, women, and children of all different nationalities fell in step behind them.

The people's palace was a two-story, square-shaped building with seven massive pillars supporting the overhang of the second floor. It's set atop 150 flights of marble steps which were as wide as the palace itself. The high-rise palace overlooked a fifteen-square-acre city park, featuring tailored green lawns, exotic trees, flower gardens, and fishponds. This was the Grand Square.

By the time the marchers reached the square's southern front, the number of followers had multiplied to the hundreds and, steadily, people were filtering in from the surrounding suburbs.

Wuuta led the marchers straight through the center of the square to its northern end. It seemed like a multitude of black faces instantly filled the square and spilled out into the adjoining streets and waysides.

Wuuta brought Muusamali and the others to rest at the base of the palace steps. The wide and towering flight before them was deserted and the top landing, where the palace sat back some thirty yards from the edge of the climb, was clear of any Royal Guardsmen. In Wuuta's mind, this was a very unusual occurrence. It was almost inconceivable that Captain Omarka, the Royal Guards' commander, didn't have at least fifty armed men posted along the top landing to try and turn the marchers away—using intimidation, force, or both.

Wuuta didn't like the "quiet before the storm" atmosphere. But he was already in too far to think about turning back. So he proceeded with the plan he'd already formulated in his mind. He took the steps three at a time, bounded four giant strides, then stopped and turned around.

He looked down at Muusamali and over the crowd of noisy onlookers. He raised his hand for silence. As the crowd slowly quieted, Wuuta yelled, "I must ask for complete cooperation from each and every one of you. This is a situation which, at this juncture, concerns only the emperor's brother Prince Muusamali and the other returning exiles. I ask that everyone else, including fellow Cuuzan citizens, please remain down in the square and do not try and enter the palace." The crowd mumbled loudly but quickly fell silent.

Wuuta then motioned for Muusamali to join him. Before Muusamali took a step, he turned and placed a hand on the Oupa Ra's lower back and led her to the steps before him. "Always the perfect gentleman, aren't you?" she said. She smiled and gently raised the front of her long dress and began her climb, her two daughters at her side.

Zuuox in turn looked at Mustafa and Firok as he waved his spear in the air signaling them to follow. The two Arabs complied without hesitation. Buuk, the Cuuzan Puma Dorr, and the two Cuuzan border guards, fell in step behind them, along with the other twelve aboriginals. They began the long climb to the top of the palace steps.

Zuuox caught up with Wuuta just as the two reached the top landing. "You make a better speaker without that mask on your face, little brother," Zuuox whispered. Wuuta didn't miss a step as they walked across the open courtyard which separated the staircase from the palace building by some thirty yards. "So you were not fooled?" Wuuta said with a grin and adding, "Three years I hid behind that mask and no one within the Puma Dorr ranks ever suspected it was me. Yet I'm in your presence less than an hour and you see through it!"

I'm hardly as dumb as I look," Zuuox said seriously. Then he added, almost playfully, "You're my brother. That made it easy!" Wuuta turned and smiled at Zuuox.

As they continued their walk, Wuuta's expression turned serious, and his eyes narrowed. He was alert, expecting an ambush at any second. They were just reaching the giant pillars supporting the second-floor overhang. Beneath the supports where three sets of double doors positioned some fifty feet apart and all leading into the palace rotunda. Three of these doors were made of steel and were equipped with gun holes and lookout slots. But the space beneath the overhang was engulfed in shadows, making it impossible for Wuuta to tell, from that distance, if the gun holes were empty or if rifle barrels were pointed their way ready for a kill.

Suddenly, the sound of a latch being thrown was heard, and Wuuta spread both arms out from his side stopping Zuuox and Muusamali in their tracks. In turn, Muusamali raised his shield, bringing those to the rear to a halt as well.

Slowly, one set of double doors began to open. Wuuta flinched and began to grab the pistol holstered to his hip, but quickly fought against it. He resolved to wait it out, determined to let himself be shot before drawing his weapon and provoking violence.

As the double steel doors swung fully open, a lone figure could be seen in the shadows. Wuuta's heartbeat faster and faster as he stood waiting for the next move.

"Captain Wuuta," the shadow in the doorway said, "Captain Omarka sends his regrets for not being able to stay and greet you. An urgent crisis hit his hometown village and he was forced to abandon his post leaving me in charge of the palace guards."

A broad smile appeared on Wuuta's nervous face as he finally recognized the voice. It belonged to his young Ikeele lieutenant.

Emperor Nuumyu had been informed by the young lieutenant of Muusamali's return and presence on the palace steps. Still in a state of disbelief, he was propped up in bed against a mountain of black silk pillows, wearing a dark blue robe. Nuumyu's large gray Afro and gray beard cast a flowing sheen against the jet-black complexion of his face and pillows. Somehow, it looked as though his hair and beard were hovering in the air unsupported.

The door opened and in walked Muusamali followed by Zuuox. Instantly, Emperor Nuumyu's black face lit up! An added glow appeared on his countenance. His eyes widened and, as they did, the whites seemed to flash like glimmering pearls. He gave a huge, broad smile displaying a half-set of shiny white teeth.

Muusamali and Zuuox parked their weapons at the door, leaving their arms free to embrace the old king, Muusamali from one side of the bed and Zuuox from the other.

"I didn't think I would live to see this moment," the emperor said as he looked into Muusamali's eyes. Muusamali sat on the edge of the bed and held the emperor's hand. Zuuox stood on the opposite side, holding the other hand, and said, "This is, indeed, a great day."

The Oupa Ra stepped up, and Zuuox relinquished the old man's hand to her. "This moment was made in heaven, by your god and mine," she said as she looked tenderly upon her old friend.

Emperor Nuumyu looked up at her with surprise in his eyes. "Nomaa?" he questioned.

"Yes, you old lion. Have I changed that much in fifteen years?" she replied with a playful voice and a frown to her face which quickly changed into a broad smile. As Nuumyu held open his arms, she eased herself into the bed opposite Muusamali and embraced the emperor with tender arms.

Nuumyu was overcome with emotion, unable to speak. All he could do once she released her grip was to stare at the group surrounding his bed. He looked from her, to Muusamali, to Zuuox, and then to all those who were in his chambers. Each was a familiar face, their names easily recalled if only he could find his voice. Unable to do so, he reached out his hands in jubilation. The warriors surrounding him responded in kind by reaching out to him and stroking his frail, trembling arms. The joy Nuumyu felt gladdened his heart and further revealed itself in his moist eyes sparkling with happiness. Both crying and smiling, the old emperor resembled an ecstatic child consumed with excitement.

As the warriors in the back of the room elbowed their way to the center of this caressing baptism of the emperor, the Oupa Ra suddenly became overwhelmed by the crowd. Their hands and arms reaching to touch the emperor finally drove her from his side. She rose to her feet and, after gently patting Nuumyu on the leg, she backed her way out of the fondling frenzy. As she did, the dozens of half-naked warriors crushed ever closer to the emperor, bent on expressing their love and enthusiasm. The grinning old man was now barely visible except for his large, white Afro.

The scene brought tears to the Oupa Ra's eyes as she joined her daughters, the Arabs, Buuk, and the two Cuuzan border guards as they stood at the back of the room watching the warming display of affection.

The fondling ritual went on for a short while longer when, suddenly, Emperor Nuumyu began to show signs of fatigue. He ceased in his attempts to touch every hand within his reach. Instead, he grabbed hold of Muusamali's arm and squeezed with unusual strength. That beaming childlike grin which had been stamped on his face, relaxed into a peculiar half-smile.

As Nuumyu's other hand fell limp in his lap. Muusamali reached and picked it up. It felt lifeless and cold. And as Muusamali stared into Nuumyu's eyes, he saw an emptiness which sent chills up his spine. "Nuumyu—no!"

Muusamali pleaded as he quickly leaned an ear to the old one's heart. He listened, and listened, but heard nothing. Still, he was unable to release his grip on the emperor's frail and now-lifeless body. Muusamali kept his arms locked about him and his face buried in Nuumyu's chest. And he wept. The old Cuuzan king was dead.

The number of spectators gathered in Grand Square had risen into the thousands and the ocean of black faces were spread far and wide. They reached from the base of the palace steps to the back entrance into the park and beyond.

The sun had slowly slipped away; it was dusk. The fire crews were out in number. Wherever you looked, boys could be seen scampering up and down the fire poles igniting the park's gas lanterns. The surprising return of the emperor's exiled brother, Prince Muusamali, had caused quite a stir as rumors and speculations flew back and forth among the crew members.

Many were asking serious questions about Prince Duugawdu's present status now that his older brother had returned. Others made damning speculations that Muusamali would assume his former role as crown prince, completely stripping the younger Duugawdu of the title. All focus was concentrated on the palace. Everyone anxiously watched, uncertain of what would happen next.

From the west side of the crowded park, the crowd suddenly started to separate. All eyes turned in that direction. "Make way for the prince," a deep commanding voice was shouting. "Stand aside!"

It was Duugawdu's two shirtless and sword-carrying bodyguards. Waving naked broadswords over their heads, they used their free hands to ruthlessly push aside anyone who hesitated to clear the path they were making to the palace steps.

Duugawdu walked easily behind his two giant henchmen, avoiding all the questions the crowd were shouting. He had an angry and intense look on his face, staring straight ahead and swinging his long powerful arms freely at his side.

At that instant, the small band of Cuuzan aboriginals appeared on the top landing of the palace steps. Zuuox and Suubala carried the dead body of Emperor Nuumyu. They had strapped him into his royal chair, sitting upright. Gently, they placed the chair with their beloved emperor down near the edge of the top step. The other warriors, along with Buuk, the Cuuzan border guards, and the two Arabs spread out to the left and right of Nuumyu's body as it sat facing the spectators below.

The crowd hushed as they looked upon the old white-haired emperor, slumped slightly to one side, and the primitive looking Cuuzan warriors at his side. In spite of the obvious, the old Cuuzan king looked more peaceful in death than he had in life.

To the left of Emperor Nuumyu, the Oupa Ra and her daughters stood beside Zuuox and the Arabs. Muusamali, Suubala, and Wuuta and Guuramus flanked the right. As Muusamali looked out over the crowd, he immediately spotted Duugawdu standing directly below at the foot of the steps. Likewise, Duugawdu spotted him as well.

Muusamali was then drawn to another face, one that loomed in the distance behind Duugawdu. Father Poe's. Father Poe was dressed in his black priestly garb and was situated in the midst of a sea of black faces, like a shining star in the nighttime sky.

"Once the white man enters the land of the blacks, the land and its people will die." That old and ancient warning sounded in Muusamali's mind as he stared at the white face of the priest. He looks peculiarly out of place in the midst of so many blacks, Muusamali mused to himself. Yet strangely enough, he appears completely serene and at peace in his surroundings.

As Muusamali looked back at Duugawdu, he yelled, "Our brother, King Nuumyu, is dead!" His words had a rippling effect on the onlookers. Like a pebble bouncing cross a calm lake, the news swept through the crowd from front to back. People began to stir, to shout, to cry. Grief was overcoming them all, and many fell to their knees in weeping prayer. No one, with the exception of Duugawdu and his bodyguards, was able to contain their sorrow.

However, there was a group of about two dozen Kongolian soldiers standing near the east entrance to the park, and they, too, showed little emotion. The young lieutenant stood with them, arms crossed and wearing his ever-present smile.

Finally, after some moments, Duugawdu climbed the steps. Halfway up, he stopped and placed his left foot on the higher step while the other remained planted on the one below. He raised his right hand in the air, keeping the other resting on his knee, and waited patiently for the crowd to quiet down. He never took his eyes from Muusamali who stood on the top landing, some ninety steps above him.

When the crowd had calmed to his satisfaction, Duugawdu yelled up to Muusamali, "There's a strict law which mandates that any member of the royal family who chooses to exile himself from the tribe, for any reason . . . in your case, to avoid going to war in defense of the homeland some nineteen years ago . . . shall never be allowed to return to the homeland. And if an attempt is made to do so, the exiled shall be forcefully banished from the homeland without appeal."

Muusamali's sullen face took on a look of disbelief as he took in Duugawdu's remarks. "Have you turned blind and deaf, as well as mad with ambition?" Muusamali asked sharply. His words didn't necessarily play to the audience, yet they cut to the heart of everyone within earshot as he continued, "Our brother sits here dead. His body is not yet cold, and all you're concerned with is my return home and your interest to see that I leave again. Have you lost your heart, as well as all sense of morality in your reckless pursuit of power?"

"You're wrong, my brother. I am concerned. I am concerned about why and how the emperor died," Duugawdu replied as he smugly turned and looked at the faces in the crowd in an attempt to draw support. But he garnered none. All were grief-stricken and silent.

Duugawdu turned and faced Muusamali once more. He continued his speech, shouting this time, saying, "I personally saw the emperor less than four hours ago, and he was alive and well. His spirits were high as they usually are when I pay him a visit. Now, what could possibly have caused his sudden decline? What could have caused his death within this short period of time? That's my concern. And I am certain of one thing." Duugawdu paused as he, once more, turned to the crowd behind him. Throwing his index finger in the air, he shouted, "One thing is certain. Emperor Nuumyu was none too happy to see our cowardly brother Muusamali return to the homeland from which he fled. Muusamali would never be welcomed back! It's my guess the emperor tried to climb from his sickbed to personally remove him from his chambers and died in the attempt!"

"That is not so!" the Oupa Ra shot back. "I can bear witness to the fact that the emperor died in Muusamali's arms. And before which, he expressed his deep happiness in having him return from exile."

"I too witnessed the same," Wuuta stepped up and offered. Before the two Cuuzan border guards could speak, Duugawdu shouted back, "All of you are lying conspirators! You all conspired to kill Emperor Nuumyu. You assumed his death would ensure Muusamali's place back in the homeland."

"Watch your tongue, Duugawdu!" Zuuox shouted as he pointed his spear in the direction of Duugawdu's heart.

"Let him speak," Muusamali interrupted. In a calm, steady voice he added, "Say what you will, Duugawdu. It will be your final voice as prince of the Cuuzan. From this moment on, I am king, and my prince shall be my son."

His remarks caused the crowd to stir, and a large group began shouting their approval.

Duugawdu, however, was quick to counter. He raised his hands in the air, both feet now firmly planted on the same step, and faced the crowd. "My exiled brother Muusamali has been in the remote swamps too long. He lives in the forgotten past." Turning to look at Muusamali, he added,

"This is no longer Cuuzanland, poor lost brother. We are a federation of tribes now, a unified empire. With the unfortunate death of our brother and emperor, I am now the new emperor of Kongolia. I demand your immediate removal from Kongolia. You and the rest of—"

"Then you remove me!" Muusamali shouted, interrupting in an angry but controlled voice. He turned and reached for Suubala's spear and, without hesitation, Suubala relinquished it to him. Muusamali then turned and calmly tossed it sideways down the steps toward Duugawdu. With grace and ease, Duugawdu reached out and quickly gathered it in with one hand. Instinctively, the front section of spectators took a step backward, leaving only Duugawdu's two bodyguards standing at the base of the steps.

Duugawdu weighed the spear as he held it in his hands. Tilting his head and fixing his eyes on Muusamali, he revealed an ominous smile and as he said, "Are you challenging me to a duel?"

Muusamali hesitated a moment. He stared at his younger brother as he briefly journeyed back in time. Back to their childhood years when the two of them, along with Nuumyu, played war games together. The older Nuumyu was stronger than either of the two younger brothers and would always dominate the games. Until their father, one day, encouraged Muusamali and Duugawdu to unite as a team whenever confronted with an overpowering opponent. The outcome of their games quickly changed with the balancing of strength, and the team play bonded Muusamali and Duugawdu. They had become inseparable throughout their adolescent years. It had been Muusamali's eventual exile which had finally torn them apart. And now, to his dismay, his return was about to spell the final turn of events which would separate them forever.

Aware he was forcing a situation which could only end with one of them dying, Muusamali's mind was made up. "Yes, I am challenging you to enforce the law, Duugawdu. If you insist on banishing me from my homeland, I am prepared to take a stand. Since I refuse to leave, the matter can only be settled in combat. I am home to stay—or to die."

"You should have stayed in the swamp and lived!" Duugawdu shouted. With that, he began peeling off his clothing as his bodyguards ran to his side to retrieve them. The crowd began to move, shove, and jockey for the best position to view the coming battle.

At that moment, three men suddenly stepped from the crowd and slowly mounted the steps, about twenty yards west of where Duugawdu was standing. It was King Mwanza, King Kweisi, and Prince Jammu. They came to rest midway up the staircase. From his place, the young Ikeele Prince, Jammu, yelled, "I speak for each member on the Imperial Council when I say that Emperor Nuumyu will be greatly missed by us all. Our condolences go out to the royal Cuuzan family and the Cuuzan people as well.

"We the Imperial Council wish to make it clear that this duel will only determine the next Cuuzan king. The office of Kongolian emperor will be decided in the traditional manner: by majority vote of the seven Imperial Council members." As Jammu paused, his eyes met Duugawdu's, who appeared unimpressed by what he'd just heard. Jammu continued, saying, "To ensure the duel is fair and uninterrupted, it shall take place on the palace steps for all eyes to witness. No one . . .," Jammu paused again, fixing his gaze on Duugawdu's bodyguards, "not a single person except the two combatants shall set foot on these steps for any reason."

With that, Jammu raised his hand in the air signaling the young lieutenant and his men who had been positioned at the far end of the palace steps. The lieutenant directed his soldiers to form a long human barrier along the base of the steps to block them off from the crowd who had gathered. Another group of soldiers marched up the steps in single file and formed a barrier along the top landing in front of Muusamali's followers.

"You can take him easily, my king," Suubala encouraged as he held Muusamali's garments in one hand and his spear in the other. Muusamali's lean, wiry frame was firm and muscular, unusually so for a man his age.

Muusamali retrieved his spear from Suubala and turned without speaking. He met Zuuox as he was quietly stepping over to whisper something in his king's ear. "It may be a good idea to ask Duugawdu Tuuwee's whereabouts before you . . ." Zuuox cut off his remarks as though something were caught in his throat.

Muusamali briefly looked at his friend and said, "I understand," then fixed his full attention on the task at hand. Duugawdu was just starting to inch his way up the steps. He, too, was lean and muscular with a bit more bulk about his upper body and thighs than his older brother. He was crouched in a stalking posture, gripping his spear with both hands and fixing his eyes on the target—Muusamali.

Just as Muusamali was about to start down the steps to engage in the encounter, Wuuta leaned forward and softly said, "You might want to keep a certain fact in mind about your brother's fighting skills." Muusamali hesitated and looked back at Wuuta who continued in a serious voice, "He is a graduate of a Timbuktu military academy . . . trained and disciplined in the foreign arts of hand-to-hand combat."

For just a moment, Muusamali looked puzzled by Wuuta's words. Then he smiled and said, "Whatever you just said sounds interesting. I'd like to hear more when I return."

Again, Muusamali turned to begin his descent when Guuramas stepped between Wuuta and Zuuox. "Let me champion your cause, King Muusamali." The young warrior was big for his nineteen years, as tall as Zuuox, and with shoulders more muscular than Suubala's.

As Muusamali looked into his eyes, he felt the young man's sincerity and, suddenly, found he was pleased he had chosen this scrappy youngster to secede Zuuox and Suubala as the future commander of the warriors. "Some other time," Muusamali said as he threw Guuramas a look revealing his pleasure with this brave young warrior.

"May Igun be with you," the Oupa Ra called from her place next to Nuumyu's body. Muusamali nodded at her then glanced once again at his dead brother with sad eyes. It seemed like the old emperor was watching everything that was taking place.

Finally, Muusamali turned his eyes and attention to Duugawdu. Duugawdu was making impatient and intimidating gestures, thrusting his spear out from his body and then jerking it back to his chest, producing loud thumping noises with each maneuver.

"Squash him like an insect, King Muusamali!" Guumal yelled as he stood next to his father. Luuka placed an arm around his son's shoulders as the two of them, like the others, watched in silent anticipation.

Muusamali took the steps two at a time as he headed down toward his brother. He gripped his powerful hardwood spear in both hands and moved with fluid motion and blind determination . . . heading for Duugawdu. Duugawdu circled slowly to his left in a strategic effort to take Muusamali from his high-ground position.

Upon reaching the same step occupied by Duugawdu, Muusamali quickly moved in jabbing with his spear as he went. Duugawdu, showing exceptional speed and grace, twirled his spear briskly striking Muusamali's just in the nick of time. The impact drove the front of Muusamali's spear toward the left. However, he went with the motion and swung the spear's butt end around with his right hand . . . aiming for Duugawdu's head.

Duugawdu's alertness prevailed, however, and he ducked beneath the blow. Quickly recovering, he jumped up and positioned himself two steps above Muusamali. But Muusamali displayed a burst of speed and quick thinking. He circled around and upward at the same time Duugawdu was making his moves. In an instant, they were on equal ground again with Muusamali forever moving forward bringing the fight directly at Duugawdu.

"My son Tuuwee. Where is he?" Muusamali asked as he came within ten feet of Duugawdu's position on the step. "Someplace where he will never break the exile law again. A place of no return!" Duugawdu said as he braced himself for what was to come.

"May Cuuz have mercy on your soul," Muusamali answered and stepped boldly in on Duugawdu once again. This time, Duugawdu met the advance with an aggressive forward attack of his own. He thrust the point of his spear toward Muusamali's heart. Muusamali turned and threw his body to the side, causing Duugawdu's spear to miss its mark.

As Muusamali twisted, he swung the butt end of his spear toward Duugawdu's temple. Duugawdu ducked. Quickly, Muusamali swung the pointed end up in an effort to hook him in the face. Again, Duugawdu's swiftness caused him to miss.

Duugawdu drew back and again tried to thrust the point of his spear into Muusamali's midsection. This time, Muusamali chop-blocked the drive by bringing his own spear down hard on top of Duugawdu's. With both hands, and all his weight pressing downward, Muusamali drove Duugawdu's spear to the ground and pinned it there.

The two brothers froze in that position: Duugawdu still gripping his spear with both hands and Muusamali pressing down with all his might. Noses nearly touching, they looked into each other's eyes. Suddenly, the point on Duugawdu's spear snapped in two. The sound of it breaking rang out and Duugawdu's face twisted into a look of rage as he let out his angry protest.

Together, they straightened up and faced each other, eye-to-eye. Duugawdu went in motion first, gripping his broken spear in both hands. Abruptly, he jerked his spear out from under Muusamali's. Muusamali stumbled slightly but quickly recovered. Duugawdu, meanwhile, was already in motion. He took his spear and swung the right end toward Muusamali's head with all his might, throwing his entire body behind the swing. Muusamali just managed to duck beneath it as it whistled overhead.

Duugawdu was so certain that the swing would hit its mark that, when it missed, his momentum threw him off balance.

Muusamali was quick to capitalize and was deadly accurate as he raised his spear in both hands. He swung the butt in a vicious upper cut that caught Duugawdu under the chin and sent him reeling backward down the steps. His broken spear flew from his hands as he was tumbling, head over heels, down the steep flight of stairs. He came to rest at the bottom and laid on the ground with the crowd at his feet. The crowd backed off as they saw Muusamali racing down the steps, spear in hand, straight toward the badly shaken Duugawdu. Muusamali could easily have finished him off—right then. Instead, he took his time walking the final few paces to Duugawdu's side.

Duugawdu fought desperately to rise to his feet; however, he only managed to raise himself on one elbow. His eyes were glazed and, for a moment, all he could do was stare at the ground and vigorously shake his head in an attempt to clear his foggy mind.

Suddenly, a gleaming steel broadsword was tossed from the crowd and landed within Duugawdu's easy reach. A muffled cry came from the crowd as the front section of spectators backpedaled and pushed against other gawking onlookers in the rear.

Duugawdu grabbed the sword and again tried to scramble to his feet . . . but found it impossible to gain his balance. His right leg was broken—a twisted, mangled member it was which hung in lifeless fashion from his body.

Leaning back on his outstretched hand, he looked at his leg and then up to Muusamali as Muusamali continued his relentless charge. The sight of his leg dangling brought pain, as well as rage for his predicament.

Glaring at Muusamali like a wounded, cornered cat, Duugawdu gripped the deadly sword firmly in his fist, drew it back and waited for his chance to strike.

Realizing Duugawdu's situation, the bodyguard who held his naked sword stepped from the crowd toward his wounded master. A hand, however, reached from the crowd and rested on his bare shoulder. The bodyguard looked back to see the Ikeele prince, Jammu. The guard froze as Jammu gave him a look carrying a warning, he both understood and feared. Immediately, the guard abandoned his plans for a rescue.

Muusamali stared at the sword in Duugawdu's hand. There was no fear in Muusamali, and he bounded straight for his brother. The crowd had hushed again. The tension was building as everyone watched this daring, headlong approach.

Muusamali gripped his spear in one hand, now holding it like a long dagger. Without hesitation or breaking stride, he thrust the point at Duugawdu's face to provoke a response. As expected, Duugawdu swung his sword at the spear in a vicious, roundhouse motion. The blade met the spear, chopping it in two like a twig. Quickly Muusamali dropped the remaining portion and rushed forward . . . bare hands extended. Before Duugawdu could react, Muusamali was upon him grabbing the arm holding the sword.

A short scuffle ensued, but a battered, one-legged Duugawdu was no match for the healthy determination of Muusamali. Muusamali jerked, yanked, and finally wrestled the sword from his hands. He rose to his feet and straddled Duugawdu as he lay helpless between his legs. Without realizing it, Muusamali had drawn the sword back and was ready to end his brother's life. At that moment, he happened to catch a glimpse of Father Poe's white face looming just over the front section of spectators. Like an explosion in his head, that old ancestral warning came back to haunt him once more: "Once the white man enters the land of the blacks, the land and its people will die."

Abruptly Muusamali brought the sword slowly down to rest at his side. "Do it, coward," Duugawdu screamed. "Do it now or, so help me god, I'll kill you later with my bare hands!"

Muusamali stared at the beaten, helpless form of his brother with a look of pity on his face yet caution in his heart. Duugawdu would never accept this humiliating defeat without seeking revenge. This realization began to haunt Muusamali.

The crowd was deadly quiet now, holding their collective breath. The only sound Muusamali could hear was Duugawdu dragging his crippled body an inch or two across the ground coming to rest in a sitting position.

Muusamali remained where he was, still straddling Duugawdu's legs. Duugawdu looked at the towering form over him, eyes filled with fire and hate. Then he greedily looked at the sword hanging from his brother's side.

"You don't have the guts to do it . . . do you?" Duugawdu hissed through clenched teeth. "You'd rather die yourself than kill me. So be it," and Duugawdu reached out for the sword.

In a swift, twirling motion, Muusamali swung his sword across Duugawdu's arm, severing it in half like a ripe banana. Duugawdu screamed in pain as he held what had once been his left arm. He looked at Muusamali with that fire still blazing in his eyes and yelled, "Finish it!" As he spoke, he tried to grab hold of Muusamali's genitals in a desperate attempt to inflict some pain of his own. But the razor-sharp steel blade came down again, taking Duugawdu's other arm off at the elbow.

Again, he screamed in pain and his chilling cries froze the crowd. This time, Duugawdu fell backward, landing on his back and the bloody stumps which had once held his arms circled the air above him, as if reaching for the limbs no longer there.

Father Poe rushed from the crowd of horrified onlookers and kneeled over Duugawdu. Hurriedly, he snatched the cross from his neck and used the string as a tourniquet to stop his massive bleeding.

Muusamali stepped back, releasing the bloody sword and allowing it to fall to the ground. He was dazed as he watched the white priest ministering to Duugawdu. Father Poe began ripping strips of cloth from his robe and tying them to Duugawdu's other wounds.

"Let me die, Father. Please!" Duugawdu whispered, his life force slowing seeping from him.

"You know I couldn't do that, my son," Father Poe said, turning his gaze toward Muusamali. They exchanged stares but no words. Muusamali was captivated by this blue-eyed man's looks as well as his actions.

321

This was the closest Muusamali had ever been to a white man. Like Tuuwee and countless other Africans, they were steeped in gory superstitions about white-skinned people. But contrary to what he'd been taught to believe as a child and what he had taught his own tribespeople about the white man's inhumane thirst for blood and urge to kill the black race, this man was actually risking his own life to save a black man.

Muusamali was overcome by the same startling realization millions of other Africans have discovered when coming face-to-face with supposed evil. He realized, at that moment, that this so-called white boogeyman was an intelligent, caring human being with, perhaps, genuine moral character. Strangely, as Muusamali watched the priest caring for his wicked brother, it gave him reason to fear and distrust the white man even more.

The cold stare Father Poe met with as he looked at Muusamali was enough to make the bravest of hearts fail. Yet the priest was unwavering in his own faith that his mission here in Kongolia was ordained by God and that whatever good he could do, was a mighty strike against corruption. To this end, Father Poe was convinced good would always prevail over evil.

Father Poe looked away from both Duugawdu and Muusamali and turned his attention to the bodyguards who stood at Duugawdu's side, mouths open. No one else in the crowd approached them. "Help me get him to the mission hospital. There's not a moment to waste," Father Poe ordered and the two guards went to work gathering Duugawdu into their arms.

"I order you to kill me!" Duugawdu said. But it wasn't to be, as the two giants rushed through the crowd, Duugawdu in their grasp, heading for the mission.

Once more, Father Poe looked at Muusamali, who stood quietly engrossed in thought. He then looked toward the Oupa Ra and the two Arabs as they came down the palace steps with Zuuox. "Forgive them, Lord, for they know not what they do." With that, Father Poe turned and hurried off through the crowd.

322

Five days later, after a grueling forced march on horseback across the hot and dry western Savanna from Kongolia to the Atlantic Coast, Muusamali and the large regiment of Kongolian soldiers reached Gabon.

Mustafa and Firok, atop their camels, led Muusamali and his soldiers to a coastal village called Bota Hava. Once there, Mustafa sent for and met with an old friend and colleague: a black slave trader named Frenchy. In turn, Frenchy contacted other associates in his business concerning a cargo of eight black slaves from Kongolia.

Father Poe provided Muusamali and his people with vital information, such as the time of departure, and the name and description of the ambassador and his black interpreter Dunbar.

Kongolia was ripe, untapped territory, rich in natural resources ranging from minerals to plant and animals, and human souls. All this meant rumors spread quickly and reached far . . . rumors about the first-ever cargo of black slaves to come from Kongolia.

Frenchy had little trouble in tracking down the cargo in question. However, the buyers of Tuuwee, Luba Zandi, and the six others had booked passage aboard a slave ship, and the ship had already sailed, gone for some unknown destination across the great Atlantic. The native tribes in and around Gabon called these mysterious European ships Namba Ndombe, which means "To nowhere and forever." As far as they were concerned, such definition appropriately described Tuuwee's fate. He was gone. Gone to nowhere . . . and gone forever.

———————————————

It was a calm summer evening as the waves pounded the beach and a light breeze blew in off the Atlantic bringing with it a cool, dewy moisture Muusamali could feel on his cheeks. He had left the company of the others to come to the beach to be alone with his thoughts. He stood in the wet sand allowing the surf to run back and forth across his bare feet, something he'd never before experienced.

Holding his spear upright, butt end resting in the sand, he couldn't take his eyes off the most beautiful sunset he'd ever seen. The sun was bigger than he'd ever imagined possible, and it seemed to slowly sink into the ocean before his very eyes.

He kept his gaze fixed on the phenomena before him, not wanting to miss a moment of the unfolding beauty. When Zuuox came up behind him, he didn't turn to see who was approaching; rather, he continued to absorb the magnificence of the coastal sunset.

Zuuox came to rest at Muusamali's side. He, too, didn't speak for a long moment, instead choosing to follow Muusamali's gaze toward the ocean, the sky, and all their wonders.

Muusamali finally broke the silence. "I want to remember this sight so I can describe it to Ruuski and the other Huzza priests when I next see them," he said without turning.

With a nod of his head, Zuuox echoed Muusamali's sentiments and then said, "What will you tell Puulu about Tuuwee, my king?"

Muusamali thought for a moment and, for the first time, his eyes seemed to look beyond the sunset, beyond the beauty. "I will tell her Tuuwee went the way of the sun, to some faraway place where even though he can't be seen or touched, he still lives . . . just as the sun lives. Although it disappears from the daytime sky, its light never goes out. It's always shining somewhere."

Muusamali paused and shifted his gaze to the surf dancing over his toes, then once more turned toward his comrade and said, "My son proved to be more courageous than I, did he not, Zuuox?"

Zuuox was caught off guard by the question. Before he could think of an appropriate response, Muusamali spoke again. "Tuuwee did what I should have done years earlier. My brother, King Nuumyu, needed me and I stayed hidden in the swamps, a prisoner to the tribal law I eventually broke.

But I hesitated too long. I came too late to save my two brothers and lost my own son in the process."

"Don't be so hard on yourself, my king. That you came at all is a grand and noble deed and can never be overshadowed by the events which followed," Zuuox offered compassionately.

Muusamali faced the ocean once more and allowed himself to look again into the setting sun. He found some comfort in Zuuox's words, but nothing could ease the pain and sorrow he felt for losing Tuuwee. Where was he this very moment? Muusamali mused to himself. Wherever, he knew one thing about his son. He knew Tuuwee longed to be in Cuuzanland. Cuuzanland was his home, and he'd risked everything to reach it. In the process, however, he'd lost his dear cousin and best friend Kuula. And now . . . his precious freedom as well.

Muusamali turned to Zuuox and said, "Ah . . . if Tuuwee were to ever come home to Cuuzanland while I live, I will make him king over me and all our people." With a wistfulness to his voice, he turned his eyes toward the graying sky taking in the onset of nightfall and said, "He will be the Sun, and I will be the Morning Star.

The End

This is just the beginning, hopefully this Book #1 will reveal the untapped well of Convict creative ingenuity hidden in plain sight behind the walls of your nearest Penitintury or as close as your friendly neighborhood Ex-Convict.

Willie Hill

B-58763